"WELCOME TO METROPOLIS"
Riding Solo into the Heart of America
By
Christopher Koch

PROLOGUE

"Early this mornin'
...you knocked upon my door
And I said, 'Hello, Satan'
I believe it's time to go"
- Me and The Devil Blues, Robert Johnson

My ass is cold inside my pants as I stop to examine an electric guitar in a Plexiglass display case. Every visible surface is covered in autographs and they sprawl and crawl amongst each other, blending into near indecipherability. A museum placard at the bottom of the case says there are over a hundred including Albert King, Rufus Thomas, and Joe Willie "Pinetop" Perkins. As I'm reading it, the petulant trickle of snot I've been battling for the last few minutes finally breaches my nostril and invades my mustache. I wipe it away with the cuff of my long sleeve t-shirt and then rub that against the cold denim of my Levi's.

It's mid-November in Arkansas. The temperature is just above freezing, less than half the seasonal average, and a damp persistent wind makes it feel even worse.

The unexpected chill is the death rattle of Nuri, a super-typhoon that had ravaged the Pacific for a week before exhausting its fury on the craggy, rooster-comb edge of Alaska pushing an enormous mass of frigid air south all the way to the Gulf of Mexico. The unexpected arctic blast had sent millions of American southerners rummaging in search of long forgotten hats and gloves as local meteorologists struggled for superlatives to describe the bitter cold.

I was as unprepared as any of them and had spent the previous night in a Memphis hotel room with the electric heater turned all the way up, sweating on top of the covers as I tried to game the system by stockpiling warmth in my deep tissue. It hadn't worked, and by the time I'd made it to Helena to catch a live broadcast of the King Biscuit Time radio show, I was as cold as I'd ever been.

Like the distant storm that had delivered the weather, the town of Helena had pretty well run its course by the time I arrived, its population dwindling away since before the promise of LBJ's Great Society. Its average household income is just $23,000 per year, roughly on par with Flint, Michigan, and homes in Helena, when they can be sold, fetch only about half the already modest Arkansas norm. On the town's dilapidated Mainstreet, vacancies are more common than not.

Still, in the month before I arrived, Helena had visitors from England, Japan, Switzerland, Holland, and Australia, their names and hometowns penned in a register at the Delta Cultural Center, an unassuming brick storefront that is home to the world's longest running blues radio show, the Peabody Award winning King Biscuit Time and its host "Sunshine" Sonny Payne.

Like most of the others in the register, it was Sonny I'd come to see. A 2010 inductee into the Blues Hall of Fame, Sonny had been part of King Biscuit since before I was born. Hell, Sonny had been part of King Biscuit since before my mother was born. A display in front of his modest studio (from which King Biscuit is broadcast remotely) features photos of Sonny with BB King and a who's who of other blues legends who came up listening to him on the radio. The same display tells Sonny's story in his own words.

"In high school, when I first got the job [at KFFA], I was telling all my friends that I was going to be on the air that very first day when they opened on November 14, 1941. So, I get there, walk in, and say, 'Here I am! Boy, this is going to be great." They said, 'Here's the broom. Here's the mop. And go empty all the baskets.' So, I was a mop boy for a while, because they told me I was going to come up the hard way or I wasn't going to do it at all."

Now the patriarchal symbol of KFFA, Sonny walks with a cane, scrutinizing each step. When he enters the cultural center dressed for work in khakis and a button-down shirt, his eyes peer out from behind thick plastic-framed glasses and his hair is wispy and nearly absent at the top of his head. He's jowly and pink, regressing physically toward infancy — Yoda with a turntable and a microphone. He seems fragile as he greets the staff and makes his way slowly to his studio, stopping graciously along the way to say hello and thank me for coming. Another KFFA personality, Leon Graves, shows up to help Sonny prep for today's show. While they work Graves tells Sonny that someone will be coming by later to install a new CD player for his ads. "They don't make those mini-discs anymore," he shouts.

Before he leaves, Graves stops to ask me if I'm staying for Sonny's broadcast. "He's always happy to visit," he cautions. "But he's really hard of hearing. You have to basically yell."

I introduce myself to Sonny again and we make awkward small talk, mostly commiserating about the cold. I mention that I rode in on a motorcycle and he seems impressed. Soon he settles in behind his console and I take a seat on a hard wooden bench just outside the studio among a display of King Biscuit memorabilia. He glances around the empty room and looks over at me.

"Are you the only one?" he asks.

"Yes" I say, leaning forward and nodding.

"C'mon back here then," he says, and gestures to a couple of padded guest chairs opposite his inside the studio. "You can sit over there."

With southern hospitality, he stands and holds open the little Dutch door to his sanctum. I thank him and sit where he points. He slips me a piece of paper with ad copy at the top, "Write your name at the bottom."

My last name has been mispronounced my whole life, mostly by accident, sometimes on purpose- like when my drill sergeant in basic training called me Cootch for six weeks straight, sometimes spiraling it up into a "my hoochie coochie man". My mother likes to tell a story about how a nurse in a hospital waiting room once looked her dead in the eye called out "Crotch!" when it was her turn to go in. People often pronounce it "cock" which always boggles my mind, because even if I were shown the name "Cock" and asked to call someone by it, I'd find some other way to pronounce it. To save me and Sonny both the trouble, I write out CHRISTOPHER COKE in big block letters spelling my last name like the soft drink.

A moment later, the main KFFA studio throws the air over to Sonny and he hits the prerecorded intro to start the broadcast. "It's

12:15! You're listening to radio kay-eff-eff-ayyyyyyyyy!"

I realize with sudden dread that I haven't had anything to drink since breakfast and my mouth has gone all dry and gummy.

"Pass the biscuits, 'cause it's King Biscuit time on KFFA radio! Ladies and gentlemen, Robert "Junior" Lockwood and the King Biscuit Entertainers!"

The King Biscuit intro music is classic Delta blues and as I try to work up some saliva, I pick out the lyric, "every mornin' for my breakfast, put King Biscuit on my plate…"

Sonny introduces the show as number 17,132 of the original King Biscuit Time Program and announces the sponsors before continuing, "Hi Everyone, 'Sunshine' Sonny Payne broadcasting live from the Delta Cultural Center, right here in historic downtown – cold – Helena. We know now why we have the cold weather today. We're gonna talk to a young man that's coming through this way from Minnesota. And we know where the cold weather came from—" Sonny pauses for effect. "He brought it. We'll talk to Christopher Coke later, but first…"

With a well-practiced hand, Sonny starts the first track of the day and makes a small adjustment on the board in front of him. Then he rises and adjusts a swiveling studio mic in front of my face. "That's good," he says. "Don't move."

Sonny shuffles through his CDs, checks his short stack of papers and then makes some small talk with me about the song that's playing. There's a stack of red Solo cups behind him on his desk and ask if I have time to grab a drink of water. He nods, and I rush to the men's room and fill a cup half full of tepid water, sipping it self-consciously as I sit back down, trying to get my face back in front of the microphone exactly where Sonny wanted.

He introduces the next track, a request, and starts it up. "It's a long one," he says to me conspiratorially. "I hate the long ones."

While the song plays, I have time to relax for a few minutes. Sonny shares with me that he likes Duke Ellington as I try to steady my breathing and prepare myself to sound calm and upbeat. I've been on the road since the previous Wednesday and traveled through nine of the ten states on the Mississippi River. As concerned as I might be about how I'll sound on the radio, I'm even more concerned that I'll be stranded in Helena. My bike's high-tech security system had developed a problem the day before and stopped recognizing my key fob. I had managed to keep going by disconnecting and reconnecting a wiring harness every time I stopped, tricking the on-board computer into a hard reboot, but there was no guarantee that would keep working.

"We don't have any motorcycle shops here in Helena" the museum's curator had warned me gravely when I first arrived and shared my story with him.

It was the second warning I'd gotten about Helena. The first had been in Memphis the day before at a Beale Street bar. "You're going to Helena?" the man at the next stool asked with exaggerated astonishment. Then he'd asked me if I had a gun and laughed at his own joke.

The track faded out and Sonny started up again, his voice natural and easy. "You wondered about the cold weather; well, we tease a lot, but he rides a motorcycle this dude and he brought that cold air with him. Now dig this, his name is Christopher Coke."

Here it is. We're off to the races. Sonny looks at me incredulously across the table and asks the obvious question. "What are you doing on a motorcycle?"

The truth— and maybe he saw it in me— was that when I'd set off down the Mississippi a week before, I'd run off completely and utterly half-cocked.

CHAPTER ONE

"I should've been a cowboy
I should've learned to rope and ride"
- Should've Been a Cowboy, Toby Keith

Sometime in my late thirties and for no particular reason one Thursday afternoon, I read the obituaries in my local newspaper, the Wright County Journal Press. A small town weekly paper, the Journal Press covers things like the Miss Buffalo Pageant, the restoration of the downtown theater marquee, and the occasional car-through-the-ice story.

The obituaries are a quick read, and after I'd read them that first week, I felt obliged to read them again the next. Those people died, I told myself. You can spare ten minutes to read about their lives. And so began a weekly habit that lasted about a year. Often, I'd read the obituaries to the exclusion of the rest of the paper.

Getting the recommended daily amount of fiber and calcium, pursuing a sensible exercise program, and diligently adding to your 401k are all things you should be doing in your late thirties. Habitually reading the obituaries is not. In fact, it can be downright disconcerting.

Each obituary begins with a standard format: name, age, town, and then some gentle euphemism for having died. Not to be too dark, but I'll use myself as an example; "Christopher Koch, 43, of Buffalo, Minnesota was called home to his heavenly father…"

If the deceased had achieved something of particular public interest, this is often noted in the opening. Again, I'll use myself as an example (with obvious embellishment); "Christopher Koch, 43, beloved star of stage and film, passed away last Thursday evening in his Buffalo home."

The age of the deceased is a crucial element in a good obituary and occupies a place of honor second only to the name. There are the obviously young, those unfortunate teens and twenty-somethings whose lives were stolen away before they really begun; and the melancholy news, rarely, of a child or infant passing. And then there are the recognizably old, those who have lived sufficiently long that no one honestly feels like Father Time had dealt them a cheap shot. They are the workhorses of the obituary page, those wizened octogenarians and feisty ninety-somethings (my own great grandmother made it into this group, called to her eternal reward just shy of the hundred-year mark, so that she was born and died in the same decade a century apart), and the Obituary All Stars-- the hundred plus club, a small fraternity whose ranks I hope to someday join, after of course, being recognized in that Smucker's segment on the Today Show. I would say "being recognized by Willard Scott", but if I hit the century mark, Willard will have long since been the subject of his own obituary. "Willard Scott, TV and radio personality, author, and original Ronald McDonald…"

Between the painfully young and the mercifully old is a gray area where our own birthdays shade our view of exactly how badly the deceased may have gotten cheated, a gray area that insurance companies and actuaries have to try to define numerically. As a twenty-five-year-old, I would have thought a fifty-six-year-old, called suddenly to the front of the line by disease or tragedy, old enough to have had their day. Now I've come to a point where anything less than the national average of 75 or 80 smacks a little premature.

The seeds of midlife crisis are germinated by staring down the barrel of our own mortality, and bear fruit as the previously unfathomable value of time takes hold in our minds. We spend our youth hearing older relatives lament how quickly time passes and around age forty we start to feel it ourselves. What follows are often the most brutal self-assessments this side of the eighth grade.

That year, as I read the obituaries and saw all those lives summarized in print, I came to the sad conclusion that I wasn't doing anything I'd want to read about.

*****

My sister Shannon was born on Christmas Day, 1981, and has spent her few dozen birthdays tearing jolly snowman wrapping paper from her presents. She is a gentle brand of pretty, with big round eyes she got from our mother, and bubblegum pink hair that she got from her stylist, Ashley. A decade younger than me, she's my office manager and confidant. I jokingly call her my assisterant. Besides my ex-wife and my daughter, Shannon is the only person I've ever met that shares my biting sense of humor right down to her coal black heart. It's a good binding agent for our friendship.

I sat across the desk from her as her hand hovered over her computer mouse, her finger poised to click. "Want me to book it?"

The Delta airlines site was up on her screen. Eighteen days later, at 1:45 in the afternoon, flight 3743 would leave from New Orleans to Minneapolis with or without me. The first-class ticket I'd asked Shannon to look up would cost five-hundred-fifty dollars I really shouldn't spend but seemed a fanciful and appropriate cap to a cross-country ride whose possibility was still coalescing in my mind. Four hours earlier, I was driving back from a job-site and looking forward to a quiet afternoon. I'd had absolutely no idea I might be about to embark on a nine-day motorcycle ride.

A cross-country solo trip had been on my mind for about two years. I have little mechanical ability and had never ridden alone more than about an hour or so from my house. When I discussed the idea with people, I always said the same thing, "I'm never going to climb Mount Everest. I'm probably never going to go into outer space or to the bottom of the ocean. This is an adventure that's doable."

As a self-employed tradesman and consultant whose slow time of year runs from December through February when the cold of the upper Midwest brings most construction to a halt, I'd resigned myself to an off-season ride, most likely in the very early spring. A southern route from San Diego to the Florida Keys seemed to offer my best chance at passable weather, although I'd been warned that I could face a lot of rain.

Having thought about the trip for a couple of years without doing anything about it, I decided that I'd spend my afternoon off researching the actual logistics, considering things like mileage and budget and checking historical weather data to see if the rain warnings were true. If I didn't start planning, "someday" was a word that might settle over my trip like an old tarp growing dusty and rigid with the passage of time.

Back in my office, seated across the desk from Shannon with my laptop perched on top of her carefully arranged papers, I decided the first thing I had to do was nail down the actual route. I googled the phrase "best cross-country motorcycle trips" looking for some guidance and soon found a site featuring a story on the top five.

Route 66 from Chicago to Los Angeles was number one, but Chicago would be cold in the spring and Route 66 wasn't a true cross-country route, something that seemed important.

Second was Route 50 from Ocean City, Maryland to Sacramento, California. Route 50 ran coast to coast, but right across the middle of the country like a belt around America's waist, meaning that weather would probably be an issue.

Third place went to the Great River Road, following the route of the Mississippi River from its headwaters in Minnesota, through St. Paul to New Orleans, and on to the Gulf of Mexico. There was romance in that. I'd recently stumbled across the Great River Road on some other website about scenic drives and had filed it away in my mind as a follow up adventure to my first ride if things went well. It had the added advantage of beginning in my home state, meaning I'd only have to ship the motorcycle one way, instead of shipping it to my departure city and then back home again once I reached my destination.

Rounding out the top five were Highway 20 from Newport, Oregon to Boston and Highway 40 from San Francisco to Atlantic City both of which would probably be too cold when I wanted to travel.

Thinking I might chart my own route across the southern US, I decided to research seasonal weather patterns and quickly found my way to the Old Farmer's Almanac. Surprisingly, weather predictions across the south proved to be just as good in November as they were for late February or early March. I hadn't really thought about traveling in November, but it was a pretty quiet month for me with two holidays and the opening of deer season in Minnesota. Deer opener typically paralyzed construction for five or six days in November as most of its workforce trundled off into the woods to drink beer, play cards, and occasionally shoot at things.

With the Great River Road fresh in my mind, I checked the long-range forecast for the Midwest. Once again, November looked as good or better than late February or March. A November ride on the Great River Road was suddenly becoming a real option. Leaving in the fall would mean riding on clean roads rather than roads rimmed with sand from winter clearing efforts and the weather along the GRR would grow warmer as I rode south, giving me something to look forward to and enjoy as the miles flowed past.

Traveling in the fall would waiting an entire year though, rather than the handful of months that riding in the spring would. The dusty tarp of "someday" threatened to lower itself once again over my trip. "What if I just went right now?" I said to Shannon. "Wouldn't that be crazy?"

It was Wednesday the 29th of October. The leaves on the large maple tree outside the office window were shades of fiery red and orange. I was leaving that Friday to spend the weekend in Colorado, returning on November 3rd, the day before the midterm elections. If I was going to go in November, there would be almost no time to prepare.

Shannon looked at me across the desk. "You could."

Over the next hour we used MapQuest to approximate the daily mileage, contacted a couple of firms for bids on shipping the motorcycle back, and took a serious look at the calendar. If I left the following Wednesday, I could be gone over Veteran's Day and deer opener, and make it home on Friday, November 14th, the day before my 43rd birthday. I decided I'd need to work both Monday and Tuesday. Discounting my planned trip to Colorado, I'd have just one day to prepare.

Shannon and I were both caught up in the boldness of the plan when I asked her to pull up the Delta site and price my return ticket. "Want me to book it?" Shannon asked.

"No. I should sleep on it. If I decide to go, we can always book it tomorrow." Saying the words out loud brought a crushing wave of disappointment. I'd already grown attached to the Great

River Road and the reckless adventure of leaving on a whim. The thought of sleeping on it seemed suddenly like reaching for the safety of the dusty tarp. It was just another way of saying, "Someday".

"Push the button," I said.

"What?"

"Click on it." My voice got higher as I said it, and I flushed with excitement. "Click on it. I'm going."

With a mouse click, the die was cast. I was due to catch a flight in New Orleans in eighteen days. Everything else, we'd work out on the fly.

*****

Later that evening I reclined on my living room couch and shopped online in preparation for the trip. I'd decided that camping was a good way to add economy and color to the journey.

That February I'd been to the Daytona 500 and camped in the infield in a cramped rental RV built on the chassis of a Ford van. During the same trip, I'd spent a day at an RV park in Orlando. Later, in August, I'd camped just outside of Sturgis, again in a crowded RV. Both times, I'd been impressed at the camaraderie of campers and the easy acquaintance of strangers in RV parks.

Commercial campgrounds provide the faint whiff of roughing it even while offering hot showers and a place to charge your iPhone. I decided to camp six of the nine nights I'd spend on the road. Hadn't Peter Fonda had a bedroll strapped across his handlebars in "Easy Rider"? I could be Peter Fonda fifty years on. Peter Fonda with a USB charger.

Navigating around Amazon.com, I found a Big Agnes SL1 one-person tent for just shy of $300. It was more than I planned on spending and could have bought me two nights in a hotel. But the Big Agnes, despite the name, weighs only about three pounds and collapses down into a compact burrito about 17 inches long and five inches across.

I also found a gigantic canister of bear repellant spray for $30. Nowhere I was headed warned of rampaging bears, but in some dark corner of my mind hatched the certainty that if I didn't have it, I'd die a gruesome and bloody death wishing the whole while that I'd had the wisdom and foresight to buy a thirty dollar can of high-pressure bear spray. "Do not seek out encounters with bears" offered the manufacturer helpfully.

Not only would I be the human equivalent of a giant bear burrito for six of nine nights, but what if I broke down and had to walk for miles to the nearest town in the middle of the night in the rural south? Bear repellant spray could probably double as people repellant spray. I thought of Ned Beatty in Deliverance. Click. Bear spray added to cart.

The thought of riding for nine days on unfamiliar roads so far from home also aroused in me a fear of crashing that led me to a motorcycle accessory site, RevZilla, where I browsed body armor until I was certain it was foolhardy to travel without it. RevZilla, by the way, has helpful videos for a lot of their products and offers easy returns. After a lot of deliberation mostly centered on how quickly I was burning through the money I had supposedly saved by deciding to sleep alongside the infamous rampaging bears of Illinois, I ordered an armored shirt called the ForceField Pro that looked to combine superior crash protection with a minimum of bulk. It cost about $300 and looked like the top half of Spiderman's suit, but with built-in muscles. I hoped to be able to wear it under my clothes.

When it arrived the following Tuesday, it turned out to be everything it promised to be- lightweight, aggressively armored, and stylishly cut. I wrestled it on and looked in my bathroom mirror. It turns out my physique has nearly nothing in common with Peter Parker or the model from the catalog. We all wear shirts with two arms and a neck hole. After that, the similarities kind of taper off. I pulled a long sleeve T-shirt over the top of the Forcefield Pro, hoping it would help. It didn't.

I looked like a chubby nine-year-old with balloon muscles shoved under a one-size-fits-none drugstore Halloween costume, the kind with the plastic mask that's held on by a rubber band.

I had ordered bear spray in some small part to protect me from caricatured southerners and was standing in front of my bathroom mirror wearing an armored shirt that would pretty much guarantee I'd need it. My existing black leather motorcycle jacket, then, would have to do. RevZilla really does offer an easy return policy. Reason for return? Customer looks nothing at all like Spiderman while wearing garment.

The remainder of that evening I spent learning as much as I could about the Great River Road and the sights I might want to see along the way. The Gateway Arch seemed a must, and Beale Street, and the King Biscuit program. There was an abandoned mountain tramway outside of Louisiana, Missouri that promised to be slightly Chernobylesque, and there was the haunted town of Alton, Illinois.

The Great River Road offered numerous brewery tours and even the world's largest six pack (in LaCrosse, Wisconsin). I estimated I'd have three to four hours of daylight available each day for tourism and was slightly worried that nine days would make a laggard's pace.

It was well after midnight when I finally turned off my computer and went to sleep, having decided less than twelve hours before to make the journey I was now committed to. The following afternoon I would run my motorcycle in for a check-up and try to make it to REI to round out my camping gear. The time I had to prepare would be measured in stolen hours over the next few days.

*****

At the end of my driveway not even a full week later, I leaned awkwardly up against my idling motorcycle so Shannon could take a picture. It had drizzled off and on all morning and I'd soaked through one pair of boots already while picking the bike up from the shop where I'd left it over the weekend for servicing.

The sky was a dull gray and the wind was up. A moment before, I had used my phone to take a photo of my odometer, which read 7,884 miles. I was responsible for less than half of that, the big Kawasaki coming to me secondhand two years before, the most recent of a handful of bikes I've owned.

I got my first motorcycle at fifteen and carry a reminder of it to this day in the form of a deep scar on my right shin. Up until a few years ago, I used to brag that you could feel it through my pants, but in all fairness, that's stopped being true.

I got the scar learning how to operate the clutch on a Honda

XL185 enduro my mom and stepdad got me for Christmas. I hadn't asked for a dirt bike and would never even thought to have. My folks couldn't afford it and the bike's appearance under the tree is no proof that they could. I remember coming down the stairs that morning with my two little sisters in tow and seeing that tall, gangly, knobby-tired wonder right in the middle of our living room and being absolutely at a loss for words. I also got socks.

I ate my breakfast that Christmas morning torn between pure joy and abject terror. I would eventually be expected to mount that wonderful frightening machine which I knew would be completely indifferent to my joy or suffering. There was no protective gear to go with the bike. Not even a helmet.

I've never asked my mom and dad if they wanted to get me one and couldn't afford it or if they had simply never thought about it. This was 1988. Kids got bikes for Christmas all the time and no one felt compelled to include a helmet. My bike just happened to have a kick starter and a tailpipe, either one of which was equally capable of inflicting bodily harm without the motorcycle ever leaving the driveway, so I suppose a helmet was a worry that remained down the road a bit.

My fifteen-year-old girlfriend (who would leave me resolutely committed to never, ever again write love poetry, a resolution I would eventually break in my forties before making once again) named the Honda Max. I've never been one for naming vehicles and that's one of only two that ever ended up with a name (the other was a Porsche Boxster I dubbed Giselle in a regrettable moment of drunken, rhapsodic Teutonic pride). All but unassisted, I did eventually learn how to operate Max's clutch. My stepdad gave me the general concept not long after breakfast and then left me in the street to figure it out on my own.

It was an early failure in my trial and error clutch learning that sent me careening off the back of the bike while still holding onto the throttle. Motorcyclists will appreciate the irony of falling off a motorcycle while gravity and momentum force your frantic right hand to pull the throttle back harder and harder. As I gave it more and more gas, the Honda and I engaged in an elaborate lovers' pirouette before coming to rest together in a heap, one of Max's foot pegs biting violently into my shin, punishing me for my novice. I didn't tell my folks. Like the boy in "A Christmas Story" who nails himself in the eye with a BB on Christmas morning, I lied about the wound to keep my mom from worrying.

A brown-eyed, broad faced neighbor kid named Bob wrecked the Honda in a ditch a few months later after promising me he knew how to ride. The wreck was his own introduction to the cruel engineering of the twist throttle. His family couldn't pay to repair the damage he caused and neither could mine. Unrideable, Max was sold for a loss.

The next motorcycle I got was a year later. I had left my mom and my stepdad's home to go and live with my father in Colorado for the last two years of high school. Like a lot of teenage boys, I was an unpleasant blend of testosterone, know-it-all-ism, and ingratitude. My mom and I agreed that some time with my father might be a good idea. I don't know how eager my old man was to take me on, but it was inarguably his turn. Except for a few weeks here and there in the summer, it was the first time since I was five that we'd shared a home.

Dad set me up with a ten or twelve-year-old Suzuki 250 streetbike. We lived outside of town on a rural two-lane road at the end of a few miles of gentle uphill grade. My primary memory of the Suzuki was its utter inability to get out of its own way. By the time I'd make it to the top of that grade, I'd be unable to maintain the speed limit and would usually have acquired a comet's tail of irritated drivers eager for me to pull off.

The last time I went down on a motorcycle was on that Suzuki. I came into our gravel driveway too fast one day trying to appease yet another parade of impatient traffic that had built up behind me and the tired old Suzuki just slid peacefully out from underneath me, providing another firsthand lesson in the physics of two-wheeled transport. I don't recall there being much damage to me or the bike, but nevertheless; it didn't hang around long after.

I got a Yamaha after that, which I rode back and forth to junior college before winding up on academic probation and working night shifts at an Amoco station. Soon after that, I joined the Air Force, got married, and became a dad. When I finally earned my bachelor's degree in 2000, my father gave me his 1977 BMW R100RS. He'd bought it gently used in 1978 and it had seen him through many happy years of bachelorhood before taking up a long stint in his barn.

By the time I got the BMW in 2000, it was showing its age. The tires were ravaged by dry rot, the gas tank had a line of damp rust along the bottom seam, and the rear turn indicators were held horizontal by a lash of strategically placed black electrical tape. Between the weeping gas tank and its twin Bing carbs, riding the big Beemer always left me stained with the noxious sweet smell of gasoline.

The R100RS remains a beautiful motorcycle, BMW's first attempt at a full fairing, one that funneled air around the rider's legs. My father painted it a Porsche color, Guard's Red, and it came from the factory equipped with optional 8 spoke wheels. To my eye, it still looks fast, exotic, and purposeful- like the Concorde. I looked up a CycleWorld review of the R100RS a few years back and the article was headlined, "If you have to ask, you can't afford it."

I rode it off and on, mostly off, for another ten years after it came to me. It's an expensive bike to maintain and despite its solid feel, the tires and brakes aren't up to modern standards. The seat is flat and slippery and the way the handlebars tuck into the fairing makes it all but impossible to find a comfortable riding position.

The BMW is a hard starter and I bought my third battery for it at my local motorcycle dealer in 2010. While I was waiting for the battery to be filled with water, I spotted a new, non-current Honda Shadow 500 for something like $5,000. It was a cruiser style motorcycle, a kind of fake Harley-Davidson that offered exceptional value for the money. A trip for a battery to keep the BMW running ended with a new Honda in my driveway.

The BMW has subsequently found its way back into the barn. I sometimes go and admire it, covered with dust and nearly forty years of patina. It's still a gorgeous design and I sometimes wonder about the cost of restoring it to its original greatness before remembering the CycleWorld headline, "If you have to ask, you can't afford it".

My father invited me to Sturgis with him and my stepmother in the summer of '12. Freshly divorced and determined to say yes to opportunities to stretch my wings, I agreed to go. Although I'd ridden a motorcycle for nearly 25 years then, it was always as a casual rider. My ex-wife didn't enjoy riding with me and I didn't have any friends who rode, so on the years I rode at all, I never racked up more than a few hundred miles, mostly on short trips around the lake near my house or on errands in my small town. I was afraid of riding on the interstate, didn't have much in the way of real gear, and felt every bit like a second-class biker.

At the time of my father's invitation, I had two years and about 400 miles on the Honda, which I'd come to call my faux Fatboy. The Shadow was the first cruiser style bike I owned, and I'd never grown used to the seating position, low and back, like sitting in an easy chair. It was reliable, comfortable, and good looking, but it was too small and underpowered to ride through the Black Hills of South Dakota.

It was also so obviously a poor man's Harley-Davidson with its plastic fenders and cheap chrome, that I was concerned about being made fun of by burly leather-clad, honest-to-goodness biker types. The thought of riding the Shadow down Main Street in Sturgis brought back feelings I hadn't had since the summer before junior high, when an older friend confided in me that on the first day of school, the eighth graders initiated the sixth graders by dunking their heads in the toilets. Apparently, the faculty knew about the practice, were in on the joke, and for years had done nothing to stop it. The toilet initiation story turned out to be bullshit. That couldn't save the Honda.

A much bigger and more powerful motorcycle than the Shadow I traded away for it, the Kawasaki I bought before that Sturgis trip was more in line with what I'd grown accustomed to over years of upright riding on the BMW. A sport tourer, the Kawasaki Concours looks like the fat Elvis of Ninjas. The two are cousins beneath the skin, sharing the same 1352cc in-line four-cylinder engine. The Concours is designed for distance riding and comes from the factory with quickly detachable hard saddlebags that can be carried like luggage. It has an electrically operated windshield that raises and lowers at the push of a button, electronic tire pressure monitors, car-like sideview mirrors, and a thoughtfully placed accessory power jack in the fairing not far from where Peter Fonda would stash his bedroll.

It's also blindingly fast. The Kawi is a black 2009, and the previous owner removed all the factory badges, giving it an angry, stealthy look that I thought would be right at home in Sturgis, even if it was a far different bike than the hordes of Harleys I expected to see. If the Harley riders were going to dunk my head in a toilet, they'd have to catch me first.

I trailered the Kawasaki out to Sturgis that year and again when I went back with my dad in 2014. Even with more motorcycle underneath me, and more miles than I'd seen in years, I was still uncomfortable on the interstate and still didn't have proper gear.

Home at my Dad's for the Halloween weekend before my trip down the Great River Road, I borrowed a pair of his leather chaps. I already had a pretty good leather jacket and a pair of gauntlets. For boots, I'd rely on a newish pair of black Doc Martins.

My helmet was twenty years old when Shannon and I booked my Delta ticket and almost never worn, so when I dropped off the Kawasaki for a check-up the previous week, I ordered a new one, spending $350 on a Nolan that offered the most panoramic face shield of any model I fitted. One of the reasons I hadn't previously liked wearing a helmet was the diminished peripheral vision you typically get, and the Nolan seemed to make that an almost moot point.

It also came with an anti-fog liner that could be fitted beneath the visor, but I only picked up the helmet night before I was due to leave and never had time to figure out how to fasten the visor in before I found myself standing in my driveway posing for Shannon's photo. I'd have to make do without.

With Shannon's impromptu driveway photo out of the way and skies threatening, I pulled on a cheap, two-piece blue plastic rainsuit I'd bought at Walmart, plugged the motorcycle's speaker cord into my iPhone, hit the shuffle button on the Great River Road playlist I had compiled on the flight back from Colorado and headed off down my street. I steered in the general direction of St. Paul with no definite plan on where I'd intercept the Great River Road.

The Great River Road is a moniker affixed to a patchwork of mostly scenic byways that are commonly known by other names, and MapQuest doesn't recognize the term Great River Road. Shannon had printed out some directions to get me to the GRR in St. Paul, but I'd tucked the folded paper away inside my jacket. I knew where St. Paul was and once there, the Mississippi River couldn't be missed. I'd just have to head that direction and keep an eye out for the distinctive pilot's wheel marker signs that designated the GRR, a task at which I was soon to become adept.

*****

I'd driven away from my house and down my street hundreds of times, but never with the sense of elation and freedom that gripped me that cold November morning. Cold weather was in the mix for Minnesota for the next several days at least, so I'd scrapped my initial plan to ride north to the headwaters of the Mississippi and start from there. It was just too cold.

The Great River Road runs for over 500 miles in Minnesota and most of it I'd seen already just by living in the state for nearly twenty years. Starting in St. Paul rather than the headwaters saved me two days travel through rural Minnesota under a blanket of November cold, and would allow me some extra time to detour west from Cape Girardeau, Missouri over to Nashville, Tennessee. After a night in Nashville, I'd double back to Cape Girardeau and rejoin the GRR.

The new plan also gave my trip a little more focus. By including Nashville, I'd turn the southern half of my trip into a tour of American musical roots, including country, rock, blues, and jazz. In the north, I'd take in the boom and bust of industry and agriculture on the river.

I pondered it all as I rode south from my hometown of Buffalo, through small farming communities and into affluent exurban Victoria where the county roads I followed meandered leisurely past sleepy lakes and horse paddocks. An hour away from home I pulled into a gas station in the Twin Cities suburb of Chanhassen and climbed off the bike. My knees ached already and my feet were falling asleep.

The problem was my father's borrowed chaps— which were too tight and were gripping me like a hungry anaconda. I hadn't noticed it when I tried them on standing up in his living room, or even earlier that morning walking around in my driveway, but forty miles of riding had revealed the truth: my father has chicken legs. I do not. Once, while being fitted for my first suit, the tailor casually told me I was "husky in the thigh". The comment stuck with me. I've shopped for boy's clothes before. I know what husky means.

I needed the chaps for warmth as much as protection and there was no room for them in my saddlebags, stuffed to capacity as they were with clothes, camping gear, and various supplies. Damn it. I felt ridiculous at not having made it fifty miles before finding some fault in my planning. The chaps, thick smooth calfskin that went all the way to the arch of my foot keeping the wind from nipping my legs and ankles, fastened by way of a belt at the waist, snaps at the cuff, and a long zipper from ankle to mid-thigh. I unzipped them most of the way, opening a long vertical slit up the outside of both legs and giving my thighs some breathing room. It looked like I'd left home half-dressed or hell bent on an evening of ballroom dancing, but it would have to do.

The stop offered me a chance to use the restroom and to gulp a Red Bull through the Nolan's open face shield. Inside the station, I got curious looks from Minnesotans enduring the first unwelcome advances of a winter that would come early and hard. "It's a good day for a ride," the cashier said as she rang up my drink. She was a hearty looking redhead, mid-fifties or so, with a smoker's rasp in her voice. I couldn't decide if she was teasing me or not.

"Not really," I replied. I had only just stowed the Walmart rain suit, chancing that the drizzle was behind me and that it was only the cold grey I'd contend with for the remainder of the day.

She stopped everything, looked me dead in the eye, and smiled broadly. "Honey," she said. "Every day is a good day for a ride".

CHAPTER TWO

"I met her accidentally in St. Paul, Minnesota."
- Big River, Johnny Cash

I bumbled across the Great River Road just outside of St. Paul at the intersection of highway 55 and highway 13, spotting, to my surprise, my first Great River Road sign just outside of Lilydale. I quickly pulled onto the shoulder and snapped a roadside selfie. My visor was fogged and I was already cold, but neither could dull the obvious excitement on my face. With no fanfare and with a view of nothing more majestic than a typical busy intersection on a gray fall day, my journey had officially begun.

Having abandoned the idea of starting at the actual headwaters of the Mississippi, St. Paul still made not just a convenient starting point, but also a fitting one since the river and her legacy of steamboat commerce were so entwined. Even the logo for the Great River Road, the one I'd see on dozens if not hundreds of signs over the coming days, features a steamboat as its centerpiece.

From its headwaters to the Gulf of Mexico, the Mississippi River drops almost 1,500 feet with better than half of that coming in Minnesota. Steamboats navigating north on the Mississippi could paddle no further than St. Paul before rugged stone bluffs blocked their passage effectively making St. Paul the northern terminus of the river for commercial traffic. The rugged bluffs that block the river there were formed by the same ice age glaciers that carved out Minnesota's ten-thousand lakes (and twenty-thousand swamps).

I followed Shepard Road past the Summit Brewery and on past the brick smokestack and crenellated towers fo the former Schmidt brewery running parallel alongside the Mississippi for the first time on my trip. Near downtown, the road edged closer to the broad flatness of the water where tugs still push long flat barges laden with salt, iron, and other bulk loads serenely past luxury apartments and condominiums sprouting up in the shade of the modern glass and concrete architecture of the Science Museum and the Xcel Energy Center, while across the river stands the imposing stone pavilion and great lawn of Harriet Island Park, named for Harriet Bishop.

Bishop, a schoolteacher -and apparently the life of any party- was a leading figure in the temperance movement ("Lips that touch liquor shall never touch ours!") that would leave the Schmidt's plant struggling for churning out non-alcoholic brew and struggling for survival for more than a decade while the business of drinking went underground.

Beyond the Wabasha Bridge, the tallest buildings on the St. Paul skyline gave way to Lowertown and I passed the historic Union Depot train station, restored to its former grandeur in a near quarter billion-dollar project completed in 2012. The city fell into the background behind me as the road followed the river southeast before rising to cross over the drab and massive CP railyard, a transport hub serving the barge terminals of Childs Road, just opposite from the St. Paul airport-- four modes of transport converging on a wide elbow of the slow-moving Mississippi.

I joined Highway 10 and rode south past the hulking, industrial mammoth of the Gerdau Steel plant, beneath the clover leaf maze of 494, and on through Newport and St. Paul Park, the scenery becoming boring and prosaic, the river lost behind a maze of housing and industry. As I sped down Highway 10, semi-trucks and SUVs barreled past me at 70 and 75 miles an hour, buffeting me in their wash and I became more and more aware of the cold seeping into my hands and up my lower back as I huddled behind the Kawi's tiny windshield for protection.

With my destination for the day, Onalaska, Wisconsin still two hours ahead, I left the freeway in Cottage Grove and pulled into the parking lot of a Kohl's department store where I bought an oatmeal colored scarf to stop the wind's relentless and unwelcome intrusion down the neck of my coat. On a bench in the store's vestibule I took off my boots and shoved a chemical handwarmer into each toe. I did the same with my gauntlets before remounting the bike and heading south again.

Eighty miles from home, with my starting city behind me, I was filled with satisfaction that I had thrown back the dusty tarp of someday and was actually riding the Great River Road. In reality, I had lost the GRR almost immediately upon leaving St. Paul.

The Great River Road was originally conceived in the mid-1930s by President Roosevelt's Secretary of the Interior, Harold Ickes (father of President Bill Clinton's White House Deputy Chief of Staff), who encouraged the Governors of the Mississippi River states to form a commission to plan a public parkway along the river. Before Congress could approve funds for a feasibility study, the US entered World War II, putting progress on the Great River Road on hold until 1949.

When the feasibility study was eventually completed in 1951, it indicated that a new road along the Mississippi would be cost prohibitive and recommended instead that existing sections of road be designated a scenic route. Any funding for new construction would be used only to link existing roads which would be upgraded as necessary.

Federal funds were made available for planning which continued for almost twenty years, even as states began to place Great River Road signage on their own segments of the road. Beginning in 1973, Congress allocated more than three-hundred million dollars for development of the Great River Road over the span of a decade, with the Federal Highway Administration issuing guidelines for the road in 1976.

Although there is a single designated National Route for the Great River Road along the Mississippi in each of the ten states it passes through, the states have designated alternate State Routes (also known as the Great River Road and carrying almost identical signage) on the opposite banks of the Mississippi so that the river can be followed continuously on either the east or west side on roads designated as part of the Great River Road.

Adding to the confusion, National Route signs are absent or all but absent in some states and the GRR deviates frequently from the course of the Mississippi along its run either due to the geography of the river or the decision-making authority of the states to determine areas of scenic or cultural interest that should be part of a traveler's experience on the Great River Road. Hence, sticking to the GRR isn't merely a matter of keeping the river in view or following a single stretch of roadway. GPS is also of little help since the patchwork of highways and bi-ways that comprise the GRR each have their own individual names. In short, trying to follow the Great River Road can be quite maddening.

US Highway 61 for example, which I rode south out of Saint Paul, runs from Wyoming, Minnesota all the way to New Orleans following the Mississippi River. US 61, sometimes called "The Blues Highway" is a designated part of the Great River Road for much of its route, but not the fifteen-mile segment from St. Paul to Hastings- the part of US 61 where I stopped to buy my scarf. With some confusion and an unplanned Google stop, I rejoined the Great River Road in Hastings, where I crossed the Mississippi for the first time since joining it.

The new Highway 61 Bridge in Hastings (a $120 million, free-standing above deck arch bridge that, at nearly 2000 feet in length, is the longest of its type in North America) made for a beautiful first crossing of the Mississippi. Opened in 2013, its construction schedule was moved up after concerns that its predecessor "Big Blue", a rusty and obsolete steel truss model that had stood for over sixty years, might fail under heavy use with concerns being heightened after the failure six years earlier of another steel truss bridge in Minneapolis that killed 13 people when it collapsed into the Mississippi during the evening rush hour on August 1, 2007.

The clean modern lines of the Highway 61 Bridge stand in brilliant orange contrast to the character of Hastings; a quiet town of about 20,000 that boasts 63 buildings on the National Register of Historic Places and has specific guidelines for the maintenance of its historic commercial district.

Just north of the new bridge in Hastings, US 10 splits off and heads east over the St. Croix River near its confluence with the Mississippi and into the scenic town of Prescott, the starting point of the Great River Road in Wisconsin, the entire route of which was voted "Prettiest Drive: The Ultimate Summer Road Trip" by the Huffington Post, beating out such epic routes as the Big Sur Coastal

Drive in California and even the Hana Highway in Hawaii.

Cold, euphoric, and somewhat disoriented, I missed the opportunity to head east into Prescott, and oblivious to the opinions of the readers of the Huffington Post and the glory of the Great River Road's Wisconsin side, followed the road on the Minnesota side, heading south and east on Minnesota 316 through a rolling sea of dull post-harvest farmland before rejoining US 61 just outside of Red Wing, my first planned tourist stop (and easily accessible by bridge from the more scenic Wisconsin side of the Great River Road).

The air was damp and chilly when I rode into Red Wing and I was glad for the chance to sit and enjoy an IPA and a bacon sandwich at Marie's Underground Grill and Tap House before walking across the street to the Red Wing Shoe museum on Main Street.

The museum's main draw is "The Big Boot", a size 638 ½ Red Wing 877 work boot that dominates the building's main entrance. Made to celebrate the company's centennial in 2005, the boot (which is 20 feet long, 16 feet high, and 7 feet wide, and fitted with a lace measuring more than a hundred feet) is large enough to accommodate a wearer twelve stories tall and would actually be too big for the Statue of Liberty's comparatively dainty foot. The Big Boot is the type of "only in America" attraction whose scale cannot be truly appreciated until you've seen it in person. I wandered up to it like a slack jawed five-year-old, barely able to see over the tip, snapping pictures with my iPhone from a variety of angles. Eventually, a Red Wing employee came over and offered to take my picture for me, but by then I already had probably a dozen frenzied selfies and waved off the offer of help.

After the colossal boot, the static displays, photos, and story boards on the museum's upper level couldn't hold my attention, and within minutes I was back on the cycle headed south on US 61 with a fresh set of hand-warmers in my gloves. With 91 miles to my planned stopping spot in Onalaska, Wisconsin and a late afternoon sunset fast approaching, I was burping IPA and cursing myself for not having left my house earlier in the day.

I rode south through Frontenac before the tarmac and the river shook hands again north of Lake City on Lake Pepin. The largest lake on the Mississippi River with a surface area of over forty square miles, Lake Pepin is named for Jean Pepin, a French explorer who settled there when the area was still part of a French Colonial effort in North America known as New France, an effort that wasn't abandoned until 1763 when the French surrendered the last of their claims under the Treaty of Paris. At its zenith, New France included the colonies of Canada and Louisiana as well as the entirety of the Mississippi River.

The drive along Lake Pepin through Lake City is magnificent even in the offseason, the coastline just a Frisbee throw from even the farthest travel lane of Highway 61, the west side of the highway lined with cottages, homes, and condominiums that look to have been transplanted from the New England Cape. South of Lake City, the glacial landscape soared and dipped, with a steep tree-lined bluff on my right and a quick drop off to the water below on my left making for ten miles of the best scenery I had yet ridden through.

As the time and miles passed, however; my attention turned more and more frequently to the unpleasant sensations of the damp wind probing its way into the gaps in my jacket and how quickly the day's cold gray frigidity nibbled away the meager heat generated by the chemical hand-warmers in my gloves and boots. I had left the house that morning wearing regular underwear, a single pair of cotton socks, a long sleeve t-shirt, jeans, and a thin athletic pullover. My riding gear consisted only of my borrowed chaps, uninsulated leather boots, a thick leather motorcycle jacket with a zip-in liner, a pair of mid-weight gauntlets, and the brand-new Nolan helmet I had picked up just the day before. Without the anti-fog insert in the visor, I had to leave it open slightly at the mouth to keep it clear, giving the insistent wind one more entrance into my fragile cocoon of body heat.

By the time I stopped for fuel at a Kwik-Trip in Goodview, just outside of Winona, I was questioning my jacket decision, cursing Kawasaki for not including heated grips on a touring motorcycle, and looking forward to warmer temperatures as I rode south. Sipping hot coffee from a paper cup and staring out at the pump island as dusk settled, I consoled myself with the idea that by the time I got down to Mississippi and Louisiana, highs would be in the upper 60s.

It was full dark and misting rain when I turned east off of US 61 in a construction zone and crossed the Mississippi into "The Sunfish Capital of the World", Onalaska, Wisconsin, on Lake Onalaska. The lake, technically a reservoir, was created when Lock and Dam No. 7 was completed in 1937 and at four miles across, is the widest spot on the Mississippi.

When Shannon had been unable to find a campground near La Crosse that was still open in November, I'd booked a room at the Stoney Creek Inn in Onalaska, honoring a pledge to myself to avoid big name hotels and restaurants, instead opting for regional or local options where possible.

The Stoney Creek Inn is a North Woods themed hotel and event center just off I-90 near a row of big box stores and a shopping mall. As I pulled up under the heavy timbered canopy at the Inn's main entrance, I was greeted by a Stoney Creek landmark, Marvin the Moose. A realistic, life-sized fiberglass statue of a moose, Marvin stands just across from the hotel's entrance in a shallow pool of clear water surrounded by river rocks.

He is kitschy and wonderful at the same time and I can imagine the hundreds of family photos in which Marvin must feature prominently, his close-lipped elementary school picture day smile and gently tilted head lending him a sort of dopey Midwestern friendliness. Dozens of Twinkie-sized goldfish swam between his thick brown ankles, unimpressed.

Marvin and his hotel were just what I needed at the conclusion of my first day's ride. The cold and damp had penetrated deep inside my clothes, and the rain slicked roads, construction barriers, rush hour traffic, and poor visibility of the last few miles had frayed my nerves. In the hotel lobby a friendly middle-aged woman greeted me warmly from behind the reception desk while a fire burned in a huge stone hearth framed by inviting leather couches.

Once inside my room, I cranked the heat up as high as it would go and took a long hot shower to get warm before setting about finding something to do for the evening. My expensive one-person tent sat folded up and waiting next to the canister of bear repellent in the bottom of one of the bike's saddle bags in the corner of the room, its inaugural use postponed by a night and I couldn't have been happier about it.

An hour later as my thin, grey-bearded cabbie, Jim, carried me southward across town toward the Pearl Street Brewery in his creaking Ford Windstar, the heavy mist I'd ridden in with had turned to a fine haze of rain that streaked across the windshield creating a glare against the lights along Wisconsin 16 and making it difficult to see.

"It's not my wipers," Jim announced, unprompted. "It's the damn wax they use at the carwash." A few long seconds ticked by accompanied by the slap and smear of the enfeebled wipers before he added. "They ought to ban it."

When Jim dropped me off a few minutes later in a darkened industrial park in front of the old La Crosse shoe building, I arranged for him to come back and pick me up at 7:45, closing time being 8:00 Tuesdays through Thursdays for the Pearl Street Brewery's tasting room.

Walking to the building's sleepy front steps as the cab pulled away, its tires shushing against the wet blacktop, I wondered if I'd regret the nearly two hours I'd committed to spending there. The workmanlike four-story red brick structure seemed all but lifeless with just a handful of lights burning behind its antique looking panes.

My concerns fell away when I entered the building's vestibule and saw the Pearl Street taproom to my left through another set of double doors. A small but raucous cadre of regulars huddled near the brewery's polished, half-moon shaped bar, behind which stood a row of gleaming stainless-steel vats and kettles. It was Wednesday, the night when bicyclists who ride in get their first pint for free. A handful of bikes leaning against the wall just inside the door helped explain the lack of cars in the lot.

Opposite the bar, a rustic hand-built wooden stage was perched on kegs between two painted concrete pillars and a local band was launching into a cover of the Beatles' "Eleanor Rigby". The group, a four-piece string band called Pigtown Fling fit the tap room's feel perfectly, lending the cavernous warehouse space an intimate pub-like atmosphere and making me feel welcome among strangers as I pulled up a seat at the bar and ordered a pint of

Lederhosen Lager, an Oktoberfest style seasonal brew that went down smoothly as I settled in and took in the surroundings.

A sign behind the bar listed the tap beers available, and unable to decide between them, I chose a tasting flight and visited with the bartender as he poured, mentioning it was my first day of a nine-day ride down the Mississippi. The bartender, a broad shouldered local with a red beard, reminisced for a moment about the location and how the La Crosse shoe company used to have tent sales there when they were still in occupancy. Then he wished me luck on my trip and told me that he had once had plans to canoe the river before a job offer got in the way. One thing led to another, and then, well…

I nodded in understanding, thinking about the dusty tarp of someday that had threatened to settle over my own trip.

I was into the second beer of my flight and making notes in a little leather notebook when a mid-twenties professional type settled onto the stool next to me and started working on a project of his own, something involving markers and a map.

The beer, the music, and the warmth of the atmosphere had its effect and soon we were chatting in the amiable way of beer warmed barfellows everywhere. The subject somehow turned to running (a habit I'd adopted more than a decade before as preemptive penance for my unwavering love of French fries) and he began to fill me in on the Hash House Harriers, a sort of international underground society of beer loving runners who organize and participate in semi-secret running events led by Hares, club members who lay out a course and mark it through a series of secretive clues and cryptic signs. Over his beer, he was preparing to hare an upcoming event.

The real purpose of a run for the Hash House Harriers is social, each one culminating in drinking and singing and general foolishness, all with the air of a clandestine fraternal society where members face various embarrassing penalties for violations real or invented, of club codes.

"You have to have a good sense of humor," my new friend explained, showing me the hand-written lyrics to a "It's a small dick after all", a drinking song he'd been required to memorize as part of his initiation.

He told me proudly of his nickname, "Mr. Pink" (nickname modified to protect Mr. Pink from having to drink PBR from his own sweaty running shoe) and talked about how Hashers have to earn their nicknames which become prized tokens of acceptance even though they're often disparaging.

Hashing sounded like the Masons, only way more fun. And with running. I wanted in.

Mr. Green gave me his phone number and invited me to contact him after my trip.

Exchanging phone numbers is always an awkward proposition among men, so we quickly excused ourselves from the conversation to return to our independent scribbling, working diligently to ignore one another after that from the distance of a single barstool.

Before I was ready, it was time to go outside and wait for Jim. I settled my tab and stepped out into the misty evening, warm, buzzed, and hungry. The owners of Pearl Street Brewery, Joe Katchever and his father, Anthony seemed to be on to something. Sixteen years into the beer making business they were producing over 3,000 barrels a year and their brew was on tap and in stores all over the area and even into Minnesota.

A few blocks from the Stoney Creek, I had Jim drop me at the Texas Roadhouse, where I had a New York strip and two baskets of their signature dinner rolls. I hadn't completed even a single day on the road and had broken my self-made promise to avoid national chains. Tomorrow was another day. I'd avoid chains then.

CHAPTER THREE

"Well, I built me a raft and she's ready for floatin'
Ol' Mississippi she's callin' my name…"
- Black Water, The Doobie Brothers

I left the heat turned up in the room overnight, sleeping on top of the covers and enjoying the luxury of being overly warm. It was difficult to want to go back out into the cold and I took my time reorganizing my saddlebags before carrying them out past Marvin the Moose and remounting them to my already filthy motorcycle.

Unable to resist the temptation, I paused for a selfie with Marvin before departing the hotel and stopping at another Kwik-Trip just up the block, this time for a slice of breakfast pizza and a large Red Bull. I ate my breakfast on a picnic table by the station's entrance before turning on my stereo and heading south out of Onalaska and into La Crosse to rejoin the Great River Road on the Wisconsin side.

With my first day's travel behind me, and having entered my second state, I once again felt a surge of elation. Less than twenty minutes passed before I stopped along Rose Street at the Indian Lacrosse Players Statue, marking the northern entrance to the city of La Crosse. The twenty-foot-tall bronze-looking fiberglass statue mounted atop a decorative rock base depicts three Ho-Chunk Indians playing "The Creator's Game" as it was known by the Native Americans who developed it centuries before the first Europeans set foot on the American continent.

The Native American version of the sport, popular among Great Lakes tribes, was similar to the field Lacrosse played at high schools around the country today only in the broadest way. The netted stick (or "crosse" in French), and the general object of reaching an opponent's goal remain, but whereas today's game is played by ten players on a hundred-meter field over a period of sixty minutes, traditional Native American variations sometimes had hundreds of players competing on a field of play that could stretch for miles with a match running from sunup to sundown. Competition took on the ritual, solemnity, and celebration of combat, with rival tribes playing for religious reasons or to settle disputes.

The Ho-Chunk Nation went on to sponsor the National Lacrosse League's St. Paul franchise, the Minnesota Swarm (with games hosted in the Xcel Energy Center, the home facility of the NHL's Minnesota Wild). In a press release announcing the partnership in late 2014, Ho-Chunk Nation President Jon Greendeer seemed genuinely pleased with the partnership and the sport's revival, saying that, "This game not only has its roots in our culture and heritage, it is vastly reclaiming its place as the activity of choice in Native communities today." Before I could finish this book, the Minnesota Swarm was vastly relocated to Duluth, Georgia by its owner John Arlotta.

Continuing south through downtown La Crosse and past the Oktoberfest Hall, the Doobie Brother's "Black Water" came up on my playlist and I smiled to myself as the opening notes gave way to the first verse. It was only just above freezing, and the air was thick again with humidity, but I was grinning like mad inside my helmet. In spite of my rushed planning and the lateness of the season, I was on the road. I had only about 200 miles to cover for the day before reaching my planned stopping point, a KOA campground in Rock Island, Illinois and was in the mood to travel at a relaxed pace, snapping photos as I went.

Just past the Mississippi River Bridge at Cass Street with the Doobie Brothers filling my ears, I spotted an impressive mural of a river boat painted on the side of a two-story brick building. I pulled into the lot next door and snapped a couple more pictures, marveling at the coincidence of the Doobie Brothers lyrics and the happenstance of stumbling across the paddle boat steamer mural. The mural, maybe 15 feet high and 45 feet across, depicted the sidewheel riverboat "War Eagle" at full steam toward the viewer, the majestic bluffs of the shore arching around her on the right like a protective hand. In the lower right corner, the mural gave her service dates as 1854-1870, just 16 years.

Built in Fulton, Ohio in 1854, the War Eagle was 219 feet long and had 46 staterooms. Luxuriously appointed, she served duty as a transport during the Civil War, escaping injury with the exception of a bullet hole to one of her smokestacks. Following the war, she returned to routine service carrying passengers and freight on the upper Mississippi until May 14th, 1870, when, while she was docked at the railroad depot less than a mile upstream from the site of her commemorative mural, a leaking barrel of kerosene was accidentally ignited by the ship's carpenter as he attempted to repair it. The fire quickly spread, dooming the War Eagle as well as a nearby barge and damaging two other riverboats. Seven people were killed in the accident and the fire quickly spread to the dock, the depot, and several neighboring buildings.

An article by Andrew Jalbert published in Big River magazine notes that the victims "included two children, two deckhands, James Geene, Felix Spiller (the ship's barber) and Mary Ulrich" who was on her way to her sister's wedding. Jalbert's article claims the value of the loss at over $360,000 and records that the wreck of the War Eagle was largely undisturbed until low water levels exposed her in 1931, allowing artifacts including silverware and dishes to be retrieved from the wreck.

The War Eagle was then left alone again until the early 1960's when scuba gear became available to the general public. Jalbert, who dived the wreck himself, says that although she has sunk into the muddy river bottom, nearly 200 feet of the War Eagle is still locatable. A marker from the Wisconsin Historical Society describes visibility in the water around the War Eagle as "near zero" and adds solemnly that her wreck remains "among a tangle of wood, metal and bricks from the burned buildings."

I hadn't known the fate of the War Eagle when I stopped to photograph her mural, only that she was compelling and beautiful there on that wall with the river sliding quietly past just a short distance away. Sometimes in our gentle ignorance, we're given the opportunity to see the beauty of something without the burden of some blacker truth, and so with the Doobies still singing their jaunty river song, I pulled back out onto the Great River Road and traveled less than half a mile before stopping again at a La Crosse landmark of an entirely different flavor.

    With a holding capacity that would fill over seven-million twelve-ounce cans, The World's Largest Six Pack stands somewhat less majestically than you might imagine just north of Mississippi Street at La Crosse's City Brewing Company, formerly the G. Heileman Brewery.

    Originally painted to resemble giant cans of Heileman's Old Style Lager, the six large holding tanks are now wrapped in a generic label that features a red diagonal ribbon with the words "La Crosse Lager" in a white Germanic font against a backdrop of running water, trees, and river rock. Near the base of each can is the slogan "Brewed with Pure Artesian Water". The old Heileman's plant now produces a variety of beverages under contract, including soft drinks, energy drinks, tea, and yes, even beer.

    Across the street, with his goblet thrust high in salute toward the mighty six pack, stands the statue of Gambrinus, the "King of Beer". He looks every bit the part, with a full beard, long flowing hair, a golden crown, and a red cloak accented with ermine fur. His left foot rests atop a small keg, lending him a slight "Captain Morgan" air, and perhaps in recognition of the King's fondness for suds, his designer endowed him with a royal paunch.

    By the time I rode out of town, with the river on my right and tree covered bluffs towering above the road on my left, it was nearly ten o'clock and had been almost an hour since I'd taken my selfie with Marvin the Moose. In that time, I'd covered just fifteen miles.

*****

Riding around in cars our whole lives spoils us to the reality of speed. We sit comfortably behind glass, interior temperature set just to our liking, our hands busy eating and drinking and texting, and our minds completely divorced from the brutality of the velocity with which we're hurtling along. That isn't the case on a motorcycle.

    Traveling at sixty miles an hour on a motorcycle, the air you're smashing your way through becomes a physical thing pushing back against the insult. It's hectoring and harassing and ceaselessly noisy. Vehicles passing from the opposite direction leave behind turbulent wakes that jostle the bike and semi-trucks push great bow waves of compressed air that dash into your exposed body like surf. You brace for them in anticipation, body tense, hands tight on the grips, willing the assault to be over quickly.

At sixty miles an hour on a motorcycle, you are keenly aware of the road. Its ridges and bumps and contours are felt in your hands and feet as it whooshes by underneath, naked and abrasive; ready to exact a toll if you become overconfident, inattentive, or just unlucky. At just sixty miles an hour, raindrops become stinging projectiles and insects pop like party favors against your clothes leaving behind paintball smears of their insides.

At sixty miles per hour on a bike, you don't eat or text or fiddle with the radio. Instead you are constantly aware of the majesty and wonder of motor travel and just how truly, blindingly fast you're moving compared to your own natural capacity. You're a fragile sack of organs hurtling down a ribbon of manufactured rock on a steel calliope horse, a metal bowl of gasoline nestled against your groin. It's wonderful and intoxicating and scary as hell all at the same time.

By the time I arrived in Prairie du Chien sixty miles and one hour out of La Crosse, I was cold and beaten. The temperature hovered just above freezing and the air was thick and wet. Gusts of wind up to twenty miles per hour hurled freezing wet air across the river at me and I was eager to switch to the opposite bank where hopefully, I would be somewhat better protected from its icy fingers.

I was grateful to spot a Cabela's on the outskirts of town. I walked around inside, helmet still on, prowling the menswear section for some kind of relief. I bought heavy duty thermal underwear and put them on under my clothes in a men's room stall. They were tight and black and made me feel like an eight-year-old ninja getting ready for bed. I also bought a fresh supply of chemical hand warmers and a pair of thin nylon gloves to slip inside my uninsulated gauntlets. The gloves had little metallic patterns on the thumb and forefinger, so I wouldn't have to go completely bare handed when I wanted to stop and take a picture with my phone.

There wasn't much to look forward to that day. All the best stuff was further down the river and I wasn't fully warm when I walked out of the cozy cabin feel of Cabela's and into the cold gray morning. I willed the sun to break through the clouds and comforted myself yet again that warmer weather waited further down the river. With only one way to get there, I climbed back on the Kawasaki, turned on the music and headed west across the Mississippi where I was welcomed to Iowa by a pink fiberglass elephant wearing a top hat.

If you look closely enough, the American roadside is practically littered with pink fiberglass elephants. There are pink elephants in Huntington, West Virginia, DeForest, Wisconsin, Roseville, Kentucky, Fenton, Missouri, Inverness, Florida, Cookeville, Tennessee, Hardeesville, South Carolina, Haubstadt. Indiana, Owego, New York, and (of course), Las Vegas, Nevada. Some carry cocktails in their trunks while others wear bikinis or Buddy Holly glasses. They serve as cheerful kitschy mascots for gas stations, car washes, RV centers, and liquor stores, but only one has waterskied for a president.

"Pinky" the Elephant stands outside the Lady Luck Casino in Marquette, Iowa on a spot that used to house the Pink Elephant Supper Club. Although there's a story online that describes Pinky as a discard from the 1964 Republican National Convention in San Francisco, she was most likely purchased new from a company called Sculptured Advertising in nearby Sparta, Wisconsin as a means to promote the Pink Elephant Supper Club by its owner Bob Ries[1].

Opened in 1963, The Pink Elephant Supper Club was a favorite among locals who called it simply "Pink's" and Pinky became a beloved Marquette landmark and erstwhile mascot for the town with tourists stopping for roadside pictures with the festively-colored yet tired-eyed pachyderm who stood on a roadside bluff overlooking the Mississippi River.

Enter Jimmy Carter, 39th President of the United States. In August of 1979, with his popularity badly waning and growing

---

[1] Bob Ries is often identified as Bob Reis, including on the placard that stands next to Pinky in front of the Lady Luck. Articles in the Des Moines Register from 1979 and 1980, as well as the Marquette Depot Museum both spell his last name Ries. Another article from the October 26, 1980 edition of the Des Moines Register references Virginia Ries and identifies her as the operator of the Pink Elephant Supper Club.

interest among his own party to replace him on the 1980 ticket with Senator Ted Kennedy, the President embarked on a weeklong riverboat vacation and whistle stop tour, cruising down the Mississippi from St. Paul to St. Louis. The first family and about thirty staff traveled aboard The Delta Queen alongside ordinary fare-paying vacationers like Charles Kaltmayer, a Missouri mailman who was impressed at how seemingly normal and approachable the President was.

There were multiple scheduled stops along the way where the President talked up the importance of energy conservation and tried to rally voters in advance of the coming elections. One such scheduled stop was in Prairie du Chien, directly across the river from the town of Marquette, Pinky the Elephant, and enthusiastic marketer Bob Ries.

When Ries got word of the President's scheduled stop at Prairie du Chien, he lugged Pinky down from her perch on the bluff and mounted her on a pair of pontoons. When the Delta Queen, carrying the President, his entourage, and a happy star-struck barber from Missouri ("[Carter's] just like one of us, and he dresses like one of us.") chuffed into port at Prairie du Chien on August 19th, Ries greeted "Steamboat One" towing Pinky the Waterskiing Elephant behind a sleek speedboat.

The following day, the Des Moines Register memorialized the feat reporting that when the Delta Queen arrived in Prairie du Chien, "The president was greeted by several pleasure boats in the river. Among them was a boat towing a huge pink elephant on a raft." Another Register article from the following spring says, "Ries and friends took the elephant water skiing on the river during President Carter's vacation here last summer. Secret Service men were not amused…"

"The Daily Diary of President Jimmy Carter" a White House document available on PDF and most notable for its minute-to-minute detailed chronology of even the most banal presidential activity, fails to give Pinky any mention whatsoever, simply recording that at 12:26 pm on August 19th, 1979[2] "The Delta Queen

---

[2] Internet versions of Pinky's water skiing escapade usually place it in 1978, or even during the 1976 campaign. The sign next to Pinky in front of the Lady Luck misidentifies the year as 1978 which probably led to the widespread discrepancy.

arrived at Prairie du Chien, Wisconsin."

The following November, Carter would suffer a landslide loss to former actor and California Governor Ronald Reagan while Pinky would go on to serve another nine consecutive presidential terms as the unofficial mascot for Marquette. She's still there today standing along 1st Street, top hat slightly askew, tired eyes looking out over the spot on the river she once shared with a President.

*****

Cresting the bluffs just south of Marquette in McGregor, I followed the Great River Road to the entrance of Pike's Peak State Park. As a native of Colorado Springs, nestled at the foot of the Rockies just east of Pike's Peak (14,110'), I was curious to learn about Iowa's own downscale version and ventured up the access road to take in the scenery and read the informational placards about the park and how it got its name.

Pike's Peak State Park is best known for its view from atop a five-hundred-foot bluff overlooking the confluence of the Mississippi and Wisconsin Rivers. The bluff is actually a Paleozoic Plateau, a piece of the original landscape left unscathed when Ice Age glaciers ground and flattened most of the surrounding area. Even in November, the park was beautiful and offered a view so majestic that I took multiple pictures of the water below disappearing off into the distant horizon in both directions, the bridge linking Prairie du Chien and Marquette still discernible in the Northern distance.

Explored by Father Jacques Marquette and Louis Joliet in 1673, the site was later reconnoitered in 1805 by Zebulon Pike who was tasked with determining its suitability for a fort. Although its fitness was obvious, the fort (Fort Crawford) was eventually built down in the Mississippi's floodplain near Prairie du Chien and was later moved three times due to repeated flooding; proving that government then was just as likely as government now to make poor decisions at great expense in the face of well-reasoned advice commissioned, paid for, and then completely ignored.

The park boasts over eleven miles of trails and paths, but with lunchtime approaching and nearly two-thirds of the day's ride still ahead, I felt the need to press on having explored little more than the main parking lot and a short section of the bluff.

Riding south from McGregor on the GRR gave me great expansive views of the Mississippi as it meandered and flowed far down below to my left, while pastoral farmland now bare for the season slipped quietly past on my right. The wind blew against me in the same angry gusts it had earlier in the morning and by the time I neared Sherrill, Iowa just outside of Dubuque and about 45 miles south of Pike's Peak State Park, it had stolen away a lot of the warmth I had managed to scavenge at the Cabela's in Prairie du Chien.

Riding slightly downhill into Sherrill, hungry and chilled, I spotted a portly three-story building with gables on the roof and an awning that ran most of the length of its front. Finished in red trim, there were neon beer signs in the window and another on the front door that read, "Welcome to The Barn". There were a handful of cars lined up on the blacktop and I wheeled in among them and climbed off the Kawasaki to head inside.

The Barn, profiled in a column called "Argosy's Food for Thought" on dubuque365.com, wasn't actually a barn at all, but rather had been converted from a hotel and general store. Continuously operated by members of the Breitbach family for over half a century The Barn is warm, inviting, and offers the kind of food you'd expect from a bar and restaurant keeping Iowa farmers happy since back when doctors recommended menthol cigarettes as a cure for smoker's cough. It was exactly the kind of place I was hoping to find when I'd promised myself I'd keep clear of national chains.

I found an open spot behind the massive wood bar that occupied the center of the main room and was greeted by a smiling female bartender while I was still folding my scarf and gloves up inside my helmet. She grabbed me a glass of water and a menu before returning to her banter with an elderly farmer wearing overalls and drinking a Busch Lite at the other end of the bar.

"You want another one of those" she asked him.

He passed on the beer and asked her how her kids were doing.

She ran down the latest calamities and then said, "I send my dog to obedience school. Maybe I should send them too."

"Maybe you should go yourself," he shot back.

She called him an ornery old goat and came back over to me. I ordered a BLT and a Coors Light and she went back to visiting with the farmer— the two of them lamenting the unusual cold. I smiled over at them and took in my surroundings.

The stools were the sturdy wooden high-backed kind you'd find in someone's out of date kitchen and the walls were paneled in real wood. Coins were laminated under the bar top and a variety of beer signs dotted the walls. Fox News was playing on a big flat screen across the room and a gaggle of old ladies were eating and gossiping around a table in the next room.

The BLT came quickly and went down well. It occurred to me that I'd ordered one for lunch the day before too. This one was even better than the first, with thick smoky bacon on Texas toast. The Barn was worn-in and comfortable, a warm place to hide and hole up against the cold, but like the ornery old goat down the bar from me, I declined a second beer and in the time it took me to finish my sandwich and get my helmet back on, I was back on the road and heading south.

To my delight after two days of riding through gray rain and mist, the sun had finally shaken off the clouds, bringing color and vibrancy to the chilled autumn countryside and allowing me to bask in the illusion of warmth as I rode through picturesque Dubuque and followed US-52 through St. Donatus joining the river again just outside of Bellevue.

In Sabula, US-52 wandered east across the river and I turned on to US-67 and followed it through the bucolic Iowa countryside down through the sleepy mid-western town of Clinton where the front lawns on the north side of town pitch upward from the sidewalks and little concrete stairways lead up to covered porches and where two-story brick facades line the old main street.

On the south end of town, US-67 is bordered equally by houses and small dated strip malls with discount stores and Chinese restaurants. At 11th Avenue, a newish Taco Bell kicks off a three-block festival of fast food places where Burger King, KFC, Jimmy John's, Wendy's, Subway, and McDonald's vie for business from nearby Ashford University and Mercy Medical Center.

In fact, Clinton County has one of the highest rates of death by heart disease in Iowa or the Upper Midwest, but residents can take comfort in knowing that homicide is a distant worry. The average Clinton resident is 171 times more likely to die from a heart attack than by a people attack. As recently as 2013, the state of Iowa was literally the last place in America someone could expect to be murdered. Peace through bacon.

I followed 67 down the river past grain elevators and railroad tracks and the billowing stacks of a power plant until it ran west for a short stretch, briefly becoming part of the transcontinental Lincoln Highway before dodging south again past a chemical plant and a mobile home park. The highway kept its distance from the Mississippi as the river bucked and shivered back and forth spitting out sloughs and backwaters all the way to Princeton where it finally settled down and agreed to flow straight once more.

Shannon had made me a loose itinerary for every day on the Great River Road. Each day included multiple tourist spots, more than I could possibly fit in; each day but the one in Iowa. There, she had simply recorded the information for the Rock Island Arsenal. A working military installation, the Rock Island Arsenal is home to the second oldest US Army museum and has an impressive collection of weapons on display. Among them is the M65 atomic canon.

Like something from a campy science fiction story, the atomic canon is exactly what its name implies. Developed in the early fifties and essentially obsolete not long after it was deployed, the M65 is the only canon ever to have fired an atomic weapon, a feat achieved during testing at the US Government's Nevada Test Site. A photo of the test, codenamed Grable, can be found online and features the M65 standing majestically in silhouette, long barrel pointing upward and away into the distance where an angry orange mushroom cloud roars upward against a blue sky. It's an image that would look right at home printed in the four-color Ben Day dots of a 1950's pulp comic. The original atomic canon, the one from the Grable test, is on display at Fort Sill, Oklahoma, but the Rock Island canon is one of just seven survivors of a production run that numbered only twenty.

Visitor hours on Rock Island are from sunrise to sunset, and first-time visitors must arrive by 3:00pm to be processed through the

Moline Gate. My relaxed morning pace found me over an hour late to gain access to the island and left only minutes to explore even if I had made it on, so instead I followed 67 across the Centennial Bridge from Davenport, Iowa into Rock Island, Illinois where Shannon had reserved a spot for me at the KOA on 78th Avenue.

After arriving at Onalaska the previous night after dark and in the rain, it was a relief to pull into the Rock Island KOA with the sun still up, if only just barely. The buoyant attendant (both meanings) let me have my pick of available sites in the nearly deserted campground and I chose one that backed up against a wooden privacy fence and a row of bushes which promised a little more shelter from the November wind.

I'd only tried putting up the Big Agnes once before- in my living room- and was glad to find it as easy as I had remembered. I managed to get the tidy grass campsite all set up and organized just as the last rays of that day's sun were making a slow retreat through the leaf-bare limbs of the trees. Having completed my longest ride ever and fighting against the cold for most of the way, I built a robust fire and suppered on a cold sandwich and a bag of chips from a nearby gas station washed down with a couple cans of beer.

My hips hurt and I was exhausted from the attentiveness that a day's ride on the Kawasaki had taken. With the sounds of the cracking fire all but drowning out the muffled traffic on 78th, I nestled right up against the stone fire ring and fell asleep on the patchy grass staring up at the stars and thinking about the road ahead.

CHAPTER FOUR

"I was a dam builder
Across the river deep and wide
Where steel and water did collide…
I slipped and fell into the wet concrete below"
- Highwayman, Jimmy Webb

Having fallen asleep by the fire and later crawling into my sleeping bag fully clothed, I woke up in a fragile cocoon of warmth breathing the freezing air of pre-dawn. A layer of frost had settled over the campground while I slept, leaving the windshield on the motorcycle a dusty gray.

I lingered for a while in my sleeping bag, enjoying the meager heat I'd managed to build and then showered in one of the KOA's tidy compact stalls, the water turned up almost as hot as it would go. I'd bought an extra-large camp towel from REI before the trip. It was a Kermit green people chamois and folded to fit inside a little mesh bag the size of a chewing tobacco pouch. Unable to find it amidst my tangle of clothes and supplies, I dried myself with the previous days campfire-scented t-shirt before quickly getting dressed and breaking camp.

The temperature was still below freezing when I fired up the Kawi and headed out to rejoin the Great River Road. Afraid that scraping away the frost might scratch the bike's Plexiglas windshield; I lowered it instead and rode away from the KOA with my helmet and shoulders buffeted by the crisp morning air.

In spite of the cold, the Friday morning sky was clear and the rising sun shone brightly through the trees sparkling on the river and exciting what color remained in the November landscape. At one point along Illinois 92, a construction crew was already at work and blocking one side of an intersection. Their flagman, a middle-aged black man with square shoulders and a round belly, flashed me a smile and a thumbs up as I rode past.

A few miles later, I crossed the Beckey Bridge over to the west side of the Mississippi and into Muscatine, Iowa, "The Pearl Button Capital of the World" and briefly the home of Mark Twain who spent the summer of 1855 as a writer for The Muscatine Journal, a newspaper partially owned by his brother Orion.

About the town, Twain later observed, "I remember Muscatine—still more pleasantly—for its summer sunsets. I have never seen any, on either side of the ocean, that equaled them. They used the broad smooth river as a canvas, and painted on it every imaginable dream of color... The sunrises are also said to be exceedingly fine. I do not know."

The sun was fully up on the pleasant river view as I rode into Muscatine's old downtown and along Riverside Park, where a docked riverboat caught my eye.

Diminutive compared to the large steamboats I was used to seeing hauling tourists around in St. Paul, the Pearl Button Paddlewheel is a compact and new side-wheeler. At 61 feet long and 24 feet wide, she was built in 1985 and at the time of her commissioning was the first side wheel paddleboat commissioned in over a hundred years. White and red, with ornate rails around her two passenger decks, the Pearl Button Paddlewheel ferries tourists (up to 100 at a time) on Mississippi River cruises offering a glimpse back in time with light refreshments along the way. "Beer is $3, Pop is $2," notes her website.

The ramp to the Pearl Button Paddlewheel was closed and I wandered over to look at the Mississippi Harvest statue, a 28-foot tall bronze sculpture of a Mississippi clam fisherman, paying tribute to the city's history. The thick shells of the local mussels made them perfect for button making and in 1905 Muscatine was producing a billion and a half buttons a year, which accounted for over a third of the world's entire supply. Pearl buttons as they were called, were eventually replaced by plastic ones which were faster, easier, and cheaper to produce.

As I rode out of town on Highway 61, the familiar pilot's wheel pointed me down Oregon Street and on to Stewart Road which ran past an assortment of neatly kept rural homes, old crooked farmhouses with peeling paint, and galvanized steel buildings with work trucks parked outside until it finally edged back toward the river at Coolegar Slough along the Mark Twain Wildlife Refuge.

As I followed County Road X61 down along bends and dips and over tiny concrete bridges through Port Louisa, the temperature hovered around 40 and a cruel gusting wind rose out of the south, stripping the heat from my body as I rode into it. Along Lake Odessa, a shallow backwater of the Mississippi, I decided to duck into the nearest place I could find to warm up.

Spotting a sign for Rocky's Landing, I eagerly pulled off the main road and coasted down the sloping tarmac of 97th Street toward the lakeshore. I was already fantasizing about a warm ceramic mug of coffee in my hand when I saw the sign announcing that Rocky's was closed for the season.

Dejected and cold, I got off the Kawasaki and just stood for a minute before rummaging through my saddlebag for a fresh packet of HotHands, the chemical hand warmers that were quickly becoming prized possessions. I tore open a plastic pouch, shook the two new warmers in the air to activate the charcoal inside them, shoved them deep into my gauntlets and reluctantly pushed on to the small town of Wapello across the Iowa River.

Turning left onto Highway 61 in Wapello around ten o'clock, I stumbled across the Jack and Jill, a squat country grocery store in a steel pole building next to a bank which displayed the commodity corn price out front on its digital sign. Stepping inside the Jack and Jill, I exchanged good mornings with the single cashier as my eyes took in the cracked and peeling linoleum tiles and the tired looking racks of familiar staples. Whether or not it had always been the Jack and Jill, the store had been there awhile, serving hard duty with little maintenance.

I found my way toward the back and paid for a cup of self-serve coffee at a counter that also sold fried chicken and soft serve ice cream. The counter was flanked by a little squadron of woodgrain Formica booths and I slid into one with a view of the bank and cradled my coffee like a baby chick as I tried to warm up.

The girl from the deli counter wandered over and started wiping down the other tables before asking me what I was doing riding a motorcycle on such a cold day. When I told her, she called me crazy and then added. "Iowa sucks. I want to move to Wyoming."

Matt Damon stared down at us from a nearby promo poster for The Monuments Men, his expression earnest and purposeful above an olive colored field jacket.

"What's the matter with Iowa?" I asked.

"It's too hot in the summer and too cold in the winter," she answered before wishing me well and starting back toward the counter, leaving me to my Styrofoam cup of black coffee.

I drank it slowly, flipping through a local ad circular. Then I drank another, staring out the window at my bike and wondering how cold it was in Wyoming.

*****

With a couple cups of hot coffee in me and with fresh HotHands in my gauntlets, boots, front pockets, back pockets, and the breast pockets of my jacket, I climbed back on the big Kawi and headed out of Wapello to the south, following Highway 61 until I came to County Rd H22 and turned left, headed east back toward the Mississippi and the Great River Road.

I had only been gone from the Jack and Jill about fifteen minutes when I spotted a little church beside the road. Other than a dilapidated barn a mile or so back, it looked to be the only manmade structure around. It was just a single story with whitewashed wood clapboard siding and a black shingled hip roof. A little gabled porch covered the stairs leading to the entrance and it was flanked by a white bell tower about thirty feet tall with gothic openings set into square frames at the top.

The church stood alone in the southwest corner of County H22 and 123rd Avenue, a narrow crushed gravel road. Its sparse lawn, the only green in the brown autumn landscape, was ringed by a spindly black wrought iron fence and a small cemetery with several dozen headstones occupied the side yard. A crooked wooden sign out front said, "Fairview Community Church". Another sign above the first one read,

EST 1885
NEW BUILDING 1905
NEW BEGINNING 1998

The whole scene was lovely and charming and maybe even a little spooky. Standing alone out there in the country, the Fairview Community Church reminded me of the country church from Kill Bill. Except it isn't really fair to say it was standing alone. In fact, it wasn't the church that had compelled me to stop.

Immediately across from the church, on the opposite side of the gravel road, stood a six or eight-foot-tall statue of an angry black gorilla locked in a perpetual stare with the little white building, its congregants, and all their new beginnings. The gorilla had one arm raised in an angry defiant fist, the other one low and forward, the hand open and choking.

It stood with its feet apart on a broad concrete base, its bared teeth painted a shocking white, its eyes bright yellow disks with small black pupils. The word "Fairview" had been painted across the gorilla's massive pecs and had been split in half to accommodate the beast's physique so that "FAiR" was painted on his right pec sloping down with the contour of the muscle, and "ViEW" was painted on his left, sloping up. Below that, in all caps across the barreled abs of his belly, was painted the word, "ZOO". FAiRViEW ZOO.

With no further sign or explanation, I stood on a gravel road in Southeastern, Iowa between the Fairview Church and the Fairview Zoo, which apparently was a one animal outfit featuring a single lifeless, yet still somehow remarkably animated, gorilla. I was torn between alternate visions of Fairview. On one hand, they might be a small town of god fearing animal lovers earnestly trying to gather the scratch to finish a zoo project well enough begun with the installation of a gorilla at the future site of the welcome center. On the other hand, they might be a god-fearing bunch of regular Iowans with one smartass neighbor who will remain forever unwelcome at the spring potluck.

With no idea which was the case, I sidled up under the raised arm of the gorilla and took a selfie, deciding that whether he was snarling or smiling might actually be a kind of attitudinal Rorschach test, like the fun optical illusions you sometimes stumble across online ("Do you see a beautiful woman or an old crone?").

Selfie complete, I situated my motorcycle in front of the church for a contrasting shot, the wispy clouds against a crisp blue sky framing the church and adding to its bucolic charm.[3]

Still smiling from my encounter with the Fairview gorilla, I turned back out onto County H22 and rejoined the Great River Road a few miles east at County Road 99. Here the GRR runs parallel with the Mississippi, rolling through miles and miles of Iowa farmland dotted with barns and pickup trucks. I rode through the sleepy hamlet of Kingston and followed the gentle curves and dips of 99 past more fields and farms and over Flint Creek into the city of Burlington. At the Bluff Harbor Marina, the GRR rejoined the Mississippi and followed Main Street through Burlington (which once served as first the capital of The Wisconsin Territory, and then the capital of the Iowa Territory) before rejoining Highway 61.

About 90 minutes after my stop in Fairview, I rolled into downtown Fort Madison, Iowa. A replica of the old army fort sits on the river in a park just off the GRR, its sturdy wooden buildings and walls gray with age. I was looking it over as I passed, wondering whether or not I should stop when a diner on the opposite side of the road caught my eye.

Occupying a tidy spot on the corner, The Fort Diner is a tiny white box with blue trim and an awning declaring it the "HOME OF THE WALLYBURGER". A shiny band of stainless steel frames the slanted roof and a couple of newspaper boxes mark the front entrance.

I was almost past it by the time I even registered its existence and I had to go around the block to get a second look, deciding as I did that I'd stop for lunch if they were open.

Stepping inside I found it not only open, but packed. The few small tables along the window and each of the eight or ten round vinyl stools along the counter were all occupied by people who looked like locals and probably regulars— tradesmen mostly. The whole place was small enough that each time the front door opened, pretty much everyone looked up to see who was coming or going. I

---

[3] As it turns out, the gorilla is a roadside marker for the Fairview Zoological Farm, where DeWayne and Melinda Connolly keep nearly 300 animals including lemurs, an anteater, and a Watusi steer. The zoo is open only on weekends and is located south of the Fairview Community Church down 123rd Ave.

felt like an outsider as I took the only open seat, a spot at the counter just inside the front door and directly across from the grill. On my right was a stack of 30-count egg cartons. Behind me, on the door of a white refrigerator, was a child's scribbled Crayon drawing.

The worn laminate counter was sea-foam green and sweet rolls on saucers covered with plastic wrap were placed at regular intervals there among the sugar dispensers and red plastic ketchup bottles. There were photocopied menus on green and orange paper, but the menu was also on the wall opposite the counter. The white plastic backlit sign offered four rows of items, each with a corresponding price in red plastic letters. The "WALLY" and "JAKES STEAK & EGGS" were the most expensive at $10.25. If you were looking to eat cheap, a single egg could be had for $1.20. In between were the "THUNDER BURGER", "THE THRILLER", "THE MESS", "THE BIG EASY", and the "EGG STANWICH". There was also a dry erase board with daily specials, including meatloaf, mashed potatoes, and green beans for $6.50.

As soon as I was settled, a frenzied waitress slid a plastic tumbler of ice water in front of me and asked if I was ready to order. Fresh from the cold and determined to do a better job of eating like a local, I ordered the special. While I waited, an older woman in a full-length coat stepped inside the door rubbing her hands together and clomping her feet. "Just getting warm," she announced to the room. She walked in place for a minute or so and then slipped out the front door, a rush of cold air accompanying her exit.

Across from me, the cook was working to keep pace with the lunch crowd, his movements fluid and graceful. He had thinning silver hair and wore a red t-shirt which stretched tight across his broad shoulders. The waitress called him Jake, as in Jake's steak and eggs, and Jake and Walt's Fort Diner (I had missed the "Jake and Walt's" on the sign out front). "You're Jake?" I asked. "Is this your place?" He agreed and said that he was one of the owners.

I wanted to ask more, talk to him about the diner, its history and how long he'd owned it, but he was busy cooking and there was just enough curtness to his reply to put me off.

Soon my lunch arrived— a generous slab of seasoned meatloaf seared brown at the edges, a scoop of mashed potatoes covered in brown gravy, and a side of green beans with meaty hunks of bacon mixed in. As I ate, a big-eyed girl sitting next to me struck up a conversation. She asked me where I was going and when I told her I was riding down the Mississippi to New Orleans, she eagerly recounted a trip she'd taken there including many funny details and stories about people I'd never meet. She followed up by saying she'd lived in Louisville, Kentucky for a while and was hoping to move back. She told me about her boyfriend and shared that since money was tight Louisville would have to wait, but that she was definitely going back. "Iowa's too cold," she said. In perfect punctuation to her point, a customer walked out the front door making way for a frigid wind that rushed through the gap and washed over us.

A moment later, the waitress noticed a forgotten Styrofoam container on the counter in front of the customer's vacant stool. She snatched it up and ran outside calling after them, only to return again a few seconds later with the container still in hand. Two more blasts of cold air.

"Somebody forgot their lunch," the waitress said and handed the container over to Jake who sat it behind the counter.

My check came and while I waited for my change (cash is preferred at The Fort Diner), I tried once again to strike up a conversation with the silver haired cook. Having ordered and complimented the special, made a temporary friend with a local girl, and sat through a couple of arrivals and departures, I thought Jake might be more inclined to give me a moment.

I was intrigued by some of the naming on the menu. Jake's steak and eggs were there and so was the egg Stanwich, which I thought was clever. I said as much and asked if Stan was also one of the owners. Jake didn't acknowledge the question, so I asked it again, thinking maybe he'd been distracted or hadn't heard me. This time, he excused himself and went outside to get something from the cooler.

When the waitress handed me my change, she glanced outside toward the cooler and said, "Stan was his brother that died." She looked at me with a mixture of consolation and condemnation and added, "Sore subject."

I may not have known any better, but it was time for me to go.[4]

Leaving Fort Madison, I felt awkward and a little ashamed. I hadn't meant any harm, but that didn't mean I hadn't caused any. I wanted to get back on the open road and put some distance between myself and the fumbled exchange. Instead I was stopped twice to sit on my idling motorcycle and wait as long freight trains lumbered past oblivious to me, Jake, and the big-eyed girl with the dreams of heading back to Louisville.

*****

The Great River Road follows US-61 south out of Fort Madison until turning east and joining the Mississippi River Road just north of Montrose. The transition couldn't be more dramatic. While that part of Highway 61 is a freshly-laid four-lane divided highway barreling through a nondescript landscape, the turnoff onto the Mississippi River Road leads immediately through the sleepy river town of Montrose, strolling past houses and parks and stately historical buildings at twenty miles per hour before snuggling right in against the river and disappearing uphill into a picturesque tree-lined lane, its sun-dappled surface narrow and unmarked.

After a half mile or so, county maintenance picks up the road, widening it, painting it with traffic lines, and raising the speed limit to fifty. Still, the essential character of the stretch is not lost, as the road continues to wind and dip along the lazily passing river while trees, wild bushes, and grass creep up on it from both sides.

The view was so pleasant and the gentle curves and undulations of the road so gratifying to ride that I stopped twice to take pictures; once next to a pond south of Montrose and again on a sweeping uphill s-curve just north of Keokuk that I rode up and then immediately turned and rode back down again just for the pleasure of doing it twice.

Riding between Montrose and Keokuk was like riding through a museum diorama of America- at least the Iowa part. There would be different dioramas later, on other sections of the road, telling a different American story. But in this hall, the Hall of the

---

[4] Many months later while working on this book, I looked up Stan's obituary online. It felt like snooping. One of eight siblings (including his brothers Walt and Jake), Stan was only 53 when he died.

Happy Midwest, the curator had placed crisp American flags on front yard poles to catch The Mississippi River breeze while fathers and sons fish from the banks. In Sandusky, he had placed a quaint Methodist church on a tree-lined slope inside a gentle curve. Its whitewashed wood sides were capped with a steep pitched roof and a brick chimney, and a permanent sign out front announced, "WORSHIP SERVICES - 9:00 A.M.". If you look the church up on Google Street View, you'll spot a homegrown vegetable stand on the corner across the street, its bounty overflowing a small folding table, its proprietor trusting payment to the honor system.

In Keokuk, the road makes one last dramatic sweep uphill, narrow and tree-lined once again, before cresting a bluff and opening up for an expansive view of the river to the left, with 57-acre Rand Park on the right. The park has a long row of benches facing the river and spaced at regular intervals all along its eastern boundary. Among them, gazing out over the river and across to Illinois stands a statue honoring Chief Keokuk, for whom the city was named.

Keokuk is remembered principally for his pragmatic cooperation with the U.S. Government including a role in the ceding of some six-million acres of land in Iowa following a bloody territorial dispute. As part of the settlement, Keokuk and his Sauk tribe were to be given a four-hundred-mile expanse surrounding their village. This land was eventually taken from the Sauk, and Keokuk and his people were relocated to a reservation in Kansas, where he died of dysentery in 1848 at the age of 60. In 1883, his remains were disinterred, moved to Keokuk, and placed at the memorial site in Rand Park. The statue created in Keokuk's honor by Iowa sculptor Nellie Walker, was added in 1913.

Continuing past Rand Park, the Great River Road follows a city street, wide and bordered with sidewalk on each side, into a quiet residential neighborhood where large historic homes sit well back from the curb among mature trees and broad, well-tended lawns. I followed Park Place down to the awkward cul-de-sac where it ends in a yellow concrete lip, tall for a curb, short for a wall, that keeps unwary drivers from toppling down the steep bank and into the river. It was there on a quiet residential street that I got my first look at one of Keokuk's most interesting landmarks- the Keokuk

Power Plant and Lock and Dam No. 19.

The Keokuk hydro plant wasn't on my itinerary and I had no way of expecting it as I puttered along Park Place admiring the weathered grandeur of the mansion-like homes at its south end. Having reached the end of the road, I stopped to admire the view of the river and found myself immediately thrown into boyish excitement and wonder at the marvel rising up out of the water far below to meet me nearly at eye level.

An imposing industrial age behemoth, spotting the Keokuk power station for the first time was like looking down and noticing the rusting hulk of the Titanic crawling up the Mississippi shoreline, except that the Keokuk power station is over twice as long as the great ship and still in operation, belching out electricity from enormous generators the likes of which mankind had never seen when they were placed in service in the summer of 1913.

The Keokuk Energy Center, as it's known today, rises ten stories above the water and includes one of the world's largest concrete monolith dams at nearly a full mile in length. Providing power as far away as St. Louis, the twenty-five-million-dollar engineering marvel once drew tourists from all over the country. One such eager visitor was Frank G. Carpenter, whose first-person account of his tour was published in Raleigh, North Carolina's The Farmer and The Mechanic in November of 1913, just a few months after the opening of the plant.

Carpenter's description of the power plant, gushing with amazed wonder begins,
"Think of dropping a force equal to 200,000 horses all pulling at once, right out of the skies into the center of one of the busiest populations on earth. That is what has been done at Keokuk power plant. Talk of the palace of Aladdin and the slaves of the lamp. The Aladdin of the Mississippi valley is Hugh L. Cooper, the engineer who conceived and built the Keokuk dam, and the slaves of the lamp are the waters of this great river, which for ages and ages will now go on laboring day and night for the nation."

Carpenter's astonishment at the awesome power generating potential of the plant was well founded. Before the plant opened, electricity had been generated only locally, with the farthest transmission being eleven miles. Cooper and the engineers at

Keokuk didn't just double, or triple, or even quadruple that. Instead, from its first day in operation, the Keokuk facility provided power as far as 140 miles away - over twelve times the previous record. It would be as if, years later having successfully placed a man in orbit, NASA skipped the moon entirely and decided instead to set out straightaway for Mars.

The immense powerhouse at Keokuk, largely unchanged from the day of its grand opening, is over 1,700 feet in length and 132 feet wide with its foundation moored in bedrock twenty-five feet below the natural river bottom. Referencing the length of the dam and the size of the powerhouse, Carpenter remarked on how hard it was to believe their dimensions. "It is only when we climb down the hundreds of steps and tramp our legs tired in going through the miles of construction that we realize these things are so."

Eager to get a better look at the massive concrete and brick structure, I followed 4th Street down into the old business district and turned left on Main, where just a couple of blocks down, I was able to turn off onto what used to be the entrance to the Iowa side of the Keokuk Municipal Bridge, before it was closed to car traffic in 1985 when its replacement opened immediately to the south.

A double-deck swing arm structure, the municipal bridge is still occasionally used by rail traffic, but the swing arm (which is near the entrance to the bridge on the Keokuk side) now rests in the open position with river traffic having the right of way.

The upper deck entrance to the bridge remains in place and has been converted to a public observation platform for viewing the powerhouse, lock, and dam. The original toll booth stands at the entrance, the blacktop roadway there now replaced with decorative cobblestones leading up to the bridge deck where wooden planks have been laid, giving the wide pedestrian walkway a boardwalk feel.

It was lunchtime on a colder than usual early November Friday and I had the observation deck to myself as I walked out to the end to gaze across the yawning gap between the observation deck and the open swing arm of the elderly bridge, the skeletal steel frame of the structure dark and spindly against the sky on both sides of the opening. To my left, upriver, was the mighty powerhouse and dam. In a fit of wonderment, I took about two dozen pictures of it with the Canon D-SLR that would remain otherwise almost entirely unused for the duration of my trip, its retrieval and stowage being a giant pain in the ass among the tight quarters in the Kawi's saddlebags, jammed as they were with bear repellent, hand warmers, and mysteriously disappearing REI camp towels.

Later, while searching through old newspaper articles from the time of the dam's construction, I stumbled across a familiar legend- that of a worker entombed in concrete. In the case of the Keokuk dam, the story is that a worker was discovered missing at roll call but wasn't found until weeks later when his hand was spotted sticking out of one of the dam's concrete sections after the wooden forms were removed. At that point, a rescue effort would have been in vain and any attempt to recover his remains would have meant significant damage to both the corpse and the structure of the dam, so he was simply left there, a ghastly and unintended addition to the project.

This story was published in dozens of local and regional papers as well as in the Detroit Free Press, the San Francisco Chronicle and The New York Times over the weekend of December 14th and 15th, 1912. The Moberly Weekly Monitor, which after providing the same general information as all the other articles, played the incident like a campfire ghost story- speculating that the dead worker "may haunt the dam, and at night, when a lone watchman casts his eye over the dam, he may see the ghost playing hide and seek among the piers…"

In spite of the widespread newspaper coverage from December 1912, I couldn't find any follow-up stories or any other mention of the tragedy. Similar stories have been told about unnamed workers entombed in other great engineering works, most notably the Hoover Dam. A few years before the Keokuk story, there was a rumor of worker trapped and left to die inside the double hull of the Titanic during her rapid construction, and prior to that of a worker similarly entombed in The Leviathan (later renamed the Great Eastern), a ship six times the size of any previous liner.[5]

---

[5] The Leviathan in fact was so large that she refused to enter the water. At her public launch in November of 1857, for which three-thousand spectator tickets had been sold, the steam winches that were to move her into the water were not up to the task. Two further attempts were made over the next three weeks which also

These unverified stories of entombment have been attributed to the collective fears of a generation rapidly transitioning from an agrarian to an industrial age. Certainly I felt small against the imposing stone face of the Keokuk facility, and there was something fascinatingly sinister in its hulking form. Reflecting a boldly masculine design aesthetic from a time when engineers flaunted their dominance over the natural world (Carpenter breathlessly proclaiming of the Mississippi River, "That rampageous old water-broncho has been lassoed by the cowboys of modern progress, and she is now plugging away and doing work like a cart-horse"), it's no surprise that visitors still find themselves in awe of the gigantic structure.

*****

Just outside of Keokuk I crossed the Des Moines River on US-136 and entered Missouri. The sun was brilliant in a cloudless sky and even though I was still bundled up in my freshly bought scarf and long underwear, the weather was the best I'd had. I pulled to side of the road and took a picture with the blue "Missouri Welcomes You" highway sign, feeling like I was finally beginning to put some distance between myself and the bastard cold that had chased me down the river for three days. It was 62 degrees, the highest the temperature would get that day and one of the highest I'd see on the entire journey.

The Great River Road whisked along a characterless four-lane stretch of Highway 61 until it found a way to reach for the river again just north of Canton. I followed it south across the Wyaconda River on a rusty old single-lane truss bridge and into La Grange, where I pulled into a vacant, weedy parking lot beside the road to take a shot of the Kawi against the backdrop of an abandoned brick building. Long and low and industrial looking, a number of its gridded window panes had been broken by vandals. A chain link

---

failed even after the addition of hydraulic rams. It wasn't until January 31st of 1858 that her builders finally managed to get the Leviathan into the water assisted by an unusually high tide, strong wind, and a newer more powerful set of rams. The launch effort itself cost nearly two-hundred thousand British Pounds, nearly a third of the original cost estimate for the entire ship.

fence kept out would-be explorers and after a few failed attempts to capture the upside-down beauty of decay, I fired up the bike and headed south toward Bowling Green where Shannon had booked me at the Cozy C Campground. Between rushed planning and the shaky nature of Great River Road signage, the ball got dropped entirely at the city of Hannibal.

Highway 61, for the most part, makes a wide four-lane, no-nonsense, southward plunge through the Missouri countryside, miles west of the meandering foolishness of the Mississippi River. This isn't the best recipe for a scenic byway celebrating the beauty and history of the river, so when it moves briefly eastward through Hannibal, Highway 61 passes the baton to the much better suited Missouri 79 which winds and darts and cuts through bluffs, and otherwise does its best to follow Carpenter's "rampageous old water-broncho" in a scenic and byway-ish way.

Taking no notice of the signage if there was any, I rode boring, economical Highway 61 right through the heart of Hannibal and onward toward Bowling Green, missing the turn for Missouri 79 entirely. Riding the thirty miles between Hannibal and Bowling Green on 61 and believing it still to be the GRR, I silently catalogued my annoyance with the Missouri DOT and the poor job they had done selecting that piece of unremarkable highway to be part of the Great River Road.

Hannibal, by the way, which I sped through with the efficiency of a long-haul trucker on a four day run, has the distinction of being the boyhood home of Mark Twain and the setting for The Adventures of Tom Sawyer AND The Adventures of Huckleberry Finn, sometimes called "The Great American Novel", facts on which the itinerary Shannon had prepared for me was entirely silent.

Instead I made a beeline toward Bowling Green to sample the offerings of Bankhead Chocolates, a local candy company founded in 1919. A visit to Woods Smoked Meats was also on the docket. Learning more about the man William Faulkner described as "the father of American literature" and whose fame was intimately tied with life on the Mississippi would just have to wait for my next once-in-a-lifetime solo motorcycle trip down the Great River.

In all fairness, I do like chocolate. A lot. Shannon knows

this. She's seen me go after a caramel pecan turtle like a man with a score to settle. I also like smoked meats. Hell, I'd been on the road only three days and had ordered a BLT for lunch twice. Shannon has seen me sprawled out and napping on every Christmas morning for decades, full of eggs and bacon and caramel rolls and assorted chocolates like a tired boxer between rounds just waiting to waddle back into the ring. She has never once heard me utter a word about Mark Twain.

I rode into the Cozy C campground just around 4:00 to secure my spot and get Agnes set up while I still had daylight. Clean and sparing, the Cozy C is primarily meant as an RV campground, laid out as it is in neat rows with crushed gravel drives and closely cropped grass between the hookups. The owner/manager met me near the office on a spiffy white golf cart and showed me to a tent camping spot immediately next to a large covered pavilion. There was a bonfire pit rimmed with flat stones and a stack of free wood. The spot was just across from the caretaker's house if I needed anything. Other than a single RV parked at the other end of the campground, the place was entirely deserted.

My spot was basically a lawn separated from the road by a broad gentle ditch. I wasn't worried about bears so much as someone falling asleep on highway 54, wandering off the shoulder and running me over. It would be like camping in someone's front yard-their large and well-tended front yard that happened to have a picnic pavilion, a mini-golf course, a row of RV spots, and an office/store/laundromat. Like that kind of front yard.

I quickly set up my tent and headed to town to try and catch the scene at Woods Smoked Meats before they closed for the day. Woods Smoked Meats is a family operation that's been around for over sixty years and has won over 500 state, national, and international awards. If you run by that sentence too quickly, the number 500 doesn't have a proper chance to register. Five-hundred. I have a couple of plaques in my office and the bibs from thirteen 5k races. Bibs aren't an award, mind you. They're a souvenir. They're the participation trophy for a 5k race. And technically, you can get the bib without running the race, so even with the bib; you're kind of on the honor system. I can't imagine earning 500 awards. Even spread over sixty years, that's still an award every month and a half.

Only you know they didn't come in like that. They came in little flurries and great deluges, punctuating generations of excellence.

Inside the store at Woods, framed awards cover almost every available wall space and they definitely aren't participation ribbons. They are for things like 1997 American Cured Meat Championships Reserve Grand Champion (smoked country ham), 1999 American Cured Meat Championships Reserve Grand Champion (cooked summer sausage), and 2002 American Cured Meat Championships Reserve Grand Champion (meat snack stick). And lest you think this American Cured Meat Championships thing is rigged, there is also a gold medal from the Internationaler Qualitatswettbewerb fur Schinken (boneless ham), and another from the same organization for bratwurst (that's right, the Germans gave Woods a gold medal for bratwurst). There's a framed cover of Meat & Poultry ("The industry's leading magazine") with Ed Woods on the cover in a ball cap and red apron. The awards and accolades go on and on.

It was after five when I walked through the door of the rustic wood-paneled building into Woods store and deli (1-800-I-LUV HAM), nowhere near enough time to take in all the awards and barely time to select a few different types of "SWEET BETSY from PIKE" jerky and sausage to sample and carry home for gifts. The woman who helped me was kind and patient, telling me to take my time looking around, but I'm not the guy who makes someone stay late at the end of their shift just so I can gawk. I took a handful of pictures, stared longingly at the fresh meat offerings behind the glass of the deli counter knowing I didn't have a good way to prepare them, paid for my souvenirs and left, hoping I might still have a chance to grab some chocolates from Bankhead.

Bankhead Chocolates, like Woods Smoked Meats, has been around awhile. Founded in 1919 by Thomas Jefferson Bankhead (great-grandson of THAT Thomas Jefferson), Bankhead is currently owned by April Foster whose family has kept the operation going for the last quarter century. Their current location is in a pink-painted brick building with an old fashioned white railed porch out front. Lace curtains hang in the picture windows that frame front doors with oval glass inserts.

Stepping inside is like stepping into the home of a

Midwestern grandmother. Oak tables and chairs with spindle backs offer patrons a place to sit and a gift shop with local crafts and cards and the sorts of whatnottery that late-middle-aged women like to buy fills a portion of the open space in front of Bankhead's long wooden display case.

The store was vacant when I walked in and I was already at the counter looking over a limited selection of chocolates when a teenaged girl came out of the back and seemed a little surprised to see me. Apparently, the store had just closed and she'd been putting away the inventory for the evening and had forgotten to lock the front door. I quickly apologized, but she encouraged me to look around, said an apology of her own for the reduced selection at that time of the day and introduced herself as Erica. While I picked out a peanut butter cup and a chocolate covered orange peel, she told me a little bit about the shop and gave me a business card, writing the owner's name on the back in precise curving script.

A few minutes later, standing in the parking lot out front, I tried the peanut butter cup I'd just bought. It was so smooth and creamy and tasted so authentic compared to the mass marketed peanut butter cups I'd grown used to over the years. I wondered how something so rich and indulgent had gotten reduced to the grainy, corrugated disks I knew from a hundred vending machines. And in that answer lies the explanation of how boutique chocolatiers like Bankhead are still around, lace curtains and all.

Afterward, I rode into quaint downtown Bowling Green and right across from a county building and war memorial found a crowded Mexican restaurant, Dos Primos, where I had a combination plate and a bottle of Pacifico while sitting at the bar and enjoying the sounds of people visiting all around me.

I'd been on the road for over two days and had only minimal interaction with anyone. Rather than feeling lonely, I was liberated by my solo vacation. I was in charge of when and where to stop, what to eat, and what to listen to on the radio. I'd enjoyed hours alone with my thoughts and the scenery. When I paid my tab and walked outside, the night was dark and cool, and the street was quiet except for the sound of a church bell ringing. Riding out of another small brick-fronted downtown I felt like a mysterious wanderer in a Saturday afternoon spaghetti western.

Back at the Cozy C, I got a fire going in the fire pit and carried a garbage bag of dirty clothes to the laundry room, stopping at the bathroom next door to change into the next day's clothes so I could wash what I'd worn that day. In only jeans and a t-shirt, I piled everything I'd already worn into a single machine and turned to look for the little wall-mounted vending station for detergent and softener. Only there wasn't any vending station. Assuming there always would be; I hadn't brought any detergent, just a Ziploc baggies full of quarters.

Where you'd expect to find the vending station, there was instead a sign, printed from a computer and laminated. It said:

COZY C LAUDROMAT GUIDELINES
PLEASE, DO NOT SET ON THE EQUIPMENT/SORTING TABLE
PLEASE DO NOT DYE CLOTHING IN THE WASHERS – OR WASH CLOTHING THAT HAS TAR, OIL, ETC. ON THEM – OR WASH RUGS/HEAVY ITEMS
WE ARE NOT RESPONSIBLE FOR UNATTENDED CLOTHING
FEEL FREE TO SING, TO READ, TAKE/EXCHANGE BOOKS/MAGAZINES
ALL DONE! GO SHOPPING/NAP! HAVE A DRINK! HUG ON!

Accompanying each line was a somewhere in the ballpark appropriate emoji. The line about not dying your clothes had an angry gray vampire thing with wings and fangs. "HAVE A DRINK!" featured a buzzed looking smiley inspecting a glass of wine.

I was trying to decide if Head & Shoulders would make an acceptable laundry detergent if used in the correct amount when I spotted a discarded bottle of liquid Tide in the plastic garbage bin by the door. What remained in the bottle was probably the correct amount if it had been Head & Shoulders. I used it anyway, holding the bottle upside down over the wash tub for long passing seconds before shaking it to release the last stubborn drops of viscous blue liquid still clinging reluctantly to the sides.

Feeling proud of my thrift and pluck ("Ah, that's the way they used to, Rusty"), I padded down the gravel driveway in my flip flops to settle beside the fire and wait out the wash cycle.

While the firelight danced, I sorted out my Highway 61

error on the map and drank a bottle of blue POWERADE ZERO.[6] I was concerned about becoming dehydrated from my hours on the cycle and the relatively little I was drinking during the day, so I'd bought a couple bottles at a gas station on the way back to the Cozy C. I sipped my way through the first during the wash cycle and then popped the second one and made my way through it while my clothes tumbled in the dryer.

When I returned to the laundry room to fold my load of clothes, they needed a couple more minutes so I busied myself looking through the small selection of community reading materials on the side of the EQUIPMENT/SORTING TABLE. Among issues of Our Daily Bread and EveryDay with Rachael Ray, there were heaps of nearly identical Harlequin romance novels. "The Cowboy's Healing Ways" featured a gentle looking Marlboro man (Dr. Jesse Alvarez Cooper) leaning against a tree and touching the brim of his hat in a Brad Pitt "A River Runs Through It" type of way. Above his head the publisher had added a banner that said, "LARGER PRINT". Apparently, lady RV'ers were Christian, farsighted, and a little randy, — at least the ones looking to TAKE/EXCHANGE BOOKS/MAGAZINES. They were also apparently familiar with the benefits of extra virgin olive oil.

Laundry folded and repacked, I returned to my campsite and settled in for the night. The Big Agnes was shaped like a lopsided pyramid, wide at the head and tapered at the feet. It had a couple of miniature cargo nets just inside the door and a separate rain flap that stretched over the top. It was a confident shade of military green, as if the good people at Big Agnes were looking to say that this is the tent Bear Grylls would use if he weren't prepared to make his own from the hide of a feral yak.

My sleeping bag was rated for sub-zero temperatures but I didn't like the claustrophobia of having it zipped all the way up, so I decided to sleep in my clothes again to make up the lost warmth. I climbed in, took off my jacket and shoes, slid them all the way to the bottom and tried to get comfortable on the little inflatable camp pillow I'd bought. It was about the size of a cigar box and required supplement by way of my own folded arm.

---

[6] The brand's official website spells the name in all caps. POWERADE ZERO has an Advanced Electrolyte System and doesn't truck in lowercase bullshit

Settled in, I contemplated the day, feeling satisfied. I was getting used to the road, had seen a couple cool things and had only the coolest stuff yet ahead. The weather had even begun to warm. Every item of clothing I had was clean and I'd taken responsible measures to stave off dehydration. Bear Grylls would be proud of that last bit.

Knowing that I'd probably have to pee in the middle of the night, I'd brought one of the empty wide-mouth POWERADE ZERO bottles into the tent with me. The temperature would be in the high forties overnight, but I'd had enough of the cold and wasn't looking forward to the prospect of leaving the sleeping bag once I was settled.

Hours later I woke up with a full bladder and a vigorous wind shaking the rain flap. After trying unsuccessfully to fall back to sleep for several minutes, I knew it was time to test the urinal properties of the POWERADE ZERO bottle. Half in and half out of the sleeping bag, I unbuttoned my jeans and got everything into position. Within seconds, I felt the sweet relief of a rapidly emptying bladder. Within a few more, I felt a spreading damp warmth on my thigh and groin. Abort! Abort! Docking maneuver failed!

Suddenly and fully awake, I took a moment to ponder what could possibly have gone wrong with something so seemingly simple, decided that the cause of the incident was less important than the consequence, and reached down to assess the damage, the bastard wind the whole while shaking the rain flap and threatening to blow my house down. My pants and underwear were wet, but thankfully my sleeping bag was still dry. I checked my watch to discover I'd somehow made it through to 5:00.

I got up, took a long leisurely shower, and ran my big boy pants through the washer with a delicate splash of Head & Shoulders. Returning to my site to break camp in the first weak moments of daylight, I saw that the wind had blown over my tent, baring Agnes's big ass to the world. 4,182 miles away, across the cold gray expanse of the Atlantic, Bear Grylls shuddered.

CHAPTER FIVE

"I got the St. Louis blues, blue as I can be…
I love my baby like a schoolboy loves his pie,
Like a Kentucky Colonel loves his mint & rye…"
- St. Louis Blues, W.C. Handy

I rode US-54 east for twelve miles to where it rejoined the Great River Road in the town of Louisiana near the Champ Clark Bridge. Louisiana, named for the daughter of the town founder, was once a thriving shipping center on the Mississippi and boasts the most intact Victorian streetscape in the state according to the Missouri DNR. Riding in on Mansion Street, it was the houses in Louisiana that first caught my eye.

Squat wooden structures with heavy porches gave way to two story antebellum homes, and tons and tons of red brick. There was red brick everywhere and where the brick wasn't red, it had been painted over in white and gray by people who'd grown weary of it. On Third Street, I passed a great Victorian home made all of red brick with three tall chimneys jutting into the sky.

On both sides of the road, the sidewalk and curbs were crumbling and heaved, and weeds grew up through their cracks. The vegetation seemed to be barely kept at bay by the remaining residents of a beautiful forgotten town slipping serenely into the river like a forlorn and listing barge. After days of riding in familiar surroundings, I felt the south settle over me, thick and foreign, beauty and ugliness woven together inextricably.

On the south side of town, I rode past deserted store fronts, vacant lots with driveways leading to nothing, worn and faded mobile homes, and Izola's place- a tiny garage-sized diner where a handful of locals were gathered for breakfast. I could see them through the front window as I rode past. The thick cold morning air was seeping through my gloves already and the diner looked warm and inviting.

I pressed on over railroad tracks and past a grain elevator, the road weaving back and forth along with the river, crossing narrow bridges over wide creeks. Here and there a tan gravel driveway ran off into the trees or marked a farmstead along the way, but mostly it was the railroad, the power company, and the Missouri DOT forging south together along the Mississippi toward Clarksville.

There, an official population of around 500 was served by two large red brick churches which stood like sentinels at either end of 2nd Street; the Clarksville Christian Church and the Clarksville United Methodist Church. In between were the First Baptist Church and the Green Chapel Baptist Church. If you're a Clarksville Baptist looking for a third choice (and more red brick), you can drive six miles inland to the Ramsey Creek Baptist Church where founding congregants under the leadership of Pastor Stephen Ruddell might have once debated the wisdom of Missouri Compromise over sweet tea following services while their horses nibbled in the grass out front.

Somewhere along the road between Clarksville and Bowling Green, I rode past an abandoned gas station and pulled over to take a picture. It was small and built of cinderblock, a drive-in concession building selling fuel. The last time anyone had painted the place it had been white, but the paint had been worn away by weather and time exposing the gray block underneath. Knee high weeds grew up all around the building and had begun to take over the concrete fuel island where a single pump remained, its service panel hanging open to reveal its antiquated meter. Under the awning, the rusted orange remains of a brawny steel light pole laid vagrant and blocking the entryway which was now just a rectangular hole in the front of the building, its door lost to history.

A rusted metal sign which clung to the station's aluminum canopy had the hieroglyph remains of an advertisement. There were two words and at first I thought they both were, "FUEL", but closer inspection convinced me one said "FULL". I imagined that at one time it might have been the labored catchy-kitschy name of the place; a mom and pop version of Pump-n-Munch. FULL-n-FUEL? I stared at it like one of those magic eye puzzles trying to make it out, but in the end the sign was all but rusted away and all the power of my imagining couldn't bring it back.

Maybe it was the encroaching cold and my eagerness to get to St. Louis, or maybe it was the out of sorts feeling I was nursing over the sudden transition from Midwest to South, or maybe it was just that my curiosity about abandoned places had been temporarily slaked, but when I rode into Clarksville and past her churches, I slipped right past one of the GRR's most interesting roadside oddities without so much as a second look-- which was a shame that couldn't be blamed on Shannon. She'd mentioned it to me excitedly and included it in my itinerary. I was excited about it too and having failed to notice it as I rode by or even to have remembered to look for it, I was disappointed when I stopped for gas later that morning and realized I was already well past it.

On the way into Clarksville, on the right-hand side of the Great River Road just across from the Rustic Eagle Inn and canted back toward the north camouflaging it a little bit from the road, stands the abandoned remains of the Clarksville Skyride, a chairlift that in its relatively short heyday drew 100,000 visitors a year.

Developed by Carl Mitchell with help from the Southern Pike Committee for Progress, the Clarksville Skyride opened in 1962 and carried tourists to the top of an 800-foot bluff-- the highest on the Mississippi. Once atop Lookout Point, they could enjoy a view of 1,000 square miles. An ad from the St. Louis Post Dispatch dated 25, April 1965 shows a smiling, sunglasses-wearing couple riding the lift, their legs dangling in space over the copy:

Ride the SKYLIFT!
To
LOOKOUT POINT
Clarksville, Missouri

THE WHOLE FAMILY WILL MARVEL AT THE
SMOOTH RIDE OF THE FABULOUS SKYLIFT AS
THEY LOOK OUT OVER THE MIGHTY MISSISSIPPI
RIVER AT LOCK & DAM 24.

Atop panoramic Lookout Point you will want to spend
several hours viewing the breathtaking beauty of the
landscape, a delightful Ghost Town, Country Store,
Indian Museum, Hanging Tree, Deer Park, and

fascinating Mystery House. Sandwiches, snacks, and refreshments are available for your convenience on the pinnacle.

The tagline at the bottom of the ad said, "Dedicated to wholesome family entertainment", but nearly from the start, not everyone agreed. As it turns out, families on day trips from St. Louis weren't the first people ever to marvel at the view from Lookout Point. In fact, about two-thousand years before Columbus delivered the news of the New World to Queen Isabella, ancient ancestors of the local Sac and Fox Indians had been so awed by the place that they decided it would be a fitting location to honor and bury their dead.

Area residents had been aware of the Indian graves at least since the 1950s. All the same, of the seven burial mounds on the top of the bluff, six were razed to make way for Skylift attractions; some of the two-thousand-year-old remains they contained pushed ignominiously over the hillside. The Southern Pike Committee for Progress then progressed a couple steel support beams right through the seventh mound, which made a handy base for the chairlift's top terminal and bullwheel. At some point, a Plexiglas viewing wall was put in place around some of the exposed skeletons, while additional remains and artifacts were put on display in the Skylift's Indian Museum.

Public interest in the plight of American Indians grew rapidly throughout the sixties, and in 1970, the year after the official founding of the American Indian Movement and the same year "Bury My Heart at Wounded Knee" was published, the Mitchells gifted the Skylift along with its land and buildings to Culver-Stockton College whose anthropology, archeology, and sociology departments were keenly interested in the Indian burial mound and its artifacts.

The College held on to the Skylift for about five years, operating it as a source of revenue while students studied the site, but by 1974, the board was ready to be rid of it and sold the attraction to Clarksville native Richard Boyd under the condition that students still be allowed to use the site as a field lab for anthropological studies.

Less than two years later, in 1976, the following newspaper

ad ran in the St. Louis Post Dispatch:

> CLARKSVILLE SKYLIFT, a good investment or fine
> family project, includes country store and cafeteria,
> Mystery House, Indian Museum and graves, Ghost Town,
> view of the lock and dam. Such potential – an exciting
> tourist attraction. Smooth chair lift to the top of beautiful
> Lookout Point, highest point overlooking the Mississippi.
> Only $150,000.

The original construction cost of the Skylift and its buildings, fifteen years earlier, had been over $600,000. The attraction had become an unwelcome albatross around the neck of its owners.

The slow and inevitable decline of the Clarksville Skylift continued through the 1980s, when it was operated under contract. In 1991, the Indian Museum was closed and in accordance with federal law, the remains it held were returned to local tribes for reburial at an undisclosed location. The Wild West town and other concessions were shuttered soon thereafter.

By 1996, almost 20 years to the day after the Skylift was listed for sale at the bargain basement price of $150,000, town leaders were in an open feud with then-owner Russ Moore, a truck driver from the nearby town of Louisiana. In an interview from Lookout Point, where holes in the rotting decking of the upper terminal were allowing water to erode the burial mound below, exposing new remains, Mayor Agnes Mae Taylor shared the story of a human arm bone, dragged home by a town dog the previous year and traced back to the litter strewn mound. With its rusty towers, shabby decking, and dilapidated buildings, the Clarksville Skylift had become such an embarrassment that the local tourist center had stopped recommending it to visitors.

Although owner Russ Moore insisted the chairlift was safe, annual cable inspections had stopped in 1994 and Bruce Martin, who operated the attraction throughout the late 80s, simply said "no way" when he was asked if he would take the ride. Moore's fiancé called safety concerns about the Skylift "a bunch of bull", but its fate was sealed and the Skylift closed for good shortly after the article was published.

The Skylift languished unused and unloved for several years, the damp river air of the Mississippi gnawing at its exposed towers and decking, until it was bought in 2002 by Bill McMurtrey, a Clarksville native and restauranteur who had grand plans for its revival. He embarked on an ambitious refurbishment in the face of legal challenges from the Fox and Sac Nations that had him facing felony charges in 2005 before a settlement was eventually reached. McMurtrey, then in his mid-60's, continued his plans for a multi-million-dollar revitalization of the Skylift, but a fire on the upper platform in 2006 delayed construction. Then the Great Recession hit and the project stalled. Despite McMurtrey's ongoing efforts to reopen the Skylift, it remains closed.

The story could end there, but in July 2016 the Bowling Green Times ran the following headline, "Clarksville senior citizen pleads guilty to large scale marijuana possession charge". The senior citizen in question was Skylift owner, Bill McMurtrey. When authorities raided his home, they found over thirty-thousand dollars in cash and more than a hundred pounds of marijuana. It was one of the largest drug busts in Pike County history.

At the bottom of the hill leading up to Lookout Point, the lower terminal of the Skylift sits a few feet back from the road on the other side of a low retaining wall, its placid cables stretching slackly up into the distance toward the bluff. Grass grows in an abandoned parking lot. Beside the concrete base of the Skylift is a small wooden building. Attached to its wall beneath a faded red Coca-Cola sign is a placard that reads:

"SKYRIDE LLC
NO TRESPASSING
VIOLATORS WILL BE PROSECUTED"

*****

I continued down Missouri 79 until it became Salt Lick Road at its junction with I-70 in St. Peters- a modern suburban enclave at the northwest edge of St. Louis that had been rated America's 60th Best Place to Live by Money magazine about the time the housing bubble burst. There, I pulled into the new concrete parking lot of a Phillips

66 convenience store and went inside to warm up and have breakfast.

St. Louis would be the biggest city I'd ridden through since St. Paul, and I was completely unfamiliar with its geography and roads. The confusion on my face must have been clear as I munched a Pop-Tart and studied my iPhone trying to make sense of my route, because the cashier, yet another friendly middle-aged woman (somewhere in corporate America there is a hiring template for convenience store workers that places friendly, middle-aged women at the top of a desirability pyramid), took pity on me and came to my assistance, helping me untangle a jagged mess of intersections that dropped me southward like a pachinko ball into Eureka and neighboring Route 66 state park.

Choosing the Great River Road for my solo motorcycle trip, I had decided against Route 66 and Highway 50; Route 66 for not being a true cross-country trip (it goes from Chicago to Los Angeles), and US 50 ("The Loneliest Road in America) for being too, well, lonely. As noted in Jamie Jensen's, Road Trip USA; however, St. Louis is the only city where the three routes intersect, and I was looking forward to riding Route 66 for ten or twelve miles into downtown St. Louis beginning at Route 66 State Park.

Route 66 State Park offers visitors the chance to experience a short segment of the original route, up to the now closed bridge spanning the Meramec River. The bridge was slowly euthanized by the Missouri DOT through a series of decreasing weight limits. It was closed to all traffic in 2009 as a result of advanced deterioration, and its concrete deck was removed in 2012 leaving behind a rusted skeleton. Near the eastern entrance to the former bridge is a 1930s era roadhouse that has been converted to a visitor's center and museum featuring a variety of exhibits celebrating the road and its impact on American culture.

With its sleepy museum, bucolic acres of grass and trees, and dowdy brown signs, Route 66 State Park looks as old as any other state park, but it's drinking on a fake ID. Occupying a four-hundred-acre, wedge-shaped parcel along the Meramec, the park sits on the former location of Times Beach; a town officially disincorporated in 1985 by then Missouri Governor John Ashcroft. Route 66 State Park was opened in 1999. The fourteen years in between were taken up by a massive environmental cleanup effort that bulldozed abandoned homes, incinerated thousands of tons of contaminated soil, and resigned the pious pews and hymnals of the Full Gospel Tabernacle Church to a landfill alongside the more earthly contents of The Western Lounge.

Although it required an executive order to wipe it from official existence; Times Beach was never really real to begin with. Developed rather than settled, Times Beach was named for the now-defunct St. Louis Times which in the summer of 1925 offered 10 by 100 foot lots for free with a six-month subscription to the newspaper, costing $67.50. Installment plans were offered. Due to the small size of the lots, any practical residential use required the purchase of more than one. The lowland area along the Meramec River was billed as a beach community, a convenient summer getaway for St. Louis residents.

It was a stretch— the idea that a buggy, flood-prone bend in a river some considered a creek could become a swank summer destination, and most who bought into the idea were, like Times Beach itself, aspirational. Even with easy credit terms, hundreds of lots went unsold. Then came the Great Depression. The desperation of the times is reflected over and over in classified ads. One from an August 1933 edition of the St. Louis Post Dispatch reads: "Lots - 33, on Times Beach at Meramec; must have money; $1500 will buy them all".

Rustic summer cabins became full time homes as cash dried up and desperate St. Louis families whose primary residences had been foreclosed on resettled in Times Beach. By the time it became a municipality in 1954, rather than the Hamptons-style getaway its developers had promised, Times Beach had become a working-class enclave where people could buy two lots for a couple hundred dollars and put up a modest house or anchor a mobile home. The town became a notorious speed trap as its strapped city council struggled for funding. In one year Times Beach took in $41,000 in fines and court fees— three times what it collected from real estate and property taxes and double what it made from sales tax.

In 1968, St. Louis County proposed putting an unwanted waste incinerator in Times Beach after nearby Valley Park approved funding to fight the project. It never developed. Ironically, the incinerator might have saved Times Beach by bringing in needed revenue. In 1971, with no money to pave many of its streets and summer dust becoming an increasing nuisance to residents, the city began paying 6 cents a gallon to Russell Bliss, a waste hauler, to spray used crank case oil on the roads. The thick black oil would keep the dust down for a little while and then Bliss would come and put down some more.

That same summer, Bliss had removed more than 18,000 gallons of still bottom residue from a tank at a chemical plant in Verona and began disposing of it by mixing it in with the waste oil. An employee for Bliss, David Covert, said, "We picked up everything you can imagine."

By the following August, residents were complaining to the town council about the odor from the oil Bliss was spraying on their roads — "sweetish, sort of, but strong. It like to never went away."

At a stable in nearby Moscow Hills, Judy Piatt's horses started dying after Bliss sprayed their arena. He denied the deaths had anything to do with his oil, but Piatt was having none of it and began a personal crusade to expose Bliss and the dangers of the oil he was spreading. Her efforts led the state to assign a 23-year-old veterinarian to the case. Soil samples were taken and sent to the Centers for Disease Control in Atlanta, but three years passed before the CDC was able to identify the chemical compound dioxin as the cause of the livestock deaths. Dioxin, a by-product of various chemical processes and a component in Agent Orange, is toxic enough that the CDC recommends cleanup at levels of just one part per billion. Samples taken at Piatt's stable contained more than 30,000 times that.

With no laws regulating the disposal of hazardous liquids to cite or enforce, state bureaucracies hemmed and hawed and stared at the ground for years, voicing concern about the problem while quietly buck-passing and wishing it away. The efforts that were undertaken focused on the contaminated soils removed from Piatt's farm and others that Bliss had sprayed (the CDC urged that they be "re-excavated and dumped at a remote, deep landfill") and the wildly contaminated storage tank in Verona where dioxin levels were found at 350,000 parts per billion.

Finally, in 1979, after an anonymous tip to the EPA that the plant in Verona had been secretly burying sludge filled barrels, the investigation took on some urgency and efforts were undertaken to track down all of the missing dioxin. Among a suspected 100 places the Verona dioxin ended up, was the entire town of Times Beach.

On the 3rd of December 1982, more than 12 years after Bliss had first began spraying in Times Beach, the EPA finally finished taking samples of the dioxin laced soil. The following day, the swollen Meramec River flooded the town to its rooftops, forcing the evacuation of most of its 2,000 residents, many of whom never returned to the muddy and debris strewn streets of the place they'd called home.

Just in case anyone hadn't gotten the message, the Meramec flooded the town again and again over the next few months, lifting some homes right off their foundations. The following December, the Knight-Ridder News Service ran a story about the seven families still remaining in Times Beach stubbornly waiting to be forced from the abandoned and barricaded town while guarding their homes from looters. A few months later, even they were gone.

As for Russell Bliss, the waste hauler who had sprayed the dioxin laced oil on the streets of Times Beach, he maintained an aw-shucks demeanor throughout, claiming at one point "I can't hardly read."

William D. Ruckelshaus, head of the EPA at the outset of the Times Beach cleanup, said in an interview that although a lot of people have dumped waste, "None are quite like Bliss."

At a videotaped hearing on the Times Beach matter, the waste-hauler dipped his finger in dioxin and touched it to his tongue. "I wasn't told what was in the oil. I wouldn't have known what it was if they had've told me what it was, if you want the truth," he said. "You could tell me it was some kind of a new jelly and I'd put it on toast and eat it."

In spite of his self-proclaimed simple nature, Bliss still managed to do okay for himself. Herman Chadbourne, one of Bliss's competitors, compared him to a smooth used-car salesman, while three of Bliss's former employees accused him of cheating his customers by "short measuring", taking more oil than he paid for and delivering less than he claimed. Convicted of tax fraud in 1983, Bliss at one point owned multiple properties including a 200-acre farm where he was said to keep a collection of exotic cars and rare animals. He also raised prize winning horses and hosted shows at his personal arena.

Bliss was never convicted of any criminal wrongdoing related to the Times Beach disaster and maintains that he was a convenient fall guy for larger interests. In an interview with the History Channel he said, "When you say dioxin or Times Beach, you don't think about NEPACCO. You don't think about all the other companies that were involved in it. You think of one thing— Russell Bliss. But to this day, I will say this: I didn't generate it. I didn't make it. I hauled it from there and put it over there. I was a transporter, no more, no less."

Today, the Missouri State Parks webpage understandably downplays the fact that Route 66 State Park sits on the former location of Times Beach, relegating the story to a single "oh, by the way" paragraph buried among a nostalgic reflection on the Mother Road and a description of the park's trail system and its level paths-rehabilitated streets of Times Beach, perfect for senior citizens, beginning riders, and people with disabilities. Near the picnic area is a large grassy mound where visitors might spot deer, wild turkeys, or one of the some forty species of birds that have been identified in the park. Below their feet, beneath the grass and dirt, lie the moldering remains of Times Beach.

*****

After touring the small museum in the park's visitor's center, I followed the directions of an enthusiastic but nervous ranger and soon found myself headed east on Missouri 366, a re-designated portion of the original Route 66. While the ranger had been enthusiastic about the history and significance of Route 66, he had been nervous about the potential for crime the closer I might get to the heart of St. Louis.

It was only about three months after the fatal shooting of Michael Brown by a Ferguson police officer. The shooting had ignited two weeks of protests and unrest in St. Louis (Ferguson is an incorporated city within the St. Louis metroplex) over what many thought amounted to the sanctioned murder of a young black man by a white officer. Although the riots were over, tensions were high, nerves were frayed, and the message the park ranger gave me— polite, carefully worded, and with all the first-date awkwardness an exchange about race between two well meaning, middle-aged white strangers, one in an official state uniform might have, was "don't be stupid". See the arch. Stay out of areas where you don't belong.

It was with this advice in mind that I started down old Route 66, thrilled a little where it intersected with Highway 50, and then again at each and every Historic Route 66 marker I saw. The week before, I had never ridden more than a couple of hours at a time and had mostly stayed around my house, and now I was hundreds of miles from home on Historic Route 66 riding toward downtown St. Louis. It was great. And 366 didn't seem like a road that should cause a tourist any worry.

It was for the most part a wide four-lane blacktop running between larger businesses. There were broad grassy boulevards and sidewalks on both sides, and while there was some commercial vacancy, I also passed a brand-new Walgreen's and a Kohl's department store. Whatever riots might have occurred in St. Louis over the past couple of months, they hadn't happened here.

Further east on Watson Road, the businesses became mostly tiny strip malls of four or five stores, followed by stand-alones. Kohl's and Walgreen's morphed into Napa and Checker, and small squat apartment buildings and older homes began to appear on either side of the road. Vacancies increased and I passed the Duplex Motel, a motor lodge whose courtyard was paved right up to and around its one scraggly evergreen bush. The Chippewa Motel, right next door, was more of the same minus the bush. Next came a half vacant strip mall with a title loan place on one end. As I continued east along tree lined boulevards, the buildings I passed both residential and commercial were more and more often built from red brick- the same type I'd encountered earlier that morning in Louisiana.

As it turns out, St. Louis rides atop massive deposits of high-quality clay and had been producing over 20 million red bricks a year in the 1800s when a fire destroyed a third of the city. A hastily passed ordinance in the wake of the blaze required all four sides of a building to be made of brick or stone, leading to the heavy use of red brick in building due to their abundance and economy compared to stone. The red brick construction became a hallmark of St. Louis and of the greater south, where many of her bricks were sent.

Now the demand for historic red brick by preservationists and others looking for authentic weathered bricks has led to a near epidemic of brick stealing with so called "brick rustlers" on St. Louis's north side literally devouring at least 65 buildings and nibbling away at hundreds more. 24-hour recycling centers pay a couple hundred bucks for a pickup load ("giant money" in the 4th ward according to Alderman Sam Moore) and brick thieves in blighted neighborhoods are rarely confronted by residents or police, both of whom are concerned with bigger crimes. Quoted in St. Louis Magazine, architectural historian Michael Allen says, "It's the weirdest damn thing in the world."

Beginning at Sulphur Avenue, there are blocks and blocks of well kept, modest St. Louis brick homes, apartments, and duplexes nestled onto tiny lots. With garages on alleyways in back, their porches and stoops become the prominent feature, each looking out onto a tree-lined sidewalk and curbside parking lane. These homes fall away at Kingshighway, giving way to poorer kept ones, vacant lots, and an assortment of mom and pop businesses, some with bars over their windows. A few blocks later, Historic Route 66 bears north following Gravois Avenue. There is a sign. I didn't notice it.

Across Gravois Avenue, Chippewa leads through a spate of two story apartment buildings, then across South Grand Boulevard into the Gravois Park neighborhood where the cross streets are named for states— if those states had been printed on Scrabble tiles and drawn randomly from a bag, so that Indiana falls between Texas and Missouri and California abuts Iowa. In addition to its alphabetically confusing cross streets, Gravois Heights has the distinction of having been named the fourth worst neighborhood in St. Louis. Coincidentally, St. Louis itself has been named the fourth worst city in the US. And so it was that I found myself on a crisp November Saturday, riding my motorcycle half lost through the fourth worst neighborhood in the fourth worst city in the country.

What it is that lands a place on a list of worsts? In the case of St. Louis, it's the city's violent crime rate, where it's in a virtual tie with the number-three-ranked Oakland[7]. In the case of Gravois

Park, it's a witch's brew of high crime and negative economic factors including high unemployment and low property values. Those are all numbers. They are intangibles. I didn't know the name of the neighborhood I was in, let alone any statistical data about it. What I knew was that I suddenly felt very far from home.

You don't need statistics to see when the residents of a place have adopted a siege mentality. First floor windows and doors had bars over them, and the ones that didn't were boarded up. The smallest personal spaces, tiny patches of scruffy grass, were fenced in from the street while cheap plastic signs announced the presence of non-existent security systems. "NO TRESPASSING" and "NO LOITERING" barked others. Weeds grew up unchallenged through the sidewalks and along the curbs.

One of the few businesses that remained was a carryout restaurant called H&M Best Fried Fish and Chicken. Painted bright red with yellow trim and not much bigger than a detached garage, H&M occupied a cement corner lot and displayed a health inspector's A rating card at its walkup window. There was no inside dining. Diagonally across the street, beneath red and white striped awnings stood the AC Pawnshop, its windows festooned with customer come-ons— "WE BUY SCRAP GOLD" and "OPEN SUNDAYS!"

At every intersection was a stop sign, and at each one I slowed to a walk, looked both ways, and then rolled right through driven by the anxiety of being an obvious outsider alone in a place the locals seemed afraid to be. I'd ridden three days away from the safety and familiarity of my home and everything I had was within eighteen inches of my body— my money, my ID, my phone, my motorcycle and all my supplies.

For the first time on the trip, I became preoccupied with the thought of what would happen and what I would do if I broke down or got robbed, or both. I wasn't afraid of being murdered. That

---

[7] According to the FBI's Uniform Crime Report for 2014, Oakland had 1685.39 violent crimes per 100,000 residents while St. Louis had only about seven fewer, at 1678.73. By comparison, the city in fifth place, Milwaukee, Wisconsin reported over two-hundred fewer violent crimes per 100,000, with a rate of 1476.41. Because everyone loves a countdown and you're probably curious who came in first, Detroit was the violent crime champion, with a number of 1988.63, followed by Memphis with 1740.51. I'd wait until Tuesday to ride through Memphis.

seemed melodramatic. It was after all, a sunny Saturday morning. It just didn't seem like innocent strangers got murdered while people were enjoying weekend brunch- even in bad neighborhoods. Robbery though, seemed like a legitimate concern.

I was alone on a motorcycle, and my Minnesota plates announced my status as a dumb tourist who had wandered off of Route 66. If they didn't, Siri's hectoring navigation tips coming over my speakers did. "In one half mile, turn left on South Broadway... In a quarter mile, turn left on South Broadway... In one thousand feet turn left on South Broadway." A few blocks after turning left on Broadway, the Gateway Arch appeared off in the distance, pushing its way up into the horizon like a lighthouse. With my goal in sight, I reached down with one hand and pulled the speaker cord from my iPhone.

*****

Dick Bowser never finished college. After the bombing of Pearl Harbor, Bowser left the University of Maryland to join the US Navy, having completed just one full year. He served as a fire controlman on the USS Wadsworth for three years before returning home after the war to work with his father developing, manufacturing and installing an automated parking system of their own design.

Bowser's father, Virgil, an elevator salesman, had designed a unique dumbwaiter for a Michigan church that traveled horizontally for a short segment to help it circumvent a beam that could not be relocated. Following the war, the two built on the concept that an elevator need not travel only vertically and created a parking system that lifted and stacked cars in cubbies like an office mail system, making more efficient use of limited urban space than traditional ramps or lots. Cars were then retrieved in the same manner and moved horizontally, vertically, and or diagonally back to the attendant's station when customers were ready to pick up.

The Bowser System along with its competitor Pigeon Hole, though complex and prone to mechanical failure, fit the whiz-bang futurist mood of optimism that marked the post war era and by 1957 over seventy automated parking systems had been built, half of which were Bowsers.[8]

So it was that Dick Bowser had been solving spatial and logistical problems with elevators for most of his adult life when he walked into the offices of the Montgomery Elevator Company in 1960 to visit his friend John Martin. The Montgomery Elevator Company, like several others, had been contacted by Eero Saarinen, the designer of the Gateway Arch, to provide a design for a transporter system to take visitors to the top of the 600-foot monument. No one had been able to reach a solution, including engineers from the venerable Otis Elevator Company. Martin thought Bowser might be able to help and immediately placed a call back to Saarinen's offices. Shortly thereafter, Bowser was given just two weeks to come up with a solution to an engineering problem that had stumped the prominent elevator firms of the day- how do you lift 3,500 people a day the equivalent of 63 stories, in a narrow, curved, triangular space that tapers as it goes up? This while leaving room for all the mechanicals along with maintenance and emergency access, and absolutely no exterior evidence of its presence or operation.

Bowser began by considering and rejecting the same concepts that had already been considered and rejected- elevators, escalators, and Ferris wheels - before settling on a hybrid solution. For two weeks he worked feverishly in his basement, grafting the merits of each solution into a Frankenstein hybrid that overcame the weaknesses of each. This new system would transport passengers in compact, barrel shaped cars that were suspended from an overhead rail at a boarding platform below the arch, then hoisted into an upward arc by modified elevator equipment, to ride more and more atop the rail as they neared the top of the arch. Along the way, the barrels would slowly rotate 155 degrees to remain level, their passengers unaware of the Rube Goldberg dance taking place just outside their cabin. After visiting the Gateway Arch more than thirty years later, Bowser described the wonder in his own words in a letter to Park Service Director George Hartzog, "...my wife and I were standing in a leg of the Arch watching a train go up. There were relays clicking, motors running, capsules rotating in an effort to

---

[8] Although most of these systems are now long gone, a few are rumored to be still in use, and companies with names like Parkmatic and Boomerang are keeping the dream alive with modern systems rooted in the Bowser past.

remain level, some cables were going up, others were moving down, wheels, trolleys, wires, chains, etc. I told my wife "I can't believe I was involved in all this and I don't believe I have the guts to do such a thing again."

So complex was the solution and so little time allotted for him to arrive at it, that two weeks later when it came time to pitch his idea, many of Bowser's notes were still written out in longhand. Traveling to Michigan to make his 45-minute presentation, Bowser believed himself to be meeting with just the architect and his staff.

Instead he was greeted by the mayors of St. Louis and East St. Louis, St. Louis area congressmen, and the Director of the Park Service among others. For hours, he was peppered with questions about his solution until finally someone probed his credentials by asking, "Mr. Bowser, what are you?"

Bowser, the college dropout whose unconventional ideas had just solved an engineering problem that had stymied the best engineers in the business defused the potential landmine by answering simply, "I'm 38 years old."

In the end, Bowser was awarded a lump sum of $40,000, about half a million dollars in today's money for a job that was to take two years. It took six. He then remained with the National Park Service another five years supervising the repair and maintenance of the system he designed. For his efforts, he was honored with The National Park Service Medal.

The Gateway Arch is wonder of mid-century engineering, its gleaming stainless-steel surface comprised of 142 separate sections whose seams are all but undetectable. Hoisting them into place required specialized construction techniques yet to be invented when the monument was approved. At over six-hundred feet tall, The Gateway Arch sways as much as 18 inches in high winds and was bolted and welded together by men untethered by safety harnesses or the OSHA regulations that would have required them. Sometimes they worked blind, guiding new pieces into place by feel, assisted by spotters over a staticky radio connection. The insurance company that underwrote the project estimated that thirteen men would die to raise the Arch. None did.

The monument and its grounds take up over 90 manicured acres of parkland and include a subterranean museum dedicated to the history of American westward expansion. Yet in spite of all the effort and attention that went into the architecture, construction, and cultural value of the Arch, the pressing goal of nearly all its visitors is the same. It's the question on the lips of every visiting school kid. "Can we go to the top?"

It was the whole reason I stopped. The sun was bright in the sky when I arrived and while still far enough away to capture the whole monument in a single frame, I snapped a photo of the Arch, its surface shining in hues of silver and gray against the crisp blue of the November sky. At the base of one leg, a copse of fiery autumn oaks exploded in hues of orange and red, a leprechaun's treasure at one end of a manmade rainbow.

Up close, I was surprised by the apparent simplicity of the thing. The park service has kept the Arch's base uncluttered by landscaping or fences and visitors are left to wander around the colossal stainless-steel legs, periodically stopping to stand in wonder, heads tilted back to try and take it all in.

I bypassed a line of people waiting at the front entrance to the museum, following a couple handmade signs to a side entrance where I passed quickly through a security check and walked deliberately past the exhibits to a ticket counter selling seats on Bowser's tram.

I got the last one on a trip scheduled to depart almost immediately and rushed to join the group waiting to board. With no research to prepare me, I was gobsmacked when the rectangular door at my loading station on the platform opened to reveal a 1950's vision of the future. The capsule was painted white inside and gently lit by recessed lights at the back of its smooth rounded interior. Its seats were five white molded plastic stools arranged in a tight semicircle. Each rested atop a stubby metallic strut fastened to the rounded wall and between them was an oblong strip of flooring no bigger than a small coffee table. It was as if Steve Jobs, George Jetson, and Mike Brady had gotten together and designed a transportation system for an astronaut corps of Oompa Loompas.

I boarded the car with four black women, all members of the same family who'd come to see the Arch together. The car's small dimensions left all of us touching in some way or another, and we made small talk on the way up, part of it spent comforting the oldest woman in the group- an aunt who had fifteen or twenty years on the rest of us. She made it plain that her riding to the top was simply the result of having lost a four-way vote, and with each lurching, mechanical bump as the car rotated to keep us level, she'd make a little gasping sound and grip the nearest surface- her stool, the wall, the arm of the woman next to her.

The doors on the front of the cars are windowed and we watched the utilitarian guts of the Arch's interior pass by as we rode up. Stairs and braces, wires, junctions, and access lights lurched into view and were gone just as quickly. The ride to the top took four minutes, a sentence that must feel like an eternity for visitors with claustrophobia, fear of heights, or social anxiety. At the top we exited onto a platform and followed the others in our group up the short incline to the apex of the Arch, where sound deadening gray carpet lines the floor, walls, and window openings, hushing the voices and footsteps that would otherwise echo and reverberate in the small metallic space.

The exterior walls feature thirty-two slit like windows, sixteen per side, just over two feet long and only seven inches tall, their size limited by the extreme structural loads at the top of the Arch. Visitors are welcome to stay in the observation room as long as they like, but there are no facilities and no seating. Most people linger only a couple of minutes, taking just long enough to admire the view from each side and grab a quick selfie or group shot to commemorate the moment, then it's back into the one of the tram cars for the slightly quicker gravity assisted ride back to the Arch's base.

On the day I rode to the top, there were only a couple of dozen people in the narrow space. The official capacity is 160, a number that would seem stiflingly overcrowded. As it was, I had to wait a moment or two for the chance to look through one of the prime windows at the top of the apex overlooking downtown St. Louis.

It was a clear day allowing a view of about thirty miles over the city. Busch Stadium, the Old Courthouse, and other features of the St. Louis cityscape were laid out in front of me like a model of their actual selves. Since the Arch is made of triangular sections and the windows are mounted flush with the exterior, they look out, but also down and you have to lean out into them to take in the full view, which eerily includes the tapered legs of the Arch itself disappearing into the grass six-hundred feet below.

I lingered for just a moment trying to make out the route I'd taken to get there, and then snapped a selfie of my own, a placard in the background that read "630 FEET" overlaid atop an image of the Arch, and then I returned to the loading platform for the three-minute tram ride back down.

Since Bowser's trams went into service in 1967, they have traveled more than 200,000 miles carrying over 18 million passengers driven in part by the same sense of curiosity and adventure that led to the westward expansion commemorated by the Arch itself. Dick Bowser retired in 1982 and moved to Florida with his wife. They had been married fifty-four years when he lost her in 1994. He died the day after Christmas in 2003. He was 82.

*****

I crossed into Illinois on the Martin Luther King Bridge and wound my way through East St. Louis, blindly feeling my way back toward the river until I stumbled across Mississippi Avenue in Sauget-which was known as Monsanto until the late 1960s. East St. Louis is the kind of place you'd go to shoot urban scenes for a dystopian sci-fi movie, just like director John Carpenter did for 1981's Escape from New York.

Sauget is more of the same, incorporated in 1926 as a company town for Monsanto's chemical operations, Sauget is home to multiple EPA cleanup sites including fenced off Dead Creek, known to glow in the dark and to periodically catch fire due to its high phosphorus content. The Village of Sauget got a movie of its own in 2009 when director Michael Silberman made it the subject of a documentary expose' called "In Our Backyard".

I rode south through Cahokia, the industry of East St. Louis eventually giving way to trees and creeks. The trains that carried chemicals and grain and ore and ash to and from the city traveled on rails that paralleled Illinois 3. The temperature was in the 50s when I passed through Columbia in the mid-afternoon and the sun was bright and strong. After spending the better part of the day navigating streets and freeways around St. Louis, it felt good to simply follow the Great River Road south past farm fields and through small towns where the Saturday traffic was light and unhurried.

In Red Bud, the GRR turned right and passed through a quaint historic downtown, with restored store fronts and decorative lamp posts. In Evansville, I stopped halfway across a new concrete bridge and took a photo of the sun glinting off the Kaskaskia River where a tug was moving a barge into place along the shore.

I was riding through rolling hills alongside the American Bottom, a sixty mile stretch of lowland sandwiched between the Mississippi's east bank and the wooded bluffs of Illinois, and the scenery was pastoral- made richer and more atmospheric by the high contrast and long shadows of the late afternoon.

As miles of gentle country scenery rolled by, Illinois 3 gradually crab-walked back down to the east bank of the Mississippi, the flatland separating the water and the bluffs tapering away to nothing just south of Chester, home to the Menard Corrections Center, an imposing brick and mortar prison opened in 1878. Menard is best known for housing convicted serial killer John Wayne Gacy for fourteen years before his execution in 1994 for the murder of at least 33 male victims.

If Menard weren't creepy enough in its own right, it sits on the river directly across from all but abandoned Kaskaskia, once the capitol of the Illinois Territory and briefly, the state of Illinois.

A thriving colonial center, Kaskaskia fell victim to its own success and its location on the river- a peninsula inside a bend of the Mississippi on the western border of Illinois. Deforestation of the river banks due to construction and steamboat traffic hastened erosion, widening the river and causing ever more frequent flooding, eventually allowing the river to slip around the east side of Kaskaskia, making it an island.

The great Mississippi soon took to the more easterly channel, abandoning its western course and leaving behind a bayou connecting the old Illinois capitol of Kaskaskia to the state of Missouri. Now accessible only from Missouri, Kaskaskia is a forgotten castaway, and with just 14 residents as of the 2010 census, the second least populous town in Illinois.

The ride south along the river on Illinois 3 was relaxing and scenic. The temperature was mild, and the tree-lined tarmac's gentle curves and undulations reminded me of the Great River Road along Wisconsin's river bluffs, so highly rated by the readers of the Huffington Post, where I had been too preoccupied with the cold to enjoy the view.

The posted speed limit was 55, but the afternoon was growing late and the traffic was light, so I crept first to 60 and then to 65 and soon was making little bursts of 70 as the River Road led me southward past the towns of Grimsby and Sand Ridge and through the flat, alluvial fields of Grand Tower. Dusk was settling as I sped through Wolf Lake and Ware, and with it came the growing threat of deer springing from the thickets that lined the road in places.

I slowed my pace and strained my eyes against the edges of the road, pondering again the folly of leaving on impulse with a barely made plan. Shannon had given me a rough daily mileage estimate, but it had come from MapQuest and followed a more direct route than the one I actually rode. Before I left, I'd thought there would be ample time for sight-seeing and photography, opportunities to rest and recharge throughout the day. Instead, each afternoon had become a race against the impending darkness, my daily stopping spot barely within reach, like a set of keys glinting up through the darkness of a storm grate.

It was nearly dark when I turned right onto Illinois 146 and crossed the Mississippi on the Bill Emerson Memorial Bridge into Cape Girardeau, Missouri. I picked my way across town through rush hour traffic to the Landing Point RV Park where Shannon had made a reservation for me. The office was closed by the time I arrived, but a sheet of paper had been taped to the door noting which sites were available. I rode through the park in the dark and selected one near the back separated by a couple spaces from the nearest late season RV'er, and set up my tent a few feet from the firepit before heading back out for dinner.

An hour later I was enjoying General Tso's chicken[9] at

---

[9] A product of New York as much as China, the General's chicken can be traced to two competing inventors, Chef Peng Chang-Kuei, who opened his New York restaurant in 1973 after fleeing his homeland during the Chinese Civil War. Chef

Chan's, a mom and pop Chinese restaurant with seven People's Choice Awards for Best Chinese Restaurant and a four-star Yelp! rating. Like a lot of other local Chinese places, Chan's was in a building that suggested it had once housed something else, but I couldn't decide what— maybe a Pizza Hut from the days before most people had their pizza delivered. Whatever it had been before, Chan's had occupied the space since the late 80s and it was packed with locals- always a good sign.

The food and service were both excellent and it was a pleasure to sit and eat after a day spent riding. I was sipping the last of a Sapporo when the check came along with a fortune cookie that reassured me that I approached life "philosophically and with warmth". I heeded the advice on the latter part and stopped for a bundle of firewood at an Ace Hardware store on the way back to the RV park, fastening it clumsily to the back of my seat with a couple bungees.

As I sat stretched out on the ground next to the firepit back at the campsite listening to the crackle of the burning wood and the quiet burble of a stream that ran behind my space, I thought about what I'd seen and what was yet to come. I felt masculine and independent. Staring into the fire and sipping a little shooter of whiskey while my faithful mount stood silent vigil just a few feet away, I felt like a modern-day cowboy. On the concrete slab next to the front tire of the Kawi, a half-empty bottle of POWERADE ZERO reflected the fire light, and in that moment I resolved that on that night, no matter what, I would not pee on myself. 4,182 miles away Bear Grylls was fashioning a kayak from a tattered windbreaker he'd stumbled across while chasing an adder through the underbrush.

T.T. Wang also claims to have invented the dish in 1972 at New York's Shun Lee Palace as General Ching's chicken. Ironically, when chef Peng opened a restaurant in Hunan, China in the 1990s, it failed with the locals who found the dishes too sweet.

CHAPTER SIX

"You took for granted all the times
I never let you down…
If I go crazy then
will you still call me Superman?"
- Kryptonite, 3 Doors Down

It was 27 degrees when I woke up and made my way to the showers at the Landing Point. Although I remembered buying a camp towel (read: "people chamois") at REI, it had pulled a David Copperfield and disappeared from my saddlebag, so for the third day in a row I dried myself with the previous day's t-shirt. I still felt damp in places, and the cold worked into my fingers while I broke camp in the feeble light of the early morning, bits of frost still clinging to the fabric of my tent as I rolled it up. The same frost coated the seat of the Kawasaki when I fired it up and made my way as quietly as I could out of the campground. It was just after 6:00 and no one else was up and moving yet.

I was headed to Nashville by way of Metropolis and had a distillery tour scheduled for 4:30. The afternoons had become a rush and I was determined to make it to the Corsair distillery without the last 20 miles being a scene out of Cannonball Run.

After the tour, I was looking forward to exploring the honky-tonks in the Broadway Historic District before sleeping in my first real bed since Wednesday- an attraction of its own after three nights spent trying to get comfortable on a glorified yoga mat while the icy fingers of an approaching winter kept reaching into my sleeping bag to explore around at will.

It was early on a Sunday and the streets of Cape Gerardeau were all but deserted as I traced my way back through town the way

I'd came in the night before. Nashville was a detour that would take me a couple of hundred miles east from the river, but also offer me the chance to score a musical trifecta; Nashville, Memphis, and New Orleans.

The morning air was damp and thick, and the grass was milky grey with frost. A blanket of haze hung over the river and I stopped on the Missouri side and took a photo of the Emerson Bridge with the sun in the background, a muted disk struggling to break through the frozen air. An hour out of my sleeping bag and just ten minutes on the road, the cold had already begun to gnaw away the small reserve of warmth in my gloves. It was a ninety-minute ride to Metropolis, home of the Superman Museum. I remounted the bike and pointed it east across the river into Illinois.

I headed north on the Great River Road up to the town of McClure and turned right onto County Highway 4, a quiet two-lane road that would wind for 15 miles through the Trail of Tears State Forest before meeting up with Illinois 127. McClure was poor; a mix of small run-down houses and decades old mobile homes. There was a Ten Commandments sign in front of one house and a "NO TRESPASSING" placard nailed to a tree in front of an ancient single-wide trailer wedged between two others, each no more than thirty feet away.

Outside of McClure, the road snaked up a forested bluff, twisting back and forth across the landscape, offering bountiful sweeping s-curves. There was no shoulder, and wide grassy ditches ran right up to the pavement in the places where trees didn't. In some spots, the landscape fell away and the highway department had installed guard rails to keep inattentive drivers from careening over the edge. There were streams and barns and acres of pines set against handfuls of bright orange Sugar Maples that had stubbornly held their leaves when their companions had thrown in the towel for the season.

All the while I rode, entranced and distracted by the magnificent scenery, the cold seeped into me like the quietly rising waters that had so often flooded the communities below, advancing inch by inch until it could no longer be ignored or wished away. By the time I arrived in Tamms, where County 4 ran into Illinois 127, my hands had started to hurt from the cold and the chemical warmers in my boots were being outmatched by the sub-freezing wind chill.

The frigid air was frustratingly damp and thick, which seemed to make fighting off its creeping advance even more difficult. I pulled to the roadside at the edge of town and took off my leather gauntlets to breathe warm air on my pale white fingertips. Nothing was open and I had no hope of getting indoors before I reached Metropolis, so after a minute or so, I rearranged the hand warmers in my gloves and set off once again, praying that the rising sun would offer some relief as it climbed into the sky.

At County Highway 5, I headed east again, through a broad open plain of farm fields as I tried to ignore the discomfort in my fingers and toes and around my waist and up the small of my back. After just a few miles, it became unbearable and I stopped once again to breathe on my fingers and do jumping jacks beside the road to get the blood flowing in my legs and feet.

My bladder had started to feel full from the energy drink I'd had while packing up my camp, but opening my pants was the last thing I wanted to do. Instead, I activated another couple hand-warmers and squashed them deep into my gloves, limiting the movement of my hands and compromising my ability to work the clutch, throttle, and front brake.

I rode like that until I reached Illinois 46, where I pulled over once again next to a signal hut at a railroad crossing. With four hand-warmers shoved into them over my thin smart-tech gloves, my gauntlets looked like MMA boxing gloves and were doing about as good a job at keeping my fingers warm. While the backs of my hands were doing fine, my fingertips were painfully, brutally cold and the design of the Kawasaki's fairing left them completely exposed to the wind.

The temperature had only just risen above freezing and the humidity was at 93%, lending a seeping dampness to the frigid air. Although I was trying to stoically endure the discomfort in my fingers by remaining focused on the idea that I'd be in Metropolis soon, I was growing legitimately afraid that the biting pain in my fingertips was a sign that I could be doing long term damage.

Desperate for some way to protect them, I pulled four nylon zip ties from my saddlebag and fastened two hand-warmers to the outside of the fingers of each gauntlet, making them into a pair of odd looking lobster claws. My hope was that having the hand-warmers attached to the outside of the gloves on top of the fingers would both offer a windbreak and get the meager warmth of the chemical packets down where I most needed it.

While I was busy with my project, a farmer in a weathered F-150 drove by, noticed me standing beside the cycle and slowed to see if I was okay. Embarrassed by my predicament, I gave him a friendly wave and big smile to indicate that I was alright. After he passed, I paused and took a picture of my modified gloves, proud of my own ingenuity, before setting off once again, lobster claws in place.

Turning onto US-45 south toward Metropolis, my pride was short lived. By the time I reached highway speed, the onrushing wind got between the hand-warmers and the fingertips of my gloves and simply folded them back over the first knuckles, leaving my fingertips exposed once again.

I only had about twenty minutes to go before reaching Metropolis and decided just to live with the reality I found myself in. I tucked my left hand into the crotch of my pants to shield it from the wind and rode on. Every few minutes, I'd hold the handlebars with my left and give my right hand a few seconds relief until the bike coasted down to about thirty miles an hour and then I'd switch off again. I'd lived in Minnesota for nearly twenty years, but my fingers had never been so thoroughly, miserably cold for so long as they were that November morning in Illinois and I daydreamed about the relief that afternoon would bring.

In the week and a half before I left the campground in Cape Girardeau, scientists with the Japanese Meteorological Association had been anxiously watching a developing storm that had started out as a low-pressure system southeast of Guam and gradually picked up steam over the next several days, quickly escalating from a tropical disturbance to a tropical depression and finally into a tropical storm. Early on Halloween the JMA had officially christened the storm Nuri.

The following day, Nuri began to move northward, developed an eye, and was upgraded once again, this time to typhoon- a Pacific hurricane. A variety of shipping alerts and warnings were issued, and weather buffs worldwide watched as Nuri continued to grow stronger. Orbiting satellites offered a bird's eye view of Nuri's spiraling cyclonic cloud mass as she sustained winds of first 125, then 150, and then an incredible 180 miles an hour- the latter endowing Nuri with Super Typhoon status.

As Chinese poaching vessels ran to flee the menacing storm, the Japanese government issued a warning that they would not be allowed to come ashore. In Alaska, the fishing industry steeled itself for the arrival of a storm that would surpass the fury of Hurricane Sandy.

*****

When I was a kid, my great-grandaunt Marie who had never had any children of her own, doted and fussed over me in a way I'd wish for any kid to have. One of the things I remember most strongly about her was her cigarette smoking. Marie was a smoker from the old school when airplanes and doctors' offices had ashtrays as a matter of course. She smoked constantly and dramatically. She'd cook an entire meal with a cigarette in her hand, blowing the smoke up over her shoulder at a poor tired fern in a macramé hanger.

She smoked over toast and orange juice. She smoked behind the thin steering wheel of her giant blue Oldsmobile. She smoked while watching Lawrence Welk on her black vinyl davenport, and even and maybe especially, while reading in bed before she went to sleep.

It was her dream for me to be a writer. For her, that hope for my future may only have been equaled by her zealous hatred of beards. As we'd sit at the two-person table in her tiny kitchen on the 11th floor of a seniors' high rise, she'd elicit alternating promises from me that I would become a writer, and that I would never, ever, grow disgusting facial hair. I'm one for two on keeping promises to Marie.

For all of her smoking, I don't think I ever saw here light one cigarette off of another. That might have been too low rent for Marie. Instead, she'd crush out her butt, ringed in red lipstick and stained with smoke, and take a fresh white cigarette from her little container and light it with a gold toned Zippo. The whiff of Butane and the distinctive snick of that Zippo closing were as much a part of Marie to me as the smell of her skin or the sound of her voice and easier to remember in the long run.

When I bought my first Zippo, it wasn't with the intention of smoking. It was meant to be a talisman. A little weight in my pocket to bear as a reminder of my own potential. Not my potential as anyone particularly special, but my potential to live a full life, vigilant of the gift of time we all are given and so often squander. The idea was that it would be hard to cheat myself into a life of minor distractions if every time I reached into my pocket my fingers would land on a reminder that I had better things to do.

The Zippo was simple and timeless and purpose built. It had a reassuring weight in my pocket and I liked flipping the lid open and closed, hearing that snick and catching a whiff of Butane. It was an easy talisman and a terrible tool.

Whenever I found myself in a situation where it might actually be useful to have a lighter, the Zippo would fail to produce a flame. Unlike a modern disposable lighter where the butane is kept in a sealed plastic tube, a Zippo is fed by Butane-soaked Rayon and must be routinely refilled due to evaporation. Marie was a smoker and routinely filled hers. I didn't, and my talisman was reduced to an affectation.

Next came a watch. Sometime around 2000 or 2001, I had a small windfall and used part of it to by an automatic Breitling. Like the Zippo, an automatic watch requires regular maintenance, and strictly in terms of performance isn't as good as its modern quartz alternative. After a few years, harsh use and lack of maintenance stalled the Breitling. When I traded it away for a quartz alternative, my watch became just a watch.

In 2005, the search for a talisman led me to a New Orleans tattoo shop just off of Bourbon Street. I'd never had a tattoo but had been thinking of getting a plain letter X to represent both the potential and uncertainty of life. I had come to reason that not only should we appreciate our gifts and work to lead a full life, but also recognize that our best laid plans can come undone as calamities great and small are meted out by the hand of an indifferent universe. Best not to take setbacks too personally.

I had seen a beautiful, stylized X in an upscale tattoo shop on Sunset Boulevard in Hollywood, but had been too nervous to pull the trigger. A block off Bourbon Street in the wee hours of some Tuesday morning, alcohol had overruled inhibition. The artist was obviously a novice, and his attempt to interpret my description of the elegant X I'd seen in Los Angeles was lopsided and tribal. Still, he'd spent the better part of a half an hour working on it and I didn't want to waste his time or make him feel bad.

When I returned home a couple of days later, my ex-wife looked at the result, rolled her eyes, and said, "I don't even know who you are anymore." To make matters worse, as I'd explained to the artist what the X was intended to mean, I'd used the phrase 'X-factor". In that moment, he'd encouraged me to place the word "factor" beneath the X to help other people make sense of the image. It made some kind of sense at the time. If that tattoo were a daily reminder of anything, it was simply the well-worn admonition "Marry in haste, repent in leisure."

Ten years and two tattoos after the X Factor debacle, I finally got a decent talisman just in time to decide the whole idea of a talisman was pretty harebrained to begin with. Just a few weeks before setting off down the river, I sat in well-decorated private studio inside a quality tattoo shop as a talented and experienced artist practiced his trade on my right pectoral muscle. It took him several hours and multiple shades of red to finish the job. The symbol he left behind has never required explaining.

*****

"The Superman", as he was originally conceived, sprang from the minds of two high-school friends, Jerry Siegel and Joe Shuster. Superman was just one of many characters created by Siegel and Shuster first for their own self-published magazine, Science Fiction and then for other publications. The pair divided duties, with Siegel doing the writing and Shuster doing the drawing.

Siegel and Shuster continued to develop the Superman over the next several years settling key elements of his backstory, including his being the last of a race of aliens from the dying planet Krypton sent to earth as an infant and raised by human parents. They made him a journalist in the guise of Clark Kent and introduced his love interest Lois Lane. They suited him in a caped costume with an S emblem on his chest and gave him superpowers which he used for good.

In 1938, after years of struggle to get anyone interested in the Superman, Siegel and Shuster sold all of their rights to the character to Detective Comics for $130. In April of that year, Superman appeared on the cover of Action Comics #1 which would come to be most valuable comic of all time, a pristine copy selling in 2014 for over 3.2 million dollars, another less pristine copy selling in 2011 for better than two million. On the cover of Action Comics #1, an anthology collection, Superman debuts holding a green sedan overhead, his red cape blowing in the wind behind him.

The story inside is simple and campy by modern standards, but also includes a heavy scene where Clark lets bully Butch Matson cut in on his dance with Lois and even encourages a reluctant Lois to dance with Butch to avoid trouble. When Lois stands up to Butch and flees the club alone, Butch and his gang force her taxi off the road and speed away with her in Butch's car.

It's that car we see Superman holding above his head on the cover of Action Comics #1, "smashing it to bits" as Butch flees into the foreground.

Clark Kent, the alter-ego, was humiliated in front of Lois, but the true self, Superman, came to her dashing rescue. In a sense, Superman is a revenge fantasy for the little guy.

Julien Feiffer, Pulitzer Prize winning author and cartoonist, first made the point back in 1965 in his book The Great Comic Book Heroes. The book was the first of its kind and was both a love letter to and a cerebral examination of an art form that had enjoyed commercial success, but little academic respect.

In the book's introductory essay, Feiffer describes Superman as "the first of the super-heroes".

Superman is the prototype on which all the others are built. He is both Adam and Zeus, and as Feiffer points out, he is unique from all the others in that he doesn't don a costume to become a hero, like Batman or the Green Hornet, but rather removes the costume of Clark Kent.

"Superman had only to wake up in the morning to be Superman," says Feiffer. "Clark Kent was the put on. The fellow with the eyeglasses and the acne and the walk that girls laughed at wasn't real…"

And perhaps that is why Superman has endured as an American icon for the better part of a century, in spite of lawsuits, cultural shifts, spinoffs, rip-offs, box-office bombs, and an unfortunate 1975 made-for-TV musical that was as bad as it sounds. Superman allows all of us the fantasy of our own greatness, even if the rest of the world around perceives us as weak, bumbling, or even cowardly. Superman can fly, but he chooses to walk and even to stumble.

As Feiffer puts it, "Did Superman become Clark Kent in order to lead a normal life, have friends, be known as a nice guy, meet girls? Hardly." Clark Kent exists "not for purposes of story, but for the reader."

"His fake identity was our real one," says Feiffer, "That's why we loved him so."

Those scenes with Lois and Butch in Action Comics #1 are bookended by others; Superman securing a last-minute pardon for an innocent man, Superman saving a woman from her abusive husband, and Superman taking down "the slickest lobbyist in Washington" after learning of a secret deal involving a US Senator. Each of these vignettes set the pattern for the hundreds to follow. Superman is defined by his morality as much as his muscle. In this way, Superman transcends the opportunity for revenge porn, and instead becomes an icon not just for the physically weak, but for the morally strong. Superman never presses his advantage on the innocent, but instead reserves the use of his powers purely for good, or at least good from the point of view of an immigrant raised in the American heartland.

"Why are you here?" Lois asks Christopher Reeve's Superman standing on her moonlit balcony in 1978's Superman: The Movie. "There must be a reason for you to be here."

"Yes." Reeve's Superman responds, his voice earnest, almost innocent. "I'm here to fight for truth, and justice, and the American way." It's one of the purest moments in American cinema. That motto and the particular brand of noble masculinity it represents has resonated with and inspired generations of American boys and men.

Recent attempts to update Superman for the times have tried to do so by making him more morally ambiguous, more adult, and more willing to use his powers to serve his own needs and desires. These attempts usually disappoint because they dilute the essential nature of the character. Perhaps the best example is 2016's "Batman v Superman: Dawn of Justice" which, after a strong opening based in part on a $165 million marketing campaign, faced news-worthy declines in attendance over the following weeks as it was savaged by fans and critics alike. Speaking about "Dawn of Justice" on his podcast, actor, director, and nerd-icon Kevin Smith said that the film demonstrated a "fundamental lack of understanding of what those characters are about."

Among those who do understand the character of Superman is Jim Hambrick, founder of the Super Museum in Metropolis, Illinois.[10] Hambrick's love of Superman began when his mom got him a Superman lunchbox for his fifth birthday. By the age of ten, Jim had collected enough Superman memorabilia to turn his bedroom into a mini-museum, charging his classmates a nickel apiece to check out his stuff.

Today, Hambrick's multi-million-dollar collection is the largest in the world, so large in fact that only a small portion of it is actually on display at the Super Museum. Still the storefront museum in the heart of Metropolis is crammed full of Superman merchandise, memorabilia, and artifacts including George Reeve's brown and grey 1950s TV costume and the lunchbox that Hambrick says started it all. (My own experience with a Superman lunchbox was far less productive. After enduring all of the abuse I could, I lashed out at a schoolbus bully, smacking them in the head with my metal Man of Steel lunchbox. The bully's name was Roxanne and I ended up grounded for hitting a girl. With a lunchbox. Extremely not super.)

---

[10] The small town with the big name, Metropolis was officially recognized by DC Comics as "The Hometown of Superman" in January of 1972. The Illinois legislature followed up a few months later with a resolution of its own. Although ambitious plans for a fifty-million-dollar, thousand-acre Superman theme park were never realized (Metropolis has fewer than 15,000 residents and the "Welcome to Metropolis" sign outside of town is missing an "O"), the town does have a fifteen-foot-tall bronze statue of Superman in the town square and a host of other Superman themed photo ops.

Originally from California, Hambrick was still showcasing his collection from his home when he was contacted by the producers of "Superman: The Movie" to bring his collection to New York to help promote the film. After seeing the phenomenal response his collection got, including from fans whose affection for Superman rivaled his own, Hambrick decided to turn a portion of his collection into a traveling exhibit.

The next decade saw the LA area man become one of the go-to authorities on Superman history and memorabilia with DC directing questions from collectors to him and film studios using him as a paid consultant. All the while, his collection continued to grow. In 1993, after years curating a traveling exhibit, Hambrick was excited to move his museum into its permanent home in Metropolis, Illinois. The small town with the big name, Metropolis was officially recognized by DC Comics as "The Hometown of Superman" in January of 1972. The Illinois legislature followed up a few months later with a resolution of its own. Although ambitious plans for a fifty-million-dollar, thousand-acre Superman theme park were never realized (Metropolis has fewer than 15,000 residents and the "Welcome to Metropolis" sign outside of town is missing an "O"), the town does have a fifteen-foot-tall bronze statue of Superman in the town square just a short distance from Hambrick's museum.

The Super Museum occupies a two-story redbrick building in the familiar Main Street USA style of downtowns throughout the Midwest, except this one features a triumphant larger than life Superman sculpture posed in the "up, up, and away" position, mounted to the second-floor exterior wall just above a Ma Bell phone booth where the Man of Steel might have just slipped free of his Clark Kent disguise.

The red, yellow, and blue trim on the building, along with the comic book signage out front could be garish, but they're not. They're fun and appropriate and just kitschy enough to make it clear that everyone is welcome regardless of whether they're a lifelong comic fan or just a casual passerby.

It was just after nine in the morning when I opened the red front door and stepped inside. Except for the guy behind the counter, a relaxed late-twenty-something going about the business of opening up the museum, I was alone to browse the giftshop. The motorcycle limited my souvenir selection, so I settled on a couple of magnets, a pair of socks, and a DVD on the history of Superman.

By the time I was ready to pay, the museum was ready for customers. The $5.00 entry fee was added to my total and I made small talk with the cashier for a couple minutes, learning that he was actually Hambrick's son-in-law, the Super Museum being a family business. I was clearly more excited to be there than he was, so I made my way through the doorway into the museum to begin a thirty-minute wander through way more memorabilia than I imagined could have fit into the space.

I like antiquing, and especially wandering through the larger antique bazaars you find in small towns; the types of rambling indoor spaces that used to be drugstores or small furniture outlets but are now filled floor to ceiling with a mishmash of antiques and curiosities divided into little stalls each curated by an independent vendor. It's easy to tell the sex of the individual vendors in those places by the types of things on offer. Amidst the dishes and dolls and costume jewelry, you'll stumble across a space filled with comic books and baseball cards and maybe a 70s-era Playboy. These are the stalls that always grab my attention. Many of them have a dusty commemorative box of Wheaties. The best ones don't. The best ones have pocket knives and adventure stories, and tin wind-up toys that somehow survived the decades.

That was what the Super Museum was like. Like wandering through one of those antique malls with the individual stalls- except that they're all curated by the same vendor and that vendor is mad crazy for Superman. A set of four original wigs worn by Christopher Reeve in each of his four Superman films share a display case with the June 1981 issue of Penthouse Forum with a cover photo of Penthouse Pet Corinne Alphen riding astride a flying Superman in the Slim Pickens pose from "Dr. Strangelove".

There's a 50's era Superman Golden Muscle Building Set, Superman Flying Bingo, and Superman costumes worn by George Reeves, Christopher Reeve, and Dean Cain. There are Superman belts and watches and books and posters and a cheesecake Supergirl crop top.

As I wound my way through the exhibit, pausing to check out random things that caught my attention, I was struck by the sheer volume of Superman merchandise that has been produced over the years and wondered if Hambrick has ever felt overtaken and overwhelmed by it.

There are obviously certain things in his collection that he has a deep affection for and many others that simply have to be there if one is to keep up with the responsibility of having the world's largest Superman collection. There were two display cases full of Superman shoes. Not shoes worn by actors portraying Superman. Superman shoes for the rank and file. I picture Jimmy Olsen stashing a pair of Superman flip flops in his carry-on.

Leaving the museum through the gift shop, I knew it deserved a second pass, but I was anxious about making Nashville on time for my scheduled tour of the Corsair Distillery and wanted to squeeze in a few miles of the Kentucky stretch of the GRR before heading east. I was still slightly chilled when I fired up the Kawi and wheeled it over in front of the Superman statue for a photo.

Seeing me take a picture of the bike followed by an awkward selfie, a pretty, soft-featured black woman in jeans and a pair of Converse sneakers offered to take a picture for me. As I leaned against the bike and offered my best look-happy-dammit, a-stranger-offered-to-take-a-photo-for-you smile, she took a couple of shots, before lowering the phone and telling me to relax. "Look like you're about to fly away," she coached playfully.

I played along and struck the up, up, and away pose, a genuine smile spreading across my face, my oatmeal-colored scarf dangling down past my waist; an accidental stand-in for a cape. When she handed me back my phone, she was smiling too. Two nerds sharing communion in Superman Square.

I had been in town exactly one hour and had taken 74 photos trying to capture what Metropolis was about. It was hers that nailed it.

*****

Among the ten states that border the Mississippi River, Kentucky has the shortest shoreline, and of the approximately 60 miles of Great River Road in the Bluegrass State only the scantest portion actually hugs that shoreline, most notably at Wyckliffe.

On the east bank of the Mississippi just south of its confluence with the Ohio River (which forms Kentucky's natural northern border), Wickliffe is a sleepy hamlet of only about a thousand people. Wickliffe is best known for the Fort Jefferson Memorial Cross, which, standing atop a bluff and as tall as a ten-story building, towers high above anything else in the surrounding landscape and can be seen from neighboring Missouri and Illinois.

I wasn't aware that the cross existed until I rounded a gentle S-curve south of town and saw it jutting skyward up on the right side of the road. The day had turned sunny by then and the dazzling white of the cross leapt out in contrast to the deep blue of the sky behind it. I downshifted quickly and made an unexpected detour up the access road to the cross, standing in dazed wonder at the size and placement of the memorial.

I had just ridden through a series of sleepy Kentucky towns along a smooth and winding two-lane blacktop that fell away into green grass at the roadsides. It was the sort of road where you'd expect to see people working on their cars in gravel driveways or playing a lazy game of catch in the lush green of their front yard. American flags hung from crowded porches and convenience stores maintained hours that were convenient mostly to their owners.

That a ninety-foot cross might have been wanted was easy enough to believe. That a ninety-foot cross had been financed, built, and maintained at no cost to visitors, was another. I stood in amazement for a few moments before taking a few obligatory selfies and returning to the smooth, gentle, winding road that would characterize pretty much all the roads in Kentucky. They were the nicest I had ridden to that point and would remain so at journey's end.

I rode further south than I'd planned, the midday sun shining through the leaves of the trees that lined the roadside. I could feel myself growing farther from Nashville with each passing mile, knowing I needed to turn back, but bargaining with and against myself for just a little more time on the magnificent Kentucky GRR.

The weather had warmed twenty degrees and I was lost in the simple joy of riding for the first time since just outside Keokuk two days prior. Finally, I set a hard deadline for myself based not on the scenery or the road going bad, which seemed unlikely, but by the dour passage of time on the bike's instrument cluster. Five more minutes and I'd turn back, regardless of where I was.

I got lucky and saw a pilot's wheel sign just ahead of a broad intersection right at the five-minute mark. I pulled over beside it and took a picture to remind me of the great ride I'd enjoyed, then wheeled the bike around to run the road in the opposite direction on the way back up into Kentucky toward Paducah and on toward Nashville.

*****

I've never enjoyed riding on the interstate. In theory, it should be safer for a motorcyclist. The lanes are wider. All the traffic is moving in the same direction. There are no driveways or side streets for inattentive drivers to shoot out from. In spite of all of that, it continues to unnerve me.

The speed is too fast to be comfortable. In moments of quiet distraction, I imagine my front tire blowing out or my engine seizing up and see myself going down on the ground at 65, 70, or 75 miles per hour. I picture myself rolling like a rag doll across the lanes and imagine a minivan or a semi trying to miss my tumbling body and failing.

I also hate the seams between the lanes. You never really notice them in your car, but the seams where the pavement or concrete meet provide a little annoying ridge that tends to grab and guide your tires as you ride over it, creating an unsettling feeling that rider and bike are going in two different directions. That's the norm. At their worst, those seams crumble away creating miles of jagged irregular craters; some as big as a KitchenAid mixing bowl.

As a rider, managing those seams is easy enough when lane changes are up to you. You can watch for a smooth patch and transition quickly, decisively, minimizing the unsettling feeling of riding up or down the little ridge. But a lot of lane changes just aren't up to you. Sometimes highway work shifts the lanes and to maintain the new one, you have to ride along over the decimated seam between the old ones.

The interstate is also where the Wholefoods-shopping mom in the Subaru Outback who would never think of murdering you voluntarily, absent-mindedly wanders into your lane while reaching into the backseat to give Madison another orange slice.

Outside of St. Louis, the day before, I was accelerating up an on-ramp in a construction zone, boxed in by other traffic and a Jersey barrier when essentially out of nowhere the weighted base of an orange plastic construction barrel appeared in the middle of my lane. With little time to react and practically nowhere to go, I instinctively rose up on my footpegs and rode right over the top of it, the way they teach you to do with a board in motorcycle safety training. It was big and heavy and I worried for a few miles about my front tire and wheel. This is why I dislike the interstate.

Whereas my ride along the Kentucky Great River Road had been idyllic and relaxing, the hours I spent cruising across Kentucky and down into Tennessee on I-24 had jangled and frayed my nerves. I spent those miles on high alert, my eyes flitting from lane to lane, my hands and feet at the ready to brake, accelerate, or change lanes based on the ever-evolving traffic around me.

It was Sunday, which helped, but still, by the time I made it to the bluffs north of Nashville, traffic had thickened and I felt hemmed in by guardrails and rushed along by the herd of vehicles which seemed frenzied and overfast as it wound down the Highland Rim and into the Nashville Basin, cars and trucks filled with locals who no longer saw the scenery racing by. Down the side of the basin and entering Nashville proper, I rode into yet another construction zone, struggling to hear my GPS instructions over the sound of wind and traffic, trying to make sense of them against the impromptu lane changes and exit closures.

When I finally exited the interstate, a few blocks from the Corsair Distillery and only about a mile from my hotel, I was eager to be off the road and off the bike. I was jumpy from the ride and exhausted from sleeping on the ground in the cold for three days.

I would have settled for a drink and a warm bed. Nashville is no place for settlers.

*****

The 84,000-foot, block-long Phoenix Cotton Mill building had been standing at the corner of Clinton Street and Clay Street (now 12th

Avenue) for almost twenty years when the newly formed Marathon Motor Works bought it to use as a manufacturing facility. An automotive Icarus, Marathon was founded and thrived in the period between 1906 and 1912, before over-expansion and mismanagement led to the company's bankruptcy in 1914[11].

In the decades that followed, the stately two-story building was reoccupied by the mill industry, mostly for use as a warehouse. It was vacant, derelict, and slated for demolition when it was bought in 1992 and eventually brought back to life as an adaptive reuse community of artistic businesses and retail outlets known as Marathon Village. Home to over 50 businesses including Antique Archaeology and Nashville's Lightning 100 radio, the stately, turn-of-the-century brick edifice was not what I expected when I exited the freeway and made my way over to Clinton Street to tour the Corsair Distillery.

Rolling slowly up the asphalt street in front of Marathon Village toward a public lot on my left, I spotted a lone Honda Goldwing parked in a shallow unused loading dock cut into the mill building's streetside frontage. About half of the remaining space in the loading dock was taken up with a pop-up awning, where a photographer had set up a display table and was selling prints. Taking the unused dock for a motorcycle lot, I pulled in next to the Honda before spotting an emphatic looking "No Parking" placard fixed to the wall directly in front of me at waist level.

As I began to walk the Kawi backward out of the space, the photographer motioned for me to pull back in. The weather was as gentle as I'd seen it, a sunny 60 by that time in the afternoon, but

---

[11] Marathon was formed by Southern Engine and Boiler Works, a successful Jackson, Tennessee enterprise that decided to gamble on the burgeoning automobile industry in 1907 and doubled down on its commitment in 1910, moving its automobile manufacturing to the better-suited and fully dedicated facility in Nashville. Led by innovative designer William Henry Collier, the Marathon Motor Works grew quickly, expanding its product line to five models in 1911 and eight models in 1912 (when they built a luxurious three-story administration building immediately across the street from the old mill). In 1913, with a dozen models then on offer (all of which were essentially handmade by the firm's 400 employees), the company was sued for non-payment by three of its suppliers. By 1914, in spite of having sold thousands of cars and developed a national and international distribution dealer network, Marathon declared bankruptcy.

still he seemed underdressed in loose khakis, sneakers and a short sleeve shirt with the top couple buttons open.

He was tanned and sun-bleached, with blonde hair just long enough to tuft a little at the edges of his faded ball cap. Somewhere in his late forties or early fifties, he was the Costco version of Jimmy Buffett. "It's okay," he assured me, waving his had dismissively at the sign. "You can park here."

I shut off the bike, put the kickstand down, and chatted with him for a minute while I stowed my gloves and disgorged my pockets of now superfluous chemical hand warmers. He seemed legitimately interested when he asked where I had ridden in from and I shared a little about my trip and revealed that I had stopped specifically to tour the Corsair Distillery. He promised I'd enjoy it, and I wandered off to look around for a few minutes before my scheduled tour.

As I explored the cool barn-find artifacts on display at Antique Archaeology a low-grade paranoia settled in on me about the parking situation in the loading dock and I became fixated on the pickle I'd find myself in if the Kawi were to be towed. I'd left it-loaded with basically everything I had - right in front of a "No Parking" sign and had taken the word of some easy-going photographer that nobody would mind. Whatever else Jimmy Buffett might be, he probably isn't the go-to guy for urban parking advice. I was going to have to move it.

When I got back outside, the photographer was gone, his pop-up canopy unattended. There was a public parking lot right across the street, so I hopped on the bike and wheeled it into an open spot over there, relieved of the nagging worry I would have felt if I'd left in in front of the No Parking sign for the duration of the Corsair tour. I was walking back across the street toward the mill building when the photographer spotted me again.

"Why'd you move?" he asked.

I was immediately embarrassed at the challenge. He'd been clear that it was okay for me to park there, and I'd basically moved to the public lot across the street as soon as he turned his back. It was clear that I hadn't trusted him and had rejected his gesture of hospitality.

"I was afraid I'd get towed," I admitted sheepishly.

"You were fine." He smiled at my doubtfulness, the I-told-you-so in his voice gentle rather than chiding. "I know the owner of this whole place. You should meet him. He'd like you. Wanna grab a beer?"

The Corsair tour, which was scheduled to start in just a few minutes, was the whole reason I'd come to the Marathon site, but I didn't want to miss the opportunity to meet the owner. I asked the photographer if he'd still be available when the tour was over.

"Sure, just give me a call when you're finished, and I'll meet you back here."

I entered the photographer's number in my phone and learned that his name was Aubrey.

*****

The Corsair Distillery website, which is boldly black and white and honey colored, describes their product as "Hand crafted small batch ultra-premium booze for badasses". That pretty much says it. In less than a decade, co-owners Andrew Webber, and Darek & Amy Lee Bell have chalked up dozens of prestigious awards including 2013 Craft Distillery of the Year and Innovator of the Year by Whisky Magazine, and 2013 Artisan Whiskey of the Year by Whisky Advocate.

Their spirits won Double Gold at the San Francisco World Spirits Competition in 2010 and 2014. They've also made a host of top ten lists including Fast Company's Top Ten Innovative Companies for 2015, Top Ten Most Pioneering US Craft Distilleries, and Top Ten Distillery Visits.

With names like Rymageddon, Hopmonster, Oatrage, Buck Yeah, and Grainiac, their products are aimed at Millennials and Gen X'ers. Hipster beards and trendy coifs abound on their staff page and their label is a Tarentino-esque homage to the company's founders-an image of three swaggering figures in sunglasses and devil-may-care Rat Pack suits.

I followed the signs to the southern end of the Marathon Village complex and found my way to the convivial and bustling bar space that served as a waiting area for scheduled tour guests. After grabbing a pint of local brew, I found myself making conversation with a thirty-something couple from Memphis, Sienna and Q, who were in Nashville on a weekend getaway. We hit it off right away and when the tour started the three of us stuck together.

Distillery and brewery tours are all more similar than they are different- the processes of brewing and distillation remaining fairly constant from one manufacturer to the next, and the tour served as much a marketing tool for the interesting Corsair product line as anything else.

The distillery itself was small, even intimate, as much so as any commercial operation can be, and it was clear that the Corsair staff was proud of not only their product, but the hand crafted and socially conscious processes that produced it. As our small tour group wandered its way through the concrete floored back rooms of Corsair, where the machinery of a textile mill had once hammered away, I made small talk with Sienna and Q, garnering a recommendation for a Memphis barbecue joint.

The tour was short, and even allowing for questions, it was only about twenty minutes before our group was shown to a tasting room and given the opportunity to sample some of the Corsair line. I thanked Sienna and Q for visiting with me and left them to enjoy each other's company without having to worry about a solo tour guest interrupting their tasting experience.

I found a place near the end of the crowded bar and was quickly acknowledged and then greeted by Sean Jewett, who had been with Corsair less than a year, but was an enthusiastic ambassador for the brand. He encouraged me to try a sample of Corsair's artisan gin, eager for me to taste its cucumber notes.

It was a multiple gold winning spirit, and I studied it for a moment before taking a small sip. I've never liked gin, but it seemed subtler than others I'd sampled. I tried to ferret out the note of cucumber. It was there I think, somewhere under the Juniper.

Realizing that Sean was waiting for my reaction, I struggled to form an opinion that suited the effort that had gone into making and presenting the aromatic spirit. "It's good," I offered. "Not too piney."

Sean, good-natured and professional to the end, offered to pour me a whiskey.

*****

Back outside, I dialed up Aubrey who led me across the street to the three-story Marathon Motor Works administration building which serves as both a museum to the former Nashville automaker and the offices of the site's owner and champion, Barry Walker.

Aubrey gave me the broad strokes of Walker's story as we covered the short distance between the two buildings, relating how Walker had saved the property from near demolition and in doing so offered a haven for dreamers, artists, and outsiders— sometimes without even charging them rent. Early tenants included a Nashville reggae band, not so terrible an anomaly as one might imagine. Nashville is second only to New York City for music production of all kinds. That kind of opportunity brings artists from all over the country, a lot of whom suffer through lean times before finding success or moving on.

Walker as it turns out, understands both lean times and artistry, especially in the form of hand-craftsmanship. A native of Jackson, Tennessee, Walker moved to Nashville in 1979 to pursue his love of drumming. Back then, he had two years of college under his belt, but little else except a CB radio and a Datsun with an empty gas tank.

Dead broke, he sold the CB, filled up the Datsun and headed east. When he got to Nashville, he started taking on odd jobs including work at a plasma center. During that time, he was "living on Snickers bars and rice". Unable to afford furniture, Walker built his own.

Eventually he managed to save $150, which he invested in a wrecked motorcycle. The motorcycle, he fixed and flipped for his next project; a wrecked car. Walker fixed the car, painted it, and sold it for $3,500. Increasingly frustrated by the music business and with a knack for mechanical problem solving, he used the profits from the car sale to buy more tools and to start his own company, The Ingenuity Shop, which he ran from the basement of his rented duplex.

Walker was doing facilities engineering work for the Red Cross when someone approached him about building an AV console. One AV console led to another and soon The Ingenuity Shop was making custom office furniture and refurbishing laminate surfaces in elevators and on doors.

Barry moved the company into a modest commercial space and started taking on employees. At just twenty-six, Walker secured a quarter-million-dollar maintenance contract from Vanderbilt University. Soon after, The Ingenuity Shop would need to move once again.

After admiring what was then a derelict property in a bad neighborhood for about a year and a half, Walker finally bought the three-story, century-old Marathon Motors Administration building for less than half the price of a new house. Speaking in a televised interview for Tennessee Crossroads, Walker explained his attraction to the site, "Well, when I came down the street I saw this beautiful building, just gorgeous. It had gorgeous detail- these beams and all this brickwork and the vines covering the entire building. I thought, 'I can't believe in this part of town, this building is just sitting here vacant like this.' I was just sort of taken by it."

Walker saw in the property something no one else did. Before he stepped up to buy it, the building had been scheduled for demolition. The once stately structure was unloved and dilapidated. Abandoned and rotting, the administration building had become a haven for drug dealers, addicts, prostitutes, and urban squatters.

Stepping into its restored and polished foyer today, it's hard to imagine the thousands of hours of labor it must have taken to bring the site back from the brink. The impression is of something grand and beautiful, yet sturdy and purposeful at the same time- a symbol of another era with decades of patina still there, spared and highlighted by the loving restoration.

The rich, earthy smell of cigar smoke grew stronger and thicker as Aubrey led me down the dimly lit hallway to Barry's office. When we stepped inside, I took an involuntary half-breath, nearly choking on the haze as my lungs accustomed themselves to the smoke-filled air. Walker's desk was massive, cluttered with papers and periodicals and the stuff of a self-made businessman. Its arcing custom-made top belied his past as a console fabricator. At the end nearest the wall, a pair of mounted flat screen TVs were tuned to cable news channels, their volume turned off.

Walker introduced himself, welcomed me, and apologized

for not getting up or coming around the desk. He is, as I'm surprised to learn, confined to a wheelchair- the result of a 2008 motorcycle accident that nearly killed him. He offers me a cigar, and when I accept, he hands me two from a humidor on his side of the desk. While I go about the work of cutting and lighting the supple hand-rolled smoke, Aubrey fishes me a Bud Light out of a cooler on the floor. He and Walker were already visiting when I'd called.

In spite of the wheelchair, Walker strikes me as a big man. His voice is big and so are his expressions and gestures. He asks me about myself and my trip, each of my answers serving as a springboard for a tale from his own adventurous life. He doesn't seem like a one-upper and his habit isn't offensive. He's just an energetic man who likes to tell a good story and can't wait to share his passions. He tells me about the building and how he fell in love with it, and how it was only later, upon the discovery of a tile mosaic underneath a layer of linoleum, that he discovered the site's past as the home of Marathon Motors.

He shares tales from the bad old days, when he used to come to the site with a loaded gun, firing it at the ground to scare away the drug addicts and squatters who would light fires in the building to cook or stay warm. He tells of how he rammed a four-wheeler into a burning barrel during one such episode, knocking it over even as the he lost his balance on the machine and crashed it, tumbling to the floor in a wild avalanche of rubber, plastic, steel, and burning debris and hot ash from the barrel.

He talks about his love life, both single and married, and of the experience of fatherhood. He says he waited to marry until he was 39, waited until he was ready to tap the brakes on his hard charging bachelor lifestyle.

He maybe didn't tap hard enough. It was a few years later in the midst of his divorce when Walker crashed his Harley on a winding country road, colliding head on with a car after swerving to avoid an obstacle. He speaks with remembered fear and fresh amazement how he flatlined three times and spent months in the hospital and even longer in rehab.

He talks about life in general, and living it well in particular. Although he's been offered tens of millions of dollars now for the properties that once, not so long ago, no one wanted, he's in no mood to sell. He has active plans for additional restoration projects and serves as the world's foremost expert and curator of the Marathon brand (Walker has 4 of only 8 Marathons known to exist).

In the wandering stories of white-water-rafting and motocross and beautiful women and Jack Daniels and hard work there is a singular gleaming thread. It is the thread of passion; passion for life itself.

While Walker talks, I smoke, and Aubrey listens and drinks his Budweiser, sometimes offering a remembered detail to enrich the story. I take few notes, not wanting to break the staccato rhythm of Barry's recollections. Instead, I nod and listen and commit to memory everything I can, grateful that he's shared his time and his cigars with me. As he speaks, he glances over occasionally at the muted talking heads on his two television screens. I get the impression that Walker has transferred his tremendous physical energy into equally intense mental exercise now that his mobility is limited.

Nearing the end of my cigar, I'm afraid that although I've been a good listener, I've failed to uphold my end of the exchange and that I have somehow bored him. Conceding that it was too late to launch a volley of my own, I ask him if he has any life advice to offer. As if anticipating the question, he leans forward with purpose in his voice and says, "Live your life and do what you want to do. Don't wait." He pauses a beat and then adds for punctuation, "All these people in their forties having midlife crisises. Your midlife crisis should begin at birth."

We visit a few minutes longer before Walker reaches into his humidor and hands me another cigar. Then he motors around the desk and offers me a quick tour of his collection of Marathon memorabilia. Aubrey hangs back just a second, collecting our empty bottles and stashing them in the cooler.

As he leads me through a small sampling of the cool and eclectic things he's acquired over the years, Walker is talking quickly again, teacher and host, eager to share his appreciation of history, artistry, and craftsmanship.

He beams over his Marathons and, as we near the front door, asks me where I'm staying. When I tell him, he nods in approval. It's gotten dark while we've been talking and he's worried about me having to go too far on the cycle. He gives me directions before seeing me out and then insists on giving me his cell phone number in case I need anything while I'm in Nashville.

Back on the street, I'm left shell-shocked by the encounter. Walker had been simultaneously kind, genuine, brusque, boastful, humble, grandiose, and practical. Leaving his warm, cigar-scented sanctum left me feeling ebullient and revitalized. I had a new sense of hope and purpose for the trip and briefly felt like anything but a fool for running off down the Mississippi in mid-November on a motorcycle with three days' notice. Had my time in Nashville ended there, I would have been satisfied that I'd found the flavor and spirit of the place. Of course, it didn't end there.

*****

I was buzzed and distracted when I pulled into the valet lane at the Nashville Aloft hotel a couple of minutes later and I almost dropped the Kawasaki on its side when my foot landed on the seam between the asphalt and the curb. Arresting the Kawi's fall and hauling it back upright required an unexpected feat of strength and a rush of adrenaline was coursing through me when I walked inside the hotel's spare, modern lobby and up to the circular reception counter where two young and beautiful clerks, Audrey and Hannah greeted me.

The two of them smiled and flirted their way through my check-in process, making me feel even higher than I already did. I'd been basically alone on the road for days, and in Nashville it seemed like everyone I met was going out of their way to make me feel welcome. I was assigned a room on the sixth floor and when Audrey handed me my room key, I noticed that she'd taken the time to write their names at the bottom in a whimsical, curling script flanked by little five-pointed stars. After several days alone on the road and suspecting I looked like all of it, I found the gesture heartbreakingly warm and hospitable.

I parked the Kawi in the hotel's parking ramp and made my way up to my room. On the way, I passed vibrant and soulful portraits of John Prine and Jimi Hendrix by local artist Ray Stephenson who, besides being a talented painter, has written songs for Merle Haggard, Willie Nelson, Miranda Lambert, and others including the title tracks to Blake Shelton's "Red River Blue" and Kenny Chesney's "Hemingway's Whiskey". As my night wore on, it would become easy to think that talent, charm, and beauty were flowing like cheap tap beer in Nashville and generally offered as a two for one.

My room at the Aloft was exactly what I wanted after days sleeping outside. It was spacious and quietly luxurious, less like a hotel and more like a stylish loft. It even had hardwood floors. I quickly fenged the shui by unceremoniously dumping my saddlebags out on the bed to rummage for a good clean outfit to wear out on the town.

Within twenty-five minutes I was showered, dried and walking down Broadway past the Embassy Suites and on toward the Midtown Tavern, a local gastro-pub recommended by Hannah. It was fifty degrees and clear out, some of the best weather I'd seen on the entire trip, day or night, and I was giddy at the thought of not having to climb back into my Big Agnes when the evening was through.

The Midtown Tavern was only a few blocks away, and even though it was a balmy weekend evening, I was able to get a seat at the bar immediately. Like the hotel I'd walked from, The Midtown Tavern had a hip, modern feel, mixing concrete and steel with reclaimed wood. Above the bar, Edison lights hung from the ceiling where exposed ductwork was painted black.

The menu featured a "Ham, Jam, Bread & Butter" sandwich, Peking Hen, Loco Moco, and something called "Son of a Brown Bag" that included beef bologna and hot mayo. Artisan cocktails included the Margarita del Diablo made with Grand Marnier and jalapeño, and the Existentialist No. 2 made with Corsair gin (made with touch of cucumber and most recently described as "not too piney" by a traveling Midwesterner).

My bartender's name was Sarah. Thin and with dark shoulder-length hair, she wore a clunky large-beaded necklace that nestled between her breasts in the vee of her black Tavern t-shirt. She recommended the Tennessee fries and the fresh fish tacos and I said yes to both, starting in on a Yuengling while I waited.

After visiting one of America's newest distilleries, it seemed fitting to enjoy a lager from America's oldest brewery. German immigrant D. G. Yuengling established his brewery in Pottsville, Pennsylvania in 1829. Now, nearly two-hundred years later, the plant is overseen by fifth-generation owner Dick Yuengling Jr., while a sixth generation of Yuenglings already have roles in the plant's day-to-day operations.

Besides being America's oldest beer brewer, since 2012 Yuengling has also had the distinction of being the largest U.S. owned brewery. While it might be tempting to think that that honor would go to Anheuser-Busch, Miller, or Coors; those are all multi-national or foreign owned.[12]

Yuengling is a regional beer maker and distributes to fewer than 20 states, all in the eastern US. Among Yuengling's family of beers, their Traditional Lager is their best-selling brew (and was the 19th best selling beer in the US in 2015, wedged between Bud Ice and Bud Light Lime) and the one I'm most familiar with from business travel up and down the east coast. It's darker in color than other American lagers like Budweiser and has a touch of sweetness owing to roasted caramel malt.

Comments from the beer snobs on beeradvocate.com include the glowing yet measured, "For macro lager it doesn't get any better", the praising yet qualified, "for what it is, it's one of the best out there," and the resigned, yet dutiful, "I would definitely drink if I got caught in a place where only a lager seems to be available" from acmurphy696.

Believing that actions speak louder than snarky internet reviews (no offense acmurphy696), I was into my second glass before the Tennessee fries arrived. The hand-cut sweet potatoes with a hint of brown sugar and sea-salt complimented the Yuengling beautifully and the jalapeño ketchup necessitated a third pint, which helpfully arrived along with two fresh fish tacos.

Sarah never let me sit too long before checking up on me, and before I finally stepped away from the bar a little over an hour after coming in, she wrote out a list of recommended places for me

---

[12] Anheuser-Busch InBev is headquartered in Belgium and purchased England-based SABMiller in 2016. Molson-Coors, while based in Denver, is a multi-national partnership. The second-largest US owned brewery is The Boston Beer Company, brewer of Samuel Adams.

on the back of a strip of receipt paper, placing a hash mark in front of every one like they were bullet points in a business presentation on where to drink if you had only one night to spend in Nashville. She listed four; Piranha's, Layla's, Robert's, and Doc Holiday's. As I got up to leave, she stopped me and thoughtfully added one more; The Big Bang.

With Sarah's to-do list in hand, I made my way out into the night, full and happy and still amazed at the friendliness of everyone in Nashville.

*****

I caught a Nashville Cab down to Honkytonk Row. My driver, Abel, was a Kurdish immigrant and happy to share how grateful he was to be in Nashville. He'd come to the US in 1996 as an asylum-seeking refugee. Waves of Kurdish refugees had been making their way to the Nashville area since the mid-1970's after their opposition to Saddam Hussein made them targets of his regime. "The US is the best country in the world," Abel announced emphatically. "No one seeks asylum FROM the US."

He asked where I was from and when I told him I was visiting from Minnesota, he asked me where that was. I said it was far enough north to touch Canada. "So, it's very cold," he said.

It was a statement as much as a question. I agreed that it was and shared the story of how I'd started my morning by fastening chemical hand-warmers to the outside of my gloves in Illinois, which caused Abel to whistle through his teeth in astonishment.

His accent was thick, and I asked if he'd spoken English when he arrived in the US. "Of course," he told me. "I have an accounting degree." When he dropped me off, he told me he'd be on for most of the night and wrote his name and number down on a generic business card, placing a horizontal bar through his sevens the way Europeans do. I thanked him and promised I'd be in touch in a few hours.

Honkytonk Row, the name given to a stretch of Lower Broadway in Historic Nashville, gets packed with tourists and locals on the weekends, with shops and bars no more than twenty or twenty-five feet wide and sharing common walls the way they do on old main streets, so Abel had to let me out a short distance down from Layla's, one of the bars on Sarah's list. It was a few bars in and situated right across from Ernest Tubb's original 1947 Nashville record store.

I could hear the music coming from Layla's well before I opened the door. Like a lot of the other honkytonks on Broadway, Layla's stage is right in the front of the establishment offering passersby a view of the live music happening inside. When I came in, the four-piece Beth Garner Blues Band (a Layla's regular) was playing a soulful, bluesy song I didn't know, but gave Garner the chance to show her chops on the guitar.

I found a spot at the weathered wooden bar and ordered another Yuengling, before settling back to enjoy the sound of the band's live performance. Country is still king in Nashville, and in spite of their labeling as a blues band, the group brought out a fiddle for the next number.

Country music in general isn't my thing, but there was no denying the talent of the group, and they sounded great, playing live against the backdrop of the bar's exposed brick walls, neon signs and incandescent bulbs shining off their instruments. Like all the bands on music row, they had a tip bucket set up near the front of the stage and I dropped a five in on my way out the door, eager to make my way down Broadway to sample more acts. The bartender had recommended that I try Tootsies Orchid Lounge next. "It's the devil's butt crack," she said, "but everybody goes there".

"Everybody" once included country legends like Willie Nelson and Kris Kristofferson, before they were country legends. Hattie Louise "Tootsie" Bess bought the bar at 422 Broadway, back in 1960 when it was still called "Mom's". The name "Tootsies Orchid Lounge" came later, after a hired painter apparently surprised Tootsie by painting the whole place orchid purple. The color stayed, and Tootsies' prime location right behind the Ryman Auditorium (which was home of the Grand Ole Opry for more than 30 years and is known as The Mother Church of Country Music), ensured a steady flow of greats and aspiring greats alike.

On the Tootsies website Loretta Lynn recounts how her husband Doo used to hang out at Tootsies and drink while she worked next door at the Opry. Other artists who frequented Tootsies in Lynn's day included Charley Pride, Faron Young, and Patsy Cline. Even three decades after the Opry's departure from the Ryman, Tootsies is still a favorite stop for artists.

"Early on when we started coming to Nashville," remembers Kid Rock in an interview on Tootsies' site, "I just knew this was the spot. This is where you were supposed to go if you like to jing-jang and play some music and do some drinking." Just two weeks before I visited, Keith Urban had stopped in to jing-jang and ended doing an impromptu two-song set on one of Tootsies' three small stages.

Tootsie, who passed away in 1978, was known to routinely slip five and ten-dollar bills into the pockets of struggling musicians. "The artists just loved Mrs. Tootsie", John Taylor, an entertainment director at Tootsie's is quoted as saying in an article by Jamesha Gibson of The National Trust, "[because] she'd take care of them."

Grand Ole Opry member Tom T. Hall, who spoke at Tootsie's funeral said, "for young songwriters and musicians, she was a small finance company, a booking agent, and a counselor." She was said to have kept a cigar box behind the bar for IOUs, some of which got paid back by those who took them out, and some of which got picked up by successful artists whose good fortunes allowed them to give back both to Tootsie and to the Nashville hopefuls whose dreams never did come true.

After surviving a decades long rough patch along with the other honkytonks on lower Broadway, Tootsies was turned around by its new owner, Steve Smith. By the time I made it in, around nine, the place was packed. The crowd was younger than the one at Layla's and I managed to get a glimpse of the devil's butt crack.

Although there was live music on all three stages, the atmosphere was more frat party than concert. The floors were wet with spilled beer and there was barely room to move from one makeshift cash bar to another. On the third floor, I stopped briefly to listen to Kelsey Hickman, a Tootsies regular, before moving on in a single sweaty, jostling trip through the different rooms and levels of the place, before finding my way back to the entrance.

Before stepping back outside, I paused and joined the raucous first floor crowd in singing a line from David Allen Coe's "The Ride" which was being covered by a sturdy out of breath cowboy who was doing his best to work the rowdy room. "You don't have to call me mister, Mister. The whole world calls me HANK!"

Back on the street, I breathed in the cool evening air, glad to be free of the pressing crowd. I started east up Broadway, past the neon pink cowboy boot of Robert's Western World, another famous honkytonk whose building once housed the Sho-Bud Steel Guitar Company and paused on the corner of 4th Avenue to wait for the crosswalk.

There I met a street performer dressed in black from foot to fedora. He was in his mid-twenties and talked without ever removing a lit cigarette from nearly the exact center of his pursed lips, where it waggled over a thin and crooked soul patch. He called himself "Eye" and held up a laminated badge to prove it, flashing me an "E" sign with his other hand. A six-string acoustic guitar hung from a band across his shoulder, but he never moved to play it, but rather just wished me peace in the overly earnest way that only the truly high are capable of.

Continuing east on Broadway, I passed Jimmy Buffett's Margaritaville and the Boot Barn, stopping next at the Whiskey Bent Saloon, where I was able to settle in and enjoy a couple of songs by Hushpuppy's Daddy, an amazing cover band led by vocalist Bryan Wain.

Hushpuppy's Daddy was putting out a different vibe than the other bands I'd heard that night. None of their four members were wearing western wear. They all looked like they were wearing what they'd had on all day and the overall effect leaned hipster. The guy playing the stand-up bass was wearing dark Levi's with a cuff, and the bassist had on a pair of Van's. They had an air of cool nostalgia around them and I gave them an enthusiastic thumbs-up when I dropped a five in their tip bucket on my way out.

Around the corner and up a few blocks north on Third, I found Piranha's, another of the bars that Sarah had recommended. It was a sports bar, rather than a honkytonk and the street side of the building was painted in a vivid and playful ocean themed mural that featured the bar's namesake fish wielding knives and forks and racing toward the entrance. Compared to the bars on Broadway, it was quiet- dead even, but I suspect I was just ahead of the crowd. Piranha's is known for their greasy, delicious, southern authentic bar food (including a cheeseburger with two glazed doughnuts for a bun) and they serve the full menu all night long.

I joined a handful of people sitting at the bar, where a bearded and ponytailed server in a black t-shirt was busy frying a burger patty on a griddle against the back wall. Above the griddle, and running the length of the bar, were hundreds of stickers. Some were bumper stickers from unusual tourist spots, while others advertised bands or radio stations, and still more featured a variety of smart-ass slogans and observations.

I had only just begun reading them when the bartender turned his attention to me. I ordered another Yeungling, starting to lose count of how many I'd had, and even though I wasn't hungry, added an order of onion rings, seduced by the aroma of the frying beef on the griddle.

A few minutes later, as I ate and drank and felt generally merry and welcome, a stranger sitting next to me struck up a conversation. He had on a ball cap and a sweatshirt and had noticed the 2014 Sturgis patch on my motorcycle jacket. He'd been to the rally too and we talked a little about motorcycling in general and my trip in particular. Laying out the remainder of my itinerary, I mentioned that I'd be in Memphis on Monday.

He recoiled. "Mem-frica?" This was followed by a disgusted headshake. "Why in the fuck would you want to go to Mem-frica?"

I hadn't heard the term before but got immediately what he was driving at. At home, in Minnesota, where I'd spent the last two decades, there are probably just as many bigots as anywhere else, but the politeness of the culture keeps most people from sharing any overtly racist comments right out loud- at least most of the time, and even then, generally not to strangers. Minnesota isn't without its own racist nicknames for places. A suburb where census data for 2010 recorded the population as 31.4% black, Brooklyn Park is sometimes called Brooklyn Dark, and the suburb of St. Louis Park, where the Coen brothers filmed 2009's "A Serious Man" which included scenes filmed at the B'Nai Emet Synagogue is often called"St. Jewish Park". Aren't we clever?

I told the guy that I'd been to Memphis for work a few years before and had enjoyed seeing Graceland. This time I was eager to see Beale Street.

"Well, you should take a gun," he said, taking a sip of his beer. "Seriously, I wouldn't go there if you paid me. You'd be better off staying around here for another day."

I thanked him for the advice, settled up my tab and headed back out into the cool evening air- eager to escape the conversation and to table any further reflections on race, racism, the south, and even my own white guy awkwardness on the subject until sometime later. Not tonight, buddy. New business is not on the agenda.

I walked over a block to Second, where the sidewalks were made of brick pavers and white fairy lights had been strung in the leafy trees along the narrow avenue. Doc Holiday's Saloon was my next stop. It was beautiful inside, all brick and dark wood. The bartender offered me a shot of Fireball.

After that, it seemed reckless and rude not to finish out the list Sarah had so carefully crafted. I backtracked to The Big Bang, and on to Robert's. The music got better the more I drank, and it was nearly midnight by the time I visited my last public men's room of the evening at a bar called The Wheel. There, someone had scrawled "MN Wild Hockey Rules!" over the urinal.

I called Abel to take me back to the hotel, but he was too far away to take the call and the cab company sent someone else. Back at the Aloft, I passed the reception desk on my way to find a soda and ended up visiting for a few minutes.

Audrey and Hannah had gone off shift and been replaced by Ramona Cummings, a soft spoken and gentle middle-aged woman with kind eyes and smile lines. It wasn't surprising to learn that she was a poet and while we chatted, she wrote the title of her book on a slip of scratch paper and handed it over to me so I wouldn't forget. "Even Love Needs Sunlight". She printed her g's with little upturned arches for tails, the way I learned to make lowercase q's in Mrs. Becker's second grade class.

While we talked, another employee, Skylar joined us. He was a younger guy, 22 or 23 and just finishing his shift- a valet maybe. He asked if I'd seen the Parthenon. When I said I hadn't, he offered to take me. Nashville's hospitality had struck again.

Before I even knew what was happening, I was in the passenger seat of Skylar's Scion TC cruising down West End Avenue toward Centennial Park, a 132-acre urban park that was home to the 1897 Tennessee Centennial Exposition.

The Tennessee Centennial Exposition took place just four years after the 1893 Chicago World's Columbian Exposition and was significantly influenced by the success of that event, including the buildings, grounds, and architecture of the White City detailed in Erik Larson's 2003 novel "Devil in the White City".

All told, over a hundred buildings would be constructed for the Exposition held in Nashville and nearly all would embrace the Classical Greek style. Just like those of the White City, none of the buildings constructed for the event were intended to last beyond the six-month tenure of the fair- including the Exposition's grandest achievement, a full-scale reproduction of the Parthenon in Athens that housed the fair's Fine Arts Building.

The Parthenon replica was the centerpiece of the event and meant to celebrate Nashville's reputation as the "Athens of the South" and would offer the Exposition's 1,750,000 attendees the opportunity to view 1,175 different pieces of art stacked and fitted together as tight as Tetris tiles.

The intended temporary nature of the structure meant that it was originally constructed from wood, brick, and plaster. Following the Exposition however and faced with both the cost of demolishing the structure and its popularity with local residents, the city elected to leave the building in place.

Over the next twenty years, it would host a variety of pageants and performances before heavy weathering necessitated reconstruction in concrete in a ten-year building project that commenced in 1920 and preserved the foundation of the original building. Today, the Parthenon continues to serve as an art museum, but rather than the nearly 2,000 pieces of art which were crammed into it in 1897, holds just 63 paintings in its permanent collection, along with a 41-foot-tall gilded statue of Athena (the largest indoor statue in the western world).

As we walked along the base of the building's impressive columns, made even more impressive by contrast of light and shadow created by the exterior illumination, Skylar shared with me what he knew about the park and the Parthenon, but mostly he just let me marvel, and walk, and think, as he himself had done on many other evenings.

On the short ride back to the hotel we made small talk and he told me about his girlfriend, who was expecting. Then he fired off a text to her to let her know he was on his way home. When he dropped me off, I thanked him sincerely for taking the time to share the Parthenon with me. I might have missed it entirely if he hadn't shown me, and I certainly wouldn't have seen it at night. He knew that he said. That's why he took me.

CHAPTER SEVEN

"I guess I should've known
by the way you parked your car sideways
that it wouldn't last..."
- Little Red Corvette, Prince

I woke up around 8:00 with the bright morning sun storming into my hotel room like a conquering army. I cursed myself for not closing the curtains the night before and turned toward the opposite wall. I'd had the good sense to swallow six ibuprofen a couple of hours before, washing them down with two tumblers of tap water from the bathroom. As I watched the minutes tick by on the digital clock on the nightstand, I was grateful for that small bit of drunken foresight. Without it, I might have been stranded in bed until lunchtime.

It was two-hundred miles back to Cape Girardeau and I wanted to head up to Chevrolet's Corvette manufacturing plant in Bowling Green, Kentucky along the way, which left precious little time for dawdling around. I left the comfort of the bed and padded to the shower, letting the hot water pour over me for what seemed like hours, one minute rolling into the next with no danger of feeling the tap run cold like it might at home.

When I finally stepped out onto the bathroom floor, my skin was a brilliant sun-burned shade of pink and my fingertips were pruned. Back in the main room, I surveyed the explosion of clothes and detritus that had been crushed into wrinkled submission in the Kawi's hardbags for days.

I dressed quickly, decisively even, parlaying the relief of the shower into some kind of temporary fevered motivation, and reorganized and repacked my stuff, laying across the saddlebags as I closed them, using my body weight to force them shut. Still feeling alright, I left the room and carried the full-to-bursting saddlebags down the stairwell that adjoined the hotel to the parking garage, and reaffixed them to the sides of the bike, noticing with the light of morning how filthy it had become, a brownish grime coating it from front fender to tail light. It looked pretty much like I'd felt when the sun had come poking at me thirty minutes earlier.

I returned to the room and did a quick reconnoiter, spotting my forgotten dopp kit on the bathroom counter. I took the opportunity to drip some Visine into both of my eyes. It was the allergy kind, a bottle I'd purchased earlier in the fall to help with a bout of hay fever. The drops stung, but I hoped they'd help me look less like a hungover homeless person.

"Too bad they don't make Visine for unsightly dark circles under your eyes," I thought to myself. It was twenty minutes or so since I'd stepped out of the shower and my feeling of invigoration was giving way to one of sickness.

I resisted the urge to lay back down on the bed in the fetal position and instead bought some time by wetting a hand towel from the bathroom and carrying it, along with a dry one, out to the parking garage where I gave the Kawi a perfunctory sponge bath. Both towels were a ruined mess of black and brown when I carried them back to the room and rinsed them out. Fearing that they were too far gone to salvage, I folded them up inside a damp bath towel and deposited the whole works in the tub.

Riding the motorcycle down the ramp and out onto the street a few minutes later, I could feel the effects of the shower wearing off. I felt weak, nauseous, and a little dizzy, but it was a crisp sunny morning and I'd left the keycard to my room on the dresser when I'd walked out for the last time. I turned on the stereo, selected "You Never Even Called Me by My Name" by David Allen Coe and pointed the Concours out of downtown Nashville and north toward Kentucky.

Twenty minutes later and with Nashville behind me, I pulled into a Shell station next to the freeway. My head was throbbing, my mouth was dry, and I was near to dry-heaving. I was overtaken by a profound sense of vertigo and had zero confidence negotiating the curves as I rode north back out of the basin. I should have stayed in bed, but it was too late now. I was disappointed in my own stupidity and poor judgement.

I filled the Kawi's tank, grabbed an extra-large Red Bull and a package of peanut-butter cheddar crackers and ate them without removing my helmet as I stood next to the bike at the pump. What the fuck was I doing? I took another five of ibuprofen, finished the Red Bull and remounted the Kawi.

Back on the Interstate, I took up a position in the slow lane and focused on the mechanics of riding. After a few miles, the crackers and caffeine and painkillers were beating back the nausea and vertigo. The sun was warming the black leather of my jacket and a series of good road songs were coming out of the speakers. I relaxed a little on the seat, allowing myself to enjoy the morning scenery. I thought about Barry Walker more than once.

I arrived at the Corvette plant in Bowling Green about twenty minutes ahead of the next factory tour and got my name in the registry. Nine months prior, early on a Wednesday morning, a sinkhole had begun to open up under the National Corvette Museum, a popular tourist destination located just across from the GM manufacturing plant. The sinkhole quickly grew to 40 feet wide and about 30 feet deep, and in doing so, swallowed eight of the museum's cars including a 1984 Indy Pace Car, a 1993 one-off Spyder on loan from General Motors, and the one-millionth Corvette ever built, a white 1992 model.

Photographs published in the news showed a surreal scene: a cartoonish jagged shark's mouth opening in the museum's gray carpet tiles and pristine Corvettes lying on the rocky earth below in a jumbled toy box heap as if dumped there by some giant seven-year-old.

The museum had re-opened almost immediately, even as plans were made to repair the damage. I'd seen the museum on a previous trip to Kentucky a few years earlier, and even though I was curious to see how they were handling the sinkhole, I was more intrigued at the prospect of touring the Bowling Green plant, which had been churning out Corvettes since 1981.

With my name on the tour registry, I was shown to a large holding room that could accommodate probably 100 people. There were about fifteen there. I sat quietly for a moment, looking up at a pair of screens where a video chronicling the Corvette's history was running. The morning's headache was staging a stubborn comeback.

With at least ten minutes to go before the tour, I headed back to the bike, walking quickly. I didn't want the tour ruined for me by a growing headache, but even more importantly, I didn't want to have climb back on the cycle afterward for a westward blast across most of Kentucky while my temples kept time with the expansion strips in the concrete. When I finally reached the bike, I fished another several ibuprofen from the trunk and swallowed them dry and then began the long march back toward the factory's visitor entrance.

Whether by thuggish muscle flexing on the part of the UAW, or the pride of a couple generations of American workers in the car they produced, there was a strict hierarchy enforced in the Bowling Green Assembly Plant's parking lot. Signage was clear and unapologetic. Corvettes scored primary placement with other Chevys following them in a secondary ring. Domestics of all types came next. Foreign products, including me and the Kawasaki, could go to hell out in the back forty.

As I made the quarter of a mile trek back across a sea of empty spaces, it was made clear that the thousand or so men and women who were busy assembling Corvettes in the pale blue building ahead had no time for Japanese motorcycles, Korean SUVs, German sports cars, or Scandinavian wagons. And don't start in on how Nissan Titans were being made in Mississippi and Dodge Rams were being made in Mexico. Buy American or bye America, Smartass.

From a distance across the lot, I could hear a Corvette mule angrily completing lap after lap of the adjacent test track under the expert, but unforgiving foot of a factory test driver.

"Bbbbb-wwwaaaa-waaaa—-aappappapp!" It screamed, only to be silent for a second before proudly firing off a second verse of "Bbbb-wwaaaa-waaaa-aappappapp!' Nearing the factory's visitor entrance, to rejoin the waiting tour group— it occurred to me that Corvette test driver may be one of the best jobs on the planet. I wondered where they got to park.

Back in the big room, with its red leatherette chairs and seemingly welcoming, yet somehow curt and restricting visitor experience, I was jarred back into pedestrian reality. No cell phones, no cameras, no purses, no sandals, no children under 10, and please for the love of sweet merciful Jesus, remain behind the yellow line at all times. Every printed warning sign seemed to be accompanied by an annoyed sigh.

The factory's mascot could have been an engineering intern with his face buried in his palm in a gesture of annoyed resignation. I was asked to hand over my helmet to a teenaged attendant for safe keeping. They weren't sure where to put it. The not so subtle subtext was, "Sir, why the hell would you carry a motorcycle helmet into the Bowling Green Assembly Plant?" There would be no stray helmets allowed on the Chevrolet Corvette manufacturing tour that day or any other. Sigh. Facepalm.

Several minutes after our tour's scheduled start time, my group was shown another short video celebrating the history of the Corvette; a history, which like that of America itself, includes both legitimate power and style, as well as braggadocio and mutton chops. A supercar in spandex built in a smallish Kentucky town by people wearing cargo shorts and NASCAR t-shirts, the Corvette is a symbol of America. It's one of us.

Bruce Springsteen and Joe Biden each have one. Alan Shepard drove one (he owned at least 10 in his lifetime). So did John Wayne. You know who didn't? That guy who opened up the gluten-free, vegan, fair trade co-op up the block from your office. Well, him and John Glenn. John Glenn was a station wagon guy.

After the video, we were led carefully through the thrumming assembly process of the Bowling Green plant. As we walked past a variety of stations, our young guide provided statistics and insights as half-built Corvettes inched slowly along. He also reminded us over and over to stay behind the yellow line and to not touch anything.

About two-thirds of the way through our tour, a gray-haired guy in dark blue Levi's and white leather sneakers had had enough. After one stop, he hung back from the pack a few feet as we all started moving again, our guide about twenty feet ahead. Then with a single index finger, he reached over and traced the shiny arched flank of one of the sleek new Corvettes passing by on the assembly line. A couple of us saw him. No one ratted him out.

The line moved at a snail's pace, creeping past individual stations where seats were added, windshields installed, and wheels and tires outfitted. The process was slow enough that none of the hundreds of assembly workers seemed rushed at their task, but there was no escaping the crawling procession of the line. All hands were engaged in a drawn-out, high-stakes, slow motion ballet. By the time a model moved through an assembler's station and their small part of the process was completed, another half-assembled example was pushing into the empty space waiting to be attended to.

Overhead, a digital stat board recorded the day's production weighed against the plant's goals. That day's output would be measured in triple digits.

At the end of the process, every single new Corvette goes through a final quality inspection. It gets fired up, tested for various functionalities, and then hustles out of the factory through a large roll up door. New Corvettes leave the factory with a bellowing flourish, and a line of black skid marks leads the way to the exit.

Beyond the initial testing, a quality assurance team nabs sample specimens from among the finished cars and puts them through more rigorous exams. Gone are the days when America's sports car could leave the factory creaky or ill-tempered. If a particularly unruly example can't be tamed after routine adjustments, it is disassembled down to its component parts and sent back to the line— all of its pieces donated to younger siblings who go on to face the same post-assembly inspection. There are no "spare" Corvettes.

After the tour, I retrieved my helmet from one of the teenaged attendants and, finally feeling legitimately hungry, rode the short distance over to the Hardee's on Corvette Drive, still within sight of the assembly plant. The midday sun was strong and warm, easily the best weather I'd had on the trip so far and I sat outside alone at a concrete table eating a freshly made cheeseburger and drinking Diet Coke out of a paper cup. I lingered for a couple minutes after I finished, enjoying the sun's heat on my jacket and jeans, looking forward to the ride ahead on Kentucky's excellent roads and feeling for a few minutes, very, very American.

*****

It took me five hours to ride the 225 miles back across Kentucky to Cape Girardeau and the beautiful fall weather stayed with me the whole way. When I rolled into the Landing Point RV Park, where I had stayed two days before, the temperature was still about sixty, even as twilight settled over the campground. The spot I'd used two nights before was vacant, so I selected it again and quickly set up camp before heading downtown for dinner.

Cape Girardeau[13], which gave the world both Rush Limbaugh and Billy Preston, is home to Southeast Missouri State University and today is mostly a college town, although evidence of its past as a vibrant Mississippi river town can still be found along its downtown riverfront.

I'd missed the historic riverfront on my last stay but had been told about it this time around by a gas station attendant when I asked about a good local place to eat. They'd recommended a place called The Library and tipped me off to a downtown landmark — The Bar — which had been prominently featured in David Fincher's "Gone Girl".

It had been about seven hours since my Hardee's stop, so I made straight for The Library, an upscale bar and grill on Spanish Street just a block off the riverfront. I backed the Kawi into a slanted parking spot on the street and headed for the understated entrance, marked by a simple green awning over the door. Inside, I stepped into a surprisingly tasteful, even elegant space lined with dark wood and featuring low-key and well-placed lighting.

The Library was divided into two separate bar rooms (one smoking and one non-smoking), and several VIP dining rooms. The non-smoking space was nearest the entrance and was empty, but from the smoking area I could hear the sound of chatting locals and a television playing, so it was there that I took a seat at the bar.

A couple of the locals were drinking bottles of Stag, a beer I'd never tried, so I joined the crowd. Stag, as it turns out, was a popular local brew made just up the river across from St. Louis in the town of Belleville, Illinois. Once a top seller in its own right

---

[13] The town was named for French soldier Jean-Baptiste Girardot, who established a trading post there in the 1730's. The original spelling is gone, along with the promontory cape which was destroyed during railroad construction.

(even topping venerable Budweiser in its own hometown of St. Louis), Stag is now a Pabst brand and had recently been ranked 17th among the 23 brands in the Pabst stable according to a September 2014 piece in Esquire magazine. Esquire's fictional slogan for Stag was "We'll keep you warm when literally no one else will". Brands that beat Stag in the survey included Olympia, Old Milwaukee, Ranier, Schlitz, and Colt 45 (with the fictional slogan, "So, it's come to this."). Stag placed an impressive four slots ahead of the all but forgotten, Champale whose real life advertisers might have made a bit of a Freudian slip with their 1969 print ad campaign that included the tagline, "Celebrate nothing with it."

The Cape Girardeau contingent could have cared less where their brew had placed and once I had my own bottle of Stag, with its old-style Germanic lettering on the label, neither did I. It was malty, easy to drink, and tasted fantastic after a long day's ride, although after that morning's brush with the Irish flu and with the Kawi parked curbside out front, I put the brakes on after the first bottle.

After I ordered a hamburger (at the bartender's recommendation) an older guy who had been visiting with friends at the other end of the bar came over to introduce himself having noticed my jacket and gloves.

He was simultaneously athletic and bohemian, wearing shorts and deck shoes with a well-worn sweatshirt. He had silver hair, a trim white beard, and a full mustache and soul patch, making him look something like a younger Colonel Sanders— if Colonel Sanders had ever seen fit to kayak the Mississippi and play the conga drums in a blues band.

His name was Don Greenwood and he was a local's local, having moved to Cape Girardeau in 1966 to take a job as an artist with American Greetings, a career move that created more than a little animosity with his former employer Hallmark, especially when much of his team followed. Retired now, he spent his time volunteering and enjoying his hobbies.

He chatted with me like a friend until my food came, asking me about my trip and sharing his story with me. He spoke frankly about his passionate love for his partner, Roseanna, a communications professor at Southern Missouri State who he had been with for nearly forty years even though they'd only just married in 2012 (In an interview with the Southeast Missourian, after having received the Otto F. Dingeldein Award for his contributions to the art community in Southeast Missouri, Greenwood joked, "We didn't want to rush things").

He told me how glad he was to see me sitting at the bar as a tourist in that part of town and how he and Roseanna had bought a home in the neglected downtown riverfront decades before when nearly all the commercial spaces in that area were vacant. Like Barry Walker in Nashville, Greenwood had been a dedicated champion of revitalization and restoration of those spaces, serving as President of the Downtown Merchants Association and later on the board of Old Town Cape. The filming of "Gone Girl" in Cape Girardeau was a point of local pride and Greenwood shared that the film's cast and crew, including star Ben Affleck, had been generous and kind with the locals.

He talked playfully about his hobbies; music and kayaking-and lamented about how a recent kayaking injury had him moving a little more gingerly than usual, before immediately joking that there weren't too many 70-year-olds out there bitching about their kayaking accidents. When my burger came, Greenwood took his leave and rejoined his friends at the other end of the bar. I glanced down that way off and on while I ate, noticing that he seemed to be taking notes about their conversation.

A few minutes later, just as I was finishing, he wandered back to my end of the bar and presented me a gift; "a souvenir" he called it of my time in Cape Girardeau. It turned out he hadn't been taking notes up the bar from me, but rather working on a cocktail napkin sketch in blue ink. He shook my hand one more time and gave me a smile and a wink as he saw me glance down at the drawing he'd made.

It was a reclining woman, surrounded by half a dozen starbursts. She had great big comic strip eyes and long doe-like eyelashes. Her bob hairdo was a relic of an earlier time. The style of the line drawing reminded me of the old school single panel cartoons I'd seen in Playboy magazine over the years. That and the fact that she was completely nude.

On her left, Don had written in block capital letters, "On the Great River Road" while on her right, he had written, "Cape

Girardeau, MO". In the lower right-hand corner of the napkin, he had signed his name including the year, like he'd done on thousands of cartoons, doodles, and pieces of art spanning half a century, "Greenwood -'14".

*****

After leaving the Library, I rode down to look at The Bar, the one from Gone Girl. From the street and from the sidewalk, it looked like it should be a functioning establishment, which made sense since it had stood in for one in the film, but at the time I visited, it was trapped somewhere between set piece and reality.

In fact, in an attempt to capitalize on the recognition that the film might bring, a local neurosurgeon, Dr. Sonjay Fonn had purchased the bar and had planned an October opening to coincide with the film's release. That opening had been put back however due to some needed work on the building. The Bar would eventually open to favorable reviews, but not until about a month after I'd stopped to peer in on its dark interior.

The Bar may not have been open for business yet, but the Isle Casino, a $135 million riverboat gambling facility had opened its doors in Cape Girardeau just two years before. The casino was just about half a mile north of The Bar and it was only about 7:30, so the decision to try my luck there was an easy one. Easy decisions aren't always good ones though, and an hour and a half later and a hundred dollars poorer, I was standing in the laundry room back at the Landing Point loading my dirty clothes into a coin operating washing machine.

The laundry room at the Landing Point was considerably larger, more up to date, and less homey than the one at the Cozy Z. The last picture I took on my sixth day of riding was of a printed sign on the wall above the row of gleaming modern, front-loading washers. There were no typos, emojis, or folksy words of encouragement. It simply said,

"Any clothes left
unattended may be
removed from washers

and dryers by anyone who
needs the machine(s)."

I removed my own clothes from the dryer, folded them neatly, wedged them back into my saddlebag, and retired for the night.

CHAPTER EIGHT

"At length, upon the morning of the third day, we arrived at a spot so much more desolate than any we had yet beheld... At the junction of the two rivers, on ground so flat and low and marshy, that at certain seasons of the year it is inundated to the house-tops... a place without one single quality, in earth or air or water, to commend it: such is this dismal Cairo."
-Charles Dickens, 1843

Back in the Big Agnes after my night of luxury at the Nashville Aloft, my sleep was restless and uncomfortable. The ground seemed harder and lumpier than before, and although the temperature was easily twenty degrees warmer than it had been the last time I'd used the tent, a tenacious wind picked up around four and thrummed ceaselessly against the rain flap, making it all but impossible to stay asleep for more than a few minutes at a time. Around five-thirty, I gave up and headed to the shower house, where I finally got to dry off with my REI camp towel, having found it while reorganizing my saddlebags in Nashville.

The Landing Point was quiet and peaceful as I broke camp, rolling leaves and bits of bark up into my tarp before storing it away. Not wanting to risk waking the other campers any earlier than necessary, I held off on starting the Kawi until I was completely packed up and ready to ride out. Finally, with the site picked up and all my gear neatly packed away, I settled myself onto the bike, plugged my phone into the stereo jack, fastened the chin strap on my helmet and pulled on first my cotton gloves and then my gauntlets.

Ready to roll out, I reached down between the handlebars and turned the Kawi's thick plastic ignition switch. Instead of the usual decisive click that breathed life into the bike's electronics, the key bumped forward and then spun around dead in its socket like the pedals of a bicycle that's slipped its chain.

Filled immediately with a sense of dread and annoyance, I turned the ignition back to the off position and tried it again. Again, it clicked forward and failed to catch, spinning lamely around in its housing instead of stopping in the on position. It wasn't the first time I'd encountered this problem.

A few months prior, just before I'd left for Sturgis, I was at a friend's house and the Kawi wouldn't start when I went to leave. Thinking that I'd left the ignition on and drained the battery, I asked for a jumpstart, which got it running.

A short while later, on a rural two-lane about ten miles from my house the Kawi's information screen issued a stern warning, "Immobilizer Error", accompanied by a red blinking light on the panel. The gauges went dead and came back to life a couple times, and then as soon as I slowed to a stop, the bike abruptly died and wouldn't start again.

Thinking it might be a battery connection issue, I pushed the lifeless Kawi off the road onto an abandoned gravel driveway, removed the painted plastic body cladding and the metal battery cover from the right side of the bike, and checked the terminal connections before trying a couple more times to start it without success.

Eventually, convinced that there would be no field fix, I called Shannon, who came to my rescue about forty-five minutes later. I used her jumper cables to start the bike and had her follow me home. Once I got there, I left the Kawi idling in my driveway for a while to charge the battery and then for added security, replaced the batteries in both of the fobs before I took it out again.

A few weeks later the motorcycle dragged itself to yet another ignominious stop on another rural ride, this time in a state park outside of Sturgis, South Dakota. By that time, research on the internet had convinced me that the problem wasn't battery related, but rather a series of quirks in the Kawasaki's design.

The Concours 1400 is equipped with an electronic security system that Kawasaki calls KiPass. Instead of a traditional key, the Concours has a radio receiver that senses a coded fob at close range. In what is perhaps a draconian anti-theft measure, there is no ready manual override. Kawasaki owner forums on the web are loaded with posts from stranded Concours riders frustrated by a variety of KiPass failures.

One thread I found read like the desperate exchange between air traffic control and a layperson trying to land a jumbo jet without much hope. That rider had been stranded alone at a campsite in San Quentin, Mexico and none of the early fixes suggested to him had helped. Twenty-four frantic hours passed before he finally got the system to work by rapping on the ignition housing with a wrench.

Another owner had posted a video of a fix that consistently worked for him. It involved removing a piece on the top left side of the Concours' fairing and then reaching down inside to disconnect one of two wiring harnesses located there. A short wait with the system disconnected allowed a full reset of the onboard computer and the bike would reliably start up again after the harness was reconnected. It was sort of the motorcycle version of unplugging your modem, waiting thirty seconds, and then plugging it back in.

I'd worried about the problem off and on in the run up to the Great River Road trip, but it had been a couple of months since the Kawi had last hiccuped, which afforded me hope that its tantrums were finished for good. I also knew that the harness fix would probably work if the bike failed again and so had made sure to travel with the appropriate wrenches on hand.

Running through my limited options if the Kawi refused to start, I quickly got the appropriate section of the fairing off and fished around in the cold and the dark until my fingers seized on the correct wiring harness. It was more difficult to disconnect than I'd anticipated, and frustrating moments went by where I felt like it should be coming loose, but just plain wouldn't. The limited space and small opening meant a choice between working sighted with just one hand, or working blind with both.

More than once, I stood up from my work and took a deep angry breath, willing myself not to release a shouted torrent of curses, before reaching back into the dim recesses of the fairing to have another go. After what must have been a dozen tries, I finally got the harness apart, waited about ten seconds to make sure the sensors reset, and then plugged it back in. The ignition key immediately worked, and I quickly started the bike, half-afraid that the KiPass might arbitrarily change its mind and go into lockdown again.

By the time I got the fairing piece reattached and was set to leave the campground, I was flustered, relieved, grateful, and annoyed all at once. In all of the messing around, I placed one of the Kawi's two coded key fobs on top of the seat immediately behind the gas tank. Doing so was something I would remember clearly twelve hours later. In Memphis.

*****

I crossed the Bill Emerson Memorial Bridge for the fourth and last time around seven o'clock and headed south toward Egypt on Illinois 3. Although there is some disagreement on how the southernmost tip of Illinois got its name, it's generally accepted that early Christian settlers nicknamed the area Egypt after the similarities (both good and bad) they found between the Mississippi River there and the life-giving and cursed Nile of their bibles.

The part of Illinois called Egypt includes the towns of Thebes, Karnak, and Cairo (pronounced "CARE-oh"), each drawing their names from deepest antiquity. Memphis, Tennessee, just a little further down the river was also named for an Egyptian cousin some six-thousand miles away.

The northernmost of these Little Egyptian enclaves is Thebes. Thebes was once the capitol of Egypt, having displaced Memphis as her largest city around 1800 BC. By 1500 BC Thebes is believed to have been the largest city in the world, home to around 75,000 people (although a population of 75,000 was almost unimaginably impressive 3,500 years ago, modern cities of that size include the thriving metropolises of Scranton, Pennsylvania, Kalamazoo, Michigan, and Waukesha, Wisconsin). It was also one of the wealthiest. The Greek author Homer, writing in his epic poem The Iliad, described Thebes as a city gleaming "with heaps of precious ingots".

In its heyday, Thebes was the center of Egyptian political

and religious life. It is home to the great temple complex, Luxor; thought to be the coronation place of New Dynasty pharaohs with names like Amenhotep and Ramesses, still familiar to our ears thousands of years after their deaths thanks to their elaborate burial sites in the nearby Valley of the Kings.

A World Heritage Site, the Valley of the Kings contains dozens of royal tombs including the most celebrated archeological find of all time, tomb KV62, discovered nearly intact in 1922 by Howard Carter and holding the remains of King Tutankhamen.

The tomb of the Boy King Tutankhamen was initially believed to have been found in 1907 by Theodore M. Davis who documented the discovery of a few artifacts bearing Tut's name at KV54. That disappointing find was described in Davis's book, "The Tombs of Harmhabi and Touatânkhamanou" which declared the archeological treasures of the Valley of the Kings "all but exhausted" at that time. The tomb of Tutankhamen almost eluded even Howard Carter. In danger of losing the support of his archeological benefactor of more than a decade, Lord Carnervon; a persuasive Carter had managed to solicit funding for one last effort in 1922. The magnificent tomb discovered in that expedition would take the next eight years to empty and would captivate the world's imagination for decades.

Thebes, Illinois, by contrast, is a sleepy town of about 450 people nestled snugly between the east bank of the Mississippi River and the two-lane tarmac of Illinois 3. Its streets are mostly narrow strips of tired macadam accompanied by the crumbled remains of a sidewalk that hoists itself up through the grass at irregular intervals to crash the front yards of weathered trailers and simple single-story homes. The town's few short blocks are laid out in a classical grid with the north south streets numbered 1st through 8th and the east west streets named for trees like Poplar, Walnut, and Sycamore.

Overlooking the Mississippi from atop a bluff at 5th and Oak stands the Thebes Courthouse which was entered into the National Register of Historic Places in 1972. Designed and built in 1848 by architect Ernstt Barkhausen, the two-story Greek Revival structure cost the people of Alexander County $4,400 when new. A recent needs assessment, posted online, comes to $22,600 and includes a new roof.

Although a historical marker in front of the courthouse claims that Dred Scott was imprisoned there ("in the dungeons below"), an article from the Southeast Missourian on the 150th anniversary of the Dred Scott ruling in 2007 casts significant doubt that Scott was ever actually there.

Today, the modest building houses the Thebes Historical Society which opens the courthouse for tours on Saturdays and Sundays. On the other side of the world, after decades of incidental tourist damage to KV62, the Egyptian government has opened an exact replica of King Tut's tomb about a mile away from the original in the Valley of the Kings. Like the courthouse in Thebes, it is also open for tours on Saturdays and Sundays.

*****

Riding south from Thebes under graying skies, I came to the unincorporated town of Future City. Here, near the confluence of the Mississippi and Ohio Rivers, Illinois 3 gave way to Highway 51, The Ohio River Scenic Byway. It was also here that I entered the troubled south; the south of slavery, segregation, and a quiet racial tension that simmered just beneath the surface of the murky Mississippi, quiet and menacing like a powered subway rail in plain sight just a few feet from the platform. I felt it settle over me as I rode into it, even if I didn't yet know what it was.

On the north end of Future City stands a green highway sign on a simple wooden post announcing the name of the place. Southward, across a few hundred feet of clumpy brown grass, stands a two-story rectangular brick building with a pitched roof. Its first-floor windows have been filled in and clay colored awnings shade the eight narrow windows on the second floor of its road-facing side. Its whitewashed exterior is mottled and faded, exposing the red brick beneath and an old out-of-place Budweiser sign juts out like a flag from one end— the building's only ornamentation other than a spindly tv antenna poking up from the roof like an insistent weed.

I pulled off Highway 51 and idled the Kawi over in front of the place to snap a photo. Although tall grass grew up around the foundation, it seemed like the building (one of a handful that remained in the abandoned town) might be someone's home, and I couldn't shake the feeling that I was being watched from one of the shaded windows on the second floor.

The building, I later learned was once The Bruce School, a segregated school for the colored. I wasn't the first tourist to happen past and be captivated by its derelict creepiness. You can find a photo of it online in the "Encyclopedia of Forlorn Places" under the entry for Future City.

A suburb of nearby Cairo, Future City was reduced to little more than a refugee camp after the flood of 1912 left its population of poor and mostly black residents living in temporary shelters. Their earnest rebuilding efforts were rewarded the following year with an even worse flood that briefly saw the Ohio River flowing straight through the middle of town, sparing none of its 214 homes and buildings.

By that time, Cairo, Future City's prosperous neighbor to the south, was beginning to show signs of decline- a decline from which neither place would ever recover. By 1990, an article in The Springfield News Leader described Future City as an encampment of about 100 people. The News Leader's article is peppered with words like "ramshackle", "squalor", "filth", "dilapidated" and "decaying", as if the author, struggling to communicate the brokenness of the place, had been reduced to rummaging through the Thesaurus of Forlorn Places.

A few hundred yards down the road from Future City, I passed a monument sign welcoming me to Cairo and shortly past that, a billboard advertising the sights of historical downtown. A quarter of a mile or so later, when I came to a rusty red railroad bridge emblazoned with the word "CAIRO" in stark white, block capital letters, morning traffic was light enough for me to park the bike sideways across the middle of the road to take a picture.

In the background, just behind the railroad bridge, stood the immense Cairo levee and its imposing steel floodgate. The floodgate, installed in 1914 at a cost of about $11,000, stands sixty feet wide, twenty-four feet high, and five feet thick. Its eighty-ton mass waits suspended at the north end of the levee underpass, ready to seal the town against the rising flood waters that have threatened it over and over again for a hundred and fifty years.

Massive counterweights ensure that the floodgate, known as

"The Big Subway Gate", can be operated by just two people on each side, sealing the town off inside a sixty-foot-high earthen and concrete bowl. Since the completion of her flood wall, Cairo has never been underwater. Riding underneath the suspended iron gate and beneath the titanic earthen levee that surrounded it made me feel as if I were entering a fortified medieval keep. In reality, I was riding into a town that had been slowly suffocating to death for a hundred years.

Situated at the confluence of the two great North American rivers, the Ohio and the Mississippi, Cairo would seem to have been perfectly situated for prosperity, and for a period it was. Up through the 1880s, Cairo benefitted not only from constant steamboat traffic on the two rivers, but also a booming rail ferry business.

Her decline began in 1889 when the construction of the Illinois Central railroad bridge cut into ferry revenue and hastened in 1905 when a new railroad bridge upriver in Thebes eliminated the need for rail ferries altogether. The economy in Cairo further declined when river barges replaced steamboats. All of these factors may yet have been survived, if not for Cairo's eager embrace of a particularly virulent and self-destructive strain of racial strife that would find it at the top of national headlines again and again.

To understand why Cairo, a small river town in Illinois, would be gripped so tightly and turbulently throughout its history by racial turmoil, it helps to envision a map of the free and slave states in the Civil War.

The free state of Illinois, shaped like a crude arrowhead, plunges deep into the slave-owning south, with Cairo at its pointed tip, staring across the river into the slave states of Missouri and Kentucky and less than fifty miles upriver from Arkansas. Thus, Cairo was a city technically free, but steeped in the traditions and culture of the Confederate south.

Cairo's location made her a regional beacon for a generation of blacks fleeing to Illinois from the horrors of old Dixie, while its white residents held to the same views as their close cousins across the river. The inevitable conflict contained therein would smolder and flare for more than a hundred years in spite of all well-intended efforts to quell it.

Cairo is now a time-frozen derelict, like some ghost ship

from a bygone war found rusting in a sheltered lagoon, intact but abandoned. I rode into the depressing and oddly beautiful moonscape of Cairo on Veteran's Day morning, perhaps adding to the perception that no one was home. Empty downtown storefronts hulked silently behind weedy concrete sidewalks, their windows gray with dirt, their brick facades weathered to a murky brown.

The wide asphalt of Washington Avenue was cracked and bleached, and on the street signs that lined it, many of the names had faded into nothingness. A few blocks away, the decaying husk of the Southern Medical Center, a three-story hospital shuttered in 1986 after filing for bankruptcy, stood waiting for demolition, rotting plywood covering the windows on its lower stories, while its top floor windows were broken, jagged, and open to the elements.

I rode through the center of town on US-51, past vacant lots, an empty grocery store, and a shuttered gas station. A block or so south of the fire station, I passed an abandoned house whose facade had been all but entirely taken over by kudzu.

At Washington and 11th, I spotted a faded mural advertising Wrigley's Pepsin gum. It sprawled across the width of a three-story brick building faded into near oblivion, the finer points of its text indecipherable. I pulled into the asphalt parking lot on the building's north side and snapped a photo of the Kawi with the building as a backdrop, lying on my stomach to frame the image just right.

At 8th street, drawn by the marquee of the historic GEM Theater, I turned left onto decorative cobblestones and rode under a wrought iron arch welcoming me to "HISTORIC DOWNTOWN CAIRO". The theater had been built in 1929 for the cost of a couple modern full-size SUVs. It was closed and boarded up, rotting sheets of plywood covering the regularly spaced panes on its upper story. A length of chain was woven through the handles on its double front doors on either side of the now vacant box office and secured with a heavy padlock.

I parked the Concours alongside the curb beneath the wordless marquee, its decorative splash of filigree neon surrounding the word "GEM" which was set against a deep royal blue background, then I walked out to the middle of the street to take a couple pictures. There were no passing cars to watch out for.

A block or so east, at the intersection of 8th and

Commercial, a stop sign leaned to one side like a night clerk waiting for relief, and although I was oblivious to the significance of both the date and the location, I had positioned the Kawi for snapshots just a few hundred feet from the location of the town's most notorious event - the brutal mob lynching of William "Froggy" James, which had taken place 105 years to the day that I lingered in front of the GEM taking souvenir photos with my iPhone.

One of the darkest episodes in Cairo's long past began on Monday November 8th, 1909 when Annie Pelley, a 22-year-old white shop girl was dragged into an alley in the cool darkness on her way home from work and bound, gagged, and brutally assaulted.

Although news accounts from the time are loathe to use the word rape, there are veiled allusions to her struggling attempts to save her honor and purity as she was savaged by her attacker.

Katherine Doran, a three-year-old girl, discovered Pelley's dead body the following morning by. She was nude and had been strangled. The tattered remains of her clothes were found nearby along with her broken umbrella.

On Wednesday, the day after Pelley's body was discovered, police used ties and a gag found at the crime scene to scent bloodhounds. The baying dogs led them repeatedly to a home where William "Froggy" James, a hulking, round-faced black man was living, as well as to a series of other locations where James was known to have been throughout the day. As the primary suspect in Pelley's murder, Froggy was taken into custody and held as the investigation into her death continued.

For the white citizens of Cairo, the evidence was in and no further investigation was needed. Overnight, as word of the crime and James' incarceration spread like wildfire to neighboring communities, angry crowds gathered around the modest jail where Froggy was being held and soon there was open talk of lynching.

At least twice through the troubled night, the raucous mob was dispersed, with law enforcement imploring its members to return to their homes and wait for the legal mechanisms of justice. By early morning, it was apparent to both the Chief of Police and Sheriff Frank Davis that the mob would overrun the jail and take Froggy by force if he weren't moved to a safer location, so Davis and a deputy made a surprise getaway with their suspect, just managing to board a train north out of town.

Word of Froggy's move was relayed up the line by telephone almost immediately and growing fearful that the train would be intercepted and overrun at an upcoming stop, Sheriff Davis and Deputy Fuller escaped with their prisoner and hid out in the neighboring woods and swamps around Karnak. Unable to make any further progress north, the three were found about five o'clock Thursday evening, exhausted, hungry, and weak, lying together on the bank of a creek having been denied help everywhere it was requested.

With the growing mob then numbering in the thousands, Froggy was taken back to Cairo where the crowd attempted to hang him from the town arch at Commercial and Eighth Streets.[14] Twice, attempts were made to hoist him up by the neck, and twice the rope broke under his muscular weight. Eventually he was shot to death- hundreds of times over according to newspaper reports from the time.

The mob, its anger still at fever pitch, then dragged Froggy's remains to the alley where Pelley had been murdered. There they cut off his head, mounted it to a pole, and burned his lifeless remains. Accounts from the time record that his heart was removed, cut into pieces, and divvied out among the crowd.

The mob then returned to the jail where they hoped to grab Arthur Alexander who had been arrested along with James and who James had named as an accomplice before he was lynched. The police had, however; anticipated that the mob would come next for Alexander and had preemptively secreted him away while the crowd's attentions had been focused on Froggy.

Denied Alexander, the mob settled on Henry Salzner, a white photographer charged with killing his wife with an axe. Salzner was kidnapped from the jail and then hanged from a telegraph pole at 21st and Washington after being permitted what the Los Angeles Times called "a short religious service for the benefit of [his] soul".

---

[14] Today, all four corners of this intersection, just up the street from the now abandoned Gem Theater, are abandoned and grass covered. The arch is gone and there is no monument to William "Froggy" James, nor any other reminder of the violence that happened there.

As with Froggy James, Salzner's body was then riddled with bullets. Unlike with James, Salzner's body was left where it fell and was retrieved by his family the following day.

The horrific story of the lynchings in Cairo made national news with the media of the time easily rivaling today's in their thirst for salacious details, dramatically filling in the blanks where necessary, such as when the Associated Press reported that gunmen appeared from the crowd "almost magically" after Froggy's hanging rope broke. Most of the follow up analysis of the event centered on the righteous indignity that had spawned it.

A letter to the editor in the New York times, written by W. L. Clanahan a former Cairo resident and one-time editor of her daily paper, after laying out some figures about the disproportionately black population "massed" in Cairo went on to sympathetically explain the motivations of the mob.

"The white people of Cairo have always dealt indulgently with the negro. For years it has been the policy to keep two negroes on the small police force, and there have been negro Justices of the Peace. A negro physician once came near being elected a member of the Board of Education. While they pay but little taxes, the negroes are provided with three public schools… Yet this negro population, coddled as it is, is a constant menace to the laws. No white woman dare venture outside of the house at night alone for fear of assault. Many outrages of which the world has never heard have been attempted. This is why, as Mayor Parsons says, the effect of the recent lynching will be 'salutary'."

In Froggy James' former home state of South Carolina, The Greenwood Index put it more succinctly:

> "GREENWOOD NEGRO LYNCHED LAST WEEK
> Went to Cairo Illinois looking for justice
> AND HE GOT IT".

And from the Louisville Courier Journal in neighboring Kentucky, under the headline,

> "KENTUCKIANS MADE UP PART OF CAIRO MOB
> Delegation of 500 From Ballard County
> Assisted In Lynching James and Salzner",

the reader's local pride is appealed to with the following, "...it was learned that the nerve of the Cairo mob was furnished by about 500 Kentuckians from Ballard County, which borders on the Mississippi River across from Cairo. Many of them were already in the Illinois city, and the remainder went over early in the evening. People were heard to remark during the excitement when the lynching, shooting and burning were taking place: 'Those Kentuckians are all right, aren't they?'"

This simmering cauldron of hatred and resentment provided the fuel for Cairo's descent into oblivion with the sharp racial divide there boiling over into open conflict time and again in the decades following the lynching of Froggy James. In 1917, Cairo had the highest arrest rate in the state and by 1937, the highest murder rate.

Into the Civil Rights era, Cairo remained stubbornly bitter and segregated. In 1952, after 21 black children were integrated into Cairo's public schools with federal help, local police arrested four NAACP members and two black parents for "conspiring to injure the life and health of Negro children" — by forcing them into white schools.

In 1962, rather than granting blacks access to the city's public pool, officials instead made it a private club requiring membership. When a number of protests and sit-ins earned wide media attention and eventually led to the pool's integration, the city simply closed it, citing lack of demand.

In 1967, after nineteen-year-old Army Private Robert Hunt, a black soldier home on leave, died suspiciously while in police custody, riots in Cairo led to the deployment of the Illinois National Guard.

Following those riots, local whites formed an armed patrol called the Committee of Ten Million but known commonly as the White Hats for the white hard hats they wore on patrol. The White Hats were formally endorsed by local law enforcement and by the end of the 1960s had six-hundred members, about 10% of the town.

The White Hats notoriously harassed Cairo's black population, even helping to enforce an illegal curfew. When the Governor of Illinois ordered the group disbanded in 1969, it simply reestablished itself under a new name, eventually morphing into the

White Citizens Council.

The White Hats spawned the creation of an organized resistance movement, the United Front, led by civil rights activists and drawing its membership heavily from local black churches. With little or no institutional power, the United Front fought for Cairo's black population through the use of lawsuits and protests. The United Front's most effective weapon though, was a multi-year boycott of Cairo's white businesses.

One photo from the boycott era shows Cairo's two faces, white and black, picketing in single file opposition to one another on a downtown sidewalk beneath the storefront awning of Dotty's department store ("If it's new, Dotty has it!"). Near the curbside, a row of neatly dressed black boycotters carry hand-lettered signs. One says, "NO JUSTICE NO MONEY".

Beside them, a row of khaki-clad white supremacists carry signs of their own, each topped with a large swastika. The signs have thick, bold lettering and say things like ""WHITE YOUTH UNITE", "BACK TO AFRICA", and "SAVE CAIRO!". No one on either side is looking at the other.

In a town with a majority black population, the organized boycott eventually proved devastating. White businesses struggled and closed one by one, until all that was left of Cairo's business district was a row of abandoned storefronts.

As the town's economic engine sputtered and died, more and more of her residents were forced to leave in search of better opportunities somewhere else— anywhere else. Cairo became a ghost town.

With no obvious improvements or investment since the United Front's boycott was launched in the late 60's, the town remains basically as it was when most of its citizens up and left. It's like Chernobyl: a place poisoned decades ago by something toxic and invisible where little life remains and curious tourists come to take pictures of the decay.

*****

I rode south out of Cairo on the well-maintained asphalt of US-51 until it came to the intersection of US-62. There I turned left following the pilot's wheel signs across the Ohio River and into Ballard County, Kentucky on a steel-framed bridge erected in Roosevelt's first term.

I followed the road south through Wickliffe past the Fort Jefferson Memorial Cross, then down through Bardwell marveling again at the quality of Kentucky's roads as 62 curved and undulated softly beneath me. There was almost no traffic and I found myself dive-bombing the quiet Kentucky countryside, leaning deep into the road's gentle bends and relishing the immediacy of the Kawi's power as I accelerated out of them.

It was easy to picture moonshiners running similar Kentucky backroads generations before, and I thumbed through the playlist on my iPhone to find Steve Earle's "Copperhead Road" listening to it several times back to back as the miles fell away. After about an hour, I overtook a bicyclist heading south along the same road and did a double take as I roared past.

His bike was laden down with more gear than mine. It had saddlebags front and rear and bristled with various pieces of gear lashed, strapped, and bungeed into place. It was ridden by an old man with a gray beard, muscular legs, and a leather flap over his nose that looked like a pointy brown beak attached to his wraparound mountaineering glasses.

I pulled to the side of the road, put the Kawi in neutral (giving into my fear that if I turned it off, it wouldn't start again), and waited for him to catch up. Having spent so much time in the previous few days feeling impressed with my own daring adventure, I had to learn more about his.

Without an ounce of wasted effort, he coasted to a stop beside me and put one foot down, offering me his gloved hand and introducing himself as Gary. He was a retired math teacher from Chicago who had been riding the Mississippi River Trail south since meeting it in Davenport. He'd been on the road for weeks already and when I asked him how long he thought it might take him to get to New Orleans; he said he didn't know if he was going that far.

He was on the Forrest Gump plan. He was riding the MRT, but when he felt like he was finished, he'd stop. He wasn't finished yet, although he shared that he was on the lookout for a nice sheltered spot to set up camp and wait out the threat of rain that was growing above. It wasn't yet nine in the morning.

I asked if he just camped wherever he felt like. "People are very nice", was his reply. We spoke briefly and haltingly about the road, how the MRT was better marked than the GRR, and about the joys and woes of tent camping. We exchanged emails formally and out of a sense of mutual obligation, like Bedouins in the desert sharing provisions. I was self-conscious of the "brraapp" the Kawi's engine made as I rode away, and suddenly had a new appreciation of the luxury and speed the big bike afforded me.

A little further south, the Great River Road led me through the town of Hickman and down along Carrol Street past historic bungalows and river houses whose front walks were carved into the hillside as it rose away from the levee wall a thousand feet away. The sky was a threatening gray and the air was damp and cool. There was plenty of green left in the grass and vines that lined the narrow residential street, and I puttered along at little better than walking speed, taking in the homespun, hardscrabble flavor of the place.

It was just about there at the intersection of Carrol and Kentucky Streets that I stopped to take a photo of a simple mural someone had painted on the block wall foundation of a structure that had long since disappeared.

The mural which was done in Grandma Moses style, showed a paddlewheel steamer with curlicue blue waves lapping at its hull. From its stack, a black plume of smoke swept backward in a graceful arc. Before the end of the arc, a chunk of the wall had fallen away, but someone had set it upright against the base of the mural, a corner jigsaw piece waiting to be tucked into place. It showed the last bit of smoke, breaking into two curled strands like the stylized mane of a horse. To the right of the mural in blue block letters against a stark white background was painted, "HICKMAN, KY." The letters were all but perfectly formed right down to the little tail on the comma.

I rode south out of town on the narrow two-lane blacktop of Kentucky-94 through broad, flat, river plain with the grass growing right up against the tar on either side of road. In time, a railroad track nestled up beside the road between me and the river, and the three of us followed the Mississippi's meandering course southward into Tennessee, where Kentucky 94 became Tennessee 78.

There, a green highway sign announced simply "Tennessee State Line" and the pavement changed abruptly from charcoal gray and smooth to cedar brown and cracked as old leather. What the Tennessee highway department lacked in paving funds, it made up for in paint, with stark white lines springing up to indicate the edge of road, as if the fields on either side weren't sign enough.

I continued south on 78 through the light industrial town of Tiptonville, where having spotted no pilots wheel signs since Hickman, I became convinced that I'd lost the River Road. The Mississippi and its levee walls were now somewhere to my west, so when the opportunity came to turn right at Upper Wynnburg Road, I took it, blindly pursuing the river and hoping to spot a reassuring pilots wheel or MRT sign. It was only mid-morning and except for the growing threat of rain, I had plenty of time to make Memphis by afternoon.

What followed was an all but random series of turns and U-turns as I headed west and south in a halting convoluted shimmy, aware in general of where I was, but increasingly frustrated at the lack of a well-marked, easily identifiable river road of some kind.

I was semi-lost among a grid of farm roads hashing their way across a great westward bow in the Mississippi. The roadway was cracked and crumbling, bordered on either side by deep drainage ditches and long flat fields that had already given up their yearly harvest. In time, I found myself parked and idling, puzzled and working through the turns I'd taken. The levee wall was to my west a few hundred yards across a field, but the road I was on was anything but the GRR. It was more like someone's driveway—someone's poorly kept driveway.

As I sat brooding on my situation, the headlights of a truck appeared at the opposite end of the road, dipping and winking as they approached in the gray light of a morning that was brewing up a storm. I gave an exaggerated friendly wave when the truck grew close. It was a silver Nissan Titan driven by a thin, white-haired black man in a plaid shirt rolled up to the elbows. The denim straps of his overalls were loose on his shoulders and a green John Deere trucker's cap sat high on his head.

"You lost?" he asked, his stringy forearm on the window sill of the big Nissan.

I explained that I'd been riding the Great River Road and had gotten myself turned around.

He nodded knowingly. "That used to happen a lot. Sometimes we'd get two or three of you a day out here." He trailed off and didn't offer any explanation why the lost biker traffic had fallen away. Maybe it was the internet. "You're in a bow in the river. There's nothing out here. You've got to work your way back east to get south." He pointed eastward as he said it, a visual aid for the hopelessly lost. With the levee wall looming just across the field to the west, hemming me in, the gesture was all but unnecessary. I thanked him and put the bike in gear.

Before I could ride away, he added "If you've got some rain gear, you might want to put it on."

"Thanks," I answered. "I will." I rode about a mile and half up the road to a spot where it widened out, then pulled over and put on the blue plastic rain suit I'd gotten from Walmart. It was a 2XL and fit over the top of the rest of my clothes. No sooner than I had it on, the rain began to fall in big fat drops that exploded on impact like little fireworks of water on my windshield and visor.

*****

Explosive cyclogenesis is a meteorological term officially defined in 1980 by an MIT Professor and a weather watching colleague of his. It describes a storm system where the barometric pressure drops by more than 24 millibars in 24 hours. Their work built upon a definition first developed by Swedish meteorologist Tor Bergeron. That type of explosive deepening of a storm system is also called bombogenesis.

Meteorologists, like other scientific types, are not generally known for their excitability, but in the face of tropical storms that go batshit crazy seemingly overnight, even they resort to frenzied sandwich board shouts of biblical Armageddon.

Ratcheting up its fury by twice the amount needed to give Bergeron the willies fifty years ago, Super Typhoon Nuri forced the deployment of the seldom-used "double bomb". When the massive storm, grown by then to the size of Alaska, blew through the Aleutian Islands over the weekend of November 8th, 2014, it did so at 100 miles an hour, pushing frigid black walls of seawater as high as New England church steeples in front of it. Nuri, in short, wasn't fucking around.

Four days later, Nuri's Pacific hissy fit had all but spun itself out, the storm weakening in intensity as it neared the North American landmass, but like an overloaded freight train, it needed a lot of track to come to a complete stop.

By the time meteorologists in Alaska were beginning to relax, their counterparts across the United States and Canada were getting ginned up over Nuri's formidable death rattle. A behemoth front of cold air was pushing southeastward across the continent bringing frigid temperatures as much as forty degrees below the seasonal norm. On satellite imagery it looked like someone had spilled a mug of blueberry syrup onto a map of North America and it was flowing in a wide viscous arc toward the Gulf of Mexico.

*****

In a cold and intermittent rain, I made my way southward along the river down to Interstate 55, where I crossed the Mississippi on a big four lane bridge and entered Missouri once again. The first time I'd seen one of the jaunty blue, white and yellow "Missouri Welcomes You" signs had been on Friday, November 7th riding out of Keokuk, Iowa still in awe of the Keokuk dam and power station. I had spent some portion of each of the past five days in The Show-Me State including sleeping on its ground three out of five nights. Missouri is taller than it is wide, and has over four hundred miles of Mississippi shoreline, but still enough was enough.

It was around 11:30 when I finally rolled across the border into Arkansas, beneath a modest concrete arch. The arch, a putty colored concrete horseshoe about fifteen feet high and twenty feet wide, spans US-61 at the Missouri Arkansas border. Its design is sparing and purposeful with the words "Entering Arkansas" stamped into the concrete at the arch's crest on one side and "Entering Missouri" stamped into the same spot on the opposite side. The only other decorative features are simple, stately grooves etched along each of the arch's edges. Bronze dedication plaques on the lower right leg of the arch as you approach from either side reveal that it was built by H.H. Hall Construction using materials supplied by the Fischer Lime & Cement Company.

The arch is on the National Register of Historic Places and is significant primarily for having survived in its original location since it was erected in 1924. There are tens of thousands of structures from 1924 left standing all over the country, but few with the "come get me, I dare you" moxie of the US 61 Arch.

Its diminutive size and extremely narrow width mean that its stubby legs rest just inches from the edges of the two-lane highway, while its inwardly sloping top span poses an ominous threat to oversized truck traffic. As proof that a simple concrete highway arch is no barrier to progress, a companion structure on the opposite side of Mississippi County was unceremoniously demolished in the 1950s when the highway needed widening.

The arch and its dead companion were both erected in a fit of civic pride by Mississippi County following the paving in 1924 of their section of what was then simply known as "The North South Road", the poorly maintained dirt passage running between St. Louis and Memphis.

At that time, automobile registration in Arkansas, like elsewhere in the nation, was doubling annually and the federal government had recently come to the aid of states in a hasty effort to build a network of functional highways. The presence of an eighteen-foot-wide ribbon of fresh concrete running right through their backyards when there were only 443 miles of paved roads in the entire state of Arkansas was a source of hope and pride for the residents of Mississippi County which placed identical archways across the road at both ends of their section.

Due to lower gas and cigarette taxes on the Missouri side of the border, a host of businesses sprang up near the arch on the Missouri side including fourteen separate service stations in an area that locals called "Little Chicago".

Little Chicago thrived into the sixties when the construction of Interstate 55 gave drivers a faster and more direct route between St. Louis and Memphis, drastically reducing traffic on US-61 and by 1989 all of the businesses that had sprung up around the arch had closed.

While the Interstate killed Little Chicago, it saved the arch. Without the construction of I-55, that section of US-61 would have eventually needed to be widened and the border arch, like its counterpart at the opposite end of Mississippi County, would have been demolished. If the arch can hold out just a little longer, it'll celebrate its centennial in 2024, unheralded by the thousands of motorists passing by on I-55 about a mile away.

I rode under the arch and pulled off onto the shoulder next to the "Welcome to Arkansas" sign. It was my eighth state in seven days. The wind had picked up dramatically and it drove a cold, thin, prickly rain. I posed the bike near the sign and took a quick photo, the wind forcing its way into the openings of my rainsuit. The Welcome to Arkansas sign shivered and rattled against the storm's rapidly intensifying assault. I switched modes on my iPhone and recorded a few seconds of video. 24 hours earlier it had been 70 degrees at that spot. Now the mercury was down to fifty and falling fast as cold gusts of wind blew in from the north at up to thirty miles an hour. I climbed back on the Kawi, slipped it into gear and pressed into Arkansas at the front of the oncoming storm.

I followed US-61 as it slipped quietly south through Arkansas farmland until I spotted a bare brown field, apparently covered in brambles but speckled throughout in tufts of white, some of which gathered in the road ditch where it looked like snow drifts. The Kawi idled beside the road as I walked to the edge of the field and saw for the first time that I'm aware of, acres and acres of agricultural cotton. The crop must already have been harvested because what was left of the white fluffy bolls were stretched and desiccated.

With the wonder of an adult experiencing something entirely new for the first time, I reached down and touched a cotton boll still on the plant, the feeling of its airy fibers at once familiar from so many jars and bags of puffy white balls. My memory conjured up the smell of nail polish remover and I looked out over the dried expanse of low growing shrubs and imagined the difficulty of separating the millions of bolls from their tangled branches.

That difficulty and the costs incurred to bear it was still on my mind when I rode into the small town of Blytheville.

Riding into town from the north, 61 was smooth and wide and bordered on either side by large modern redbrick houses with arched windows and hip roofs. When I spotted an Exxon station, I pulled in to fuel up and grab a Red Bull, which I had taken to drinking through my open visor without removing my helmet.

I pulled up next to one of the pumps and unplugged the cord from my iPhone, letting the Kawi idle for a moment while I considered the consequences of shutting it off. It had been running continuously since I'd gotten it started that morning on the concrete slab next to my campsite at The Landing and I wasn't confident it would start again if I shut it off.

I considered leaving it running while I fueled up and paid. I could ride straight on through to Memphis and shut it off there. Then if I couldn't get it restarted, I'd have services at my disposal, things to do, and an easier time making my way back home. It was only about seventy miles to Memphis. Seventy miles of rural landscape that would need to be traveled through the wind and rain of a gathering storm.

Almost stubbornly, I shut the bike off. It was either going to restart, or it wasn't. The problem had come and gone before and might just as easily be gone when I turned the key again. If not, being stranded at a gas station in Blytheville seemed better than being stranded at some random location between there and Memphis if for some reason the bike shut off along the way— if I killed it pulling away from a stop, or fell, or God knows what.

I fueled up, went inside, grabbed a can of Red Bull, and paid. Back outside, I chugged the Red Bull through my visor and climbed back on the bike, willing it to start when I turned the ignition. When it didn't, I sat there in silence, freshly aware of the damp cold creeping in underneath my cheap Walmart rainsuit. I suddenly felt like the tether that had tied me to home had snapped and gone slack in my hands.

As an American I'm tremendously proud of our achievement of reaching the moon, and the Apollo missions have long been a source of fascination and wonder.

Sitting there on my lifeless motorcycle in rural Arkansas stuck somewhere in the yawing distance between home and my destination, I thought of the movie Apollo 13, which tells the story of three American astronauts who experience a mechanical failure on their way to the moon. I was nowhere even remotely in the jam that the crew of Apollo 13 had been in, but I was stuck pondering whether or not I could continue toward my intended destination, or if just getting home was going to be my new goal.

The important thing either way was to not panic, and instead focus on my options. I thought about Ed Harris in his role as Apollo 13's Director of Flight Operations, Jean Krantz. "Let's look at this thing from a standpoint of status. What do we got on the spacecraft that's good?"

The bike would run fine once it was started and unplugging the wiring harness and plugging it back in had already worked as a kind of manual reset when it failed to start. It would likely work again. "What if it doesn't", I asked myself. I could feel little jets of panic shooting up from the reservoir of fear and anxiety that I'd carried around inside me for my entire life.

I struggled to push back the what ifs. "You're worrying about something that hasn't happened yet" I told myself and climbed off the cycle to remove the black plastic cover on the fairing.

I reached down into the narrow crevice I had opened on the left of the bike and felt around until I got hold of the wiring harness and then peered into the charcoal darkness to verify that I had the one with the orange and grey connector. I slowly worked it apart, then stood and waited. I gave it probably two or three minutes, pacing back and forth around the pump island hoping the extra time would ensure the computer had reset when I reattached the harness. Then I reattached it and turned the ignition.

I immediately heard the click and hum of the instrument panel coming to life and was filled with a sense of triumph and relief. I hit the starter and fired the engine, glad to hear the familiar burble from the Kawi's exhaust. Moments later, back on 61 and pointed southward, the what ifs began to work their way back into my mind. What if the bike wouldn't start tomorrow in Memphis? What if the computer decided to shut it down while I was riding, the way it had done to me twice before back home? What if it stranded me in the middle of nowhere? Would I abandon it and walk? Should I hole up somewhere and see about having the bike shipped home? Should I try to find a mechanic, rent a different motorcycle to complete the trip, or maybe even find a dealer and trade the Kawi away for a new bike?

As I rode along out of Blytheville, I fought a battle of wills with my own unsettled mind until finally I reached a decision that gave me a roadmap forward. I simply wouldn't turn the bike off. I only had two days of travel left to get to New Orleans. In the morning, in Memphis, if the trick with the wiring harness didn't work on the first try, I'd disconnect it and try again. I'd do that as many times as necessary to get the bike to start and then I'd leave it running all day until I stopped for the night. The next day I'd do the same thing with the ride into New Orleans.

As for the remote possibility that I'd somehow stall the bike pulling away from a stop sign or something, I realized I was being unreasonable. That would stop the engine running, but the ignition would remain in the on position and the electronics would stay up. The bike should still fire. I didn't want to push that point, but it would probably be okay. As for the bike deciding out of the blue that it didn't recognize my key fob and shutting itself down automatically as it had done to me twice before at home, that was a real and significant worry, but out of my control. If that happened... Well, if that happened, we'd just have to see.

*****

On the south side of Blytheville, I stopped at a NAPA auto parts store, leaving the Kawi idling out front. Inside I bought a set of metric hex wrenches. I already had two individual hex wrenches with me- the ones I needed to remove the Kawi's battery cover and the panel on the fairing that covered the wiring harnesses, along with a small assortment of tools including a pair of pliers and a compact adjustable wrench. I didn't know what I was planning to do with them, but the idea of having a complete set suddenly brought more comfort than did the industrial sized can of bear spray stashed somewhere among my dirty underwear.

The temperature was dropping quickly as I rode out of town on US 61 and angry gusts of wind kept shoving the Kawi sideways as the road led southward toward the town of Wilson, paralleling a set of railroad tracks across a grassy road ditch to the east while

Interstate 55 cut a path through farm country a few miles to the west. On the west side of 61, just north of Wilson, I passed a stately redbrick plantation house with white columns and trim, set back from the road about a hundred and fifty yards behind a circular driveway flanked on both sides by mature pines.

As I slowed the bike for a closer look, I spied a manicured hedge row just ahead, one continuous rectangle of carefully trimmed greenery fencing off a massive flat lawn hundreds of feet wide and probably twice as deep. Set deep onto the lot and framed by small copses of leafy trees was a white house with three dormers punctuating its grey shingled roof. Smaller than the plantation house I'd just passed, the little white house would still have been at home among the large stately homes nestled up against one another around Lake Minnetonka, a wealthy enclave back home where residents had surnames like Cargill and Pilsbury.

At the end of the hedgerow there was a formal entrance to a second driveway. A whitewashed low brick wall curved inward toward the second driveway from either side of its wide mouth, a small triangular island of grass pointing the way down the long narrow ribbon of asphalt which disappeared around a bend to end at the home whose facade I'd just seen across acres of manicured lawn. The long driveway was bordered on either side by tall sturdy trees whose branches had all but shaken free of their leafy burden.

On the south side, the driveway's brick entrance gave way to hundreds and hundreds of feet of neat white wooden fence bordering an even grander lawn and leading to an identical driveway entrance, this time offering a straight on view of the stately southern mansion perhaps a quarter mile down the narrow tree lined drive.

I slowed the Kawasaki and swung back around to take a picture, staring down the driveway for a long moment. I'd been riding through scenes of poverty and decay near continuously since leaving Cape Girardeau that morning including in Blytheville. Now here, in rural Arkansas, seemingly miles from anywhere, unfolded a sprawling plantation house and its dowager sister. The two stood like defiant monuments to another era, the brick and wood equivalents of the bronzed Civil War generals gazing provincially off into the distance from atop statuary mounts in old downtowns throughout the south.

In fact, the town of Wilson, just south of where I was, was founded as a company town by Robert E. Lee Wilson- born the youngest of five children on his father's plantation just weeks before his namesake would be forced to surrender his Confederate army at Appomattox, and whose parents' sentiments regarding the war of northern aggression are easily enough inferred.

His father Josiah died without a will when Wilson was only five, leaving heirs to quarrel over a 2,300-acre plantation estate. The youngest Wilson, being ill-equipped to advocate for himself during the fray, was left with a 400-acre parcel that was more wooded swamp than fertile agricultural land. One of his brothers-in-law maintained custody over the land while Wilson and his mother Martha went to live in Memphis.

Martha died in 1878 of yellow fever when Wilson was thirteen and for a time after her death he lived with an uncle, before petitioning the court for emancipation while still a teen in order to oversee his own land and conduct his own business- which he did with zeal and tenacity, focusing his efforts on acquiring and reclaiming land that others found worthless, primarily swamps and deforested woodlands.

Over the course of his life, Wilson would go on to build the world's largest cotton operation, relying largely on the labor of freed black sharecroppers. He founded multiple company towns including not only Wilson, but also Victoria, Marie, and Armorel (named in tribute to Arkansas, Missouri, and Robert E. Lee respectively).

To imagine the scale of the late nineteenth century empire he built and the authority it had over its army of workers, it's helpful to know that Wilson once minted his own currency, which could be deposited in the Wilson family bank or spent at a Wilson owned business in the town of Wilson, under the prudent leadership of Mayor Wilson.

Described as one of the largest contiguous agricultural tracts in the Delta, the land on which the Wilson fortune was built survived intact and in Wilson hands until it was finally sold in 2010, for an estimated one-hundred-ten-million dollars, ensuring that future generations of Wilsons will have plenty of hard currency available for years to come, even if it doesn't have their name on it.

*****

A few miles south out of Wilson on US-61, I came to a set of old concrete gates, streaked and sooted with age, the elements having pitted their flat surfaces even as it smoothed their once crisp corners. They were sturdy, solemn and purposeful looking, their simple chunky design a patina of orange and gray and chalky green black.

Beyond the gates there was nothing more than a huddle of five or six shabby looking pines and acres of scrubby late autumn fields. Nearby, a weighty and serious looking historical marker stood atop a black painted steel post. Under the logo of the Cotton Highway, printed in gold against a black background was the story of Mississippi County's past as a host to eight World War II POW camps where captured German soldiers labored in the cotton fields until being returned to their homeland at war's end. Seventy years on, only the concrete columns remained.

I looked off into the distance over the fields where captured Germans toiled under the southern sun, their hands raw and chapped from picking a foreign crop. I tried to imagine their homesickness, disorientation, sadness, and spite. In four decades of exposure to the stories of World War II, I'd never heard that the US had held prisoners of war on American soil, much less as agricultural hands. It seemed King Cotton's demand for forced labor hadn't ended with slavery or even with the abysmal conditions of post reconstruction share-cropping.

A sharp pointed drizzle began to fall while I was checking out the POW monument and I wiped off the Kawi's seat with my glove before remounting the idling bike, the pavement growing shiny ahead of me as I rode with the coming storm. I tucked my body up against the bike's wide black gas tank, peering upwards through my visor and the rain spattered windshield.   It wasn't terribly far to Memphis and I decided to press on regardless of what the weather delivered. It was cold and rainy. I could endure that. It wasn't going to snow or freeze. I just had to go easy on the controls and try to distance myself from my physical discomfort and the unease of riding through the rain. This had been the whole point of the trip; challenging myself to do something both worthwhile and uncomfortable. I smiled in spite of myself.

When the storm ratcheted up its intensity, I decided to brave the Interstate. Getting to Memphis as quickly as possible supplanted any desire I had to stay true to the River Road. The country at that point was broad and featureless save for miles of rocky railbed running alongside the road across a deep and weeded ditch interrupted at intervals by stands of trees being strangled by creeping kudzu.

Interstate 55 paralleled highway 61 just a short distance to the west, far closer than the Mississippi, which looped and tangled itself haphazardly southward a few miles to the east. "Move along," I told myself. "Nothing to see here."

At the town of Joiner, a sleepy village of 500 (the birthplace of record executive Alvin "Al" Bennett after whom Alvin of Alvin and the Chipmunks was named), I hung a right on Arkansas 118 and headed west to catch I-55 south toward Memphis which promised to shave about ten minutes off the forty-mile trek. It was a short run from Joiner to the Interstate and the wind pushed and manhandled the bike as I rode 118 across tabletop-flat farm fields focused on enduring the last forty-five minutes of the day before I could climb off the bike and into a long hot shower at a luxury hotel.

The rain had soaked through my gauntlets and boots, and my hands and feet were wet and cold as I crossed the concrete overpass of Interstate 55 to make the acceleration ramp on the other side. Rain covered my visor and the windshield of the Kawi in fat drops and little streaking comet trails, and a steady hiss of it rose up from both tires as I rolled along. I'd turned down the radio to help me concentrate and was bracing myself for the sensory rush that would be the freeway as I began to brake and lean in toward my turn on the far side of the overpass.

I was leaning to my left as the Kawi's front tire began to slide on the rain-slicked pavement and I felt the handlebars go slack. The sensation is acute and panic inducing- akin to placing all of your weight on a step and then having it suddenly give way under the stress. Instinctively, I released both brakes and dropped the soles of my boots to the tarmac, using my legs as outriggers to keep me upright.

The bike was trying to go down and I fought to hold onto it like a deep-sea fisherman wrangling a thrashing Marlin as it slapped back and forth between my legs.

I'd abandoned the turn and fighting just to keep the Kawi upright, I rode helplessly up and over the low curb and right through the little triangle-shaped island of soggy weeds that separated one turn lane from the other, heading straight across the opposing traffic lane and toward the ditch on the other side. I regained control at the last possible second and managed to stop the motorcycle just as its front tire reached the tall grass of the deep roadside ditch.

My heart was racing beneath the cheap blue plastic of the Walmart rainsuit and my knees were rapidly going to rubber as a passing car slowed, the silver haired Peggy Hill in the passenger seat looking out at me through eyes wide with concern. "Are you all right?" she asked, her voice full of astonishment after watching me almost fall and then recover.

Her wide-eyed expression made me think the ride must have looked even wilder than it felt. My frightened mind fired haphazardly, the details of the two or three second slip and slide tumbling together in my memory like socks from unconnected pairs.

"I'm fine," I lied back at her. "All good now, just slid a little." The old couple rolled slowly past, sizing me up like an overturned eighteen-wheeler as I smiled broadly and tried to look nonchalant, my left hand squeezing the clutch handle so tightly I thought it might simply tear away. As soon as I could see their taillights, I looked down at the Kawasaki's display and watched for the neutral indicator as I toed the bike down and out of gear, eager to climb off and leave it idling.

I tested the soundness of the earth beneath the kickstand and then dismounted, raising my visor to gulp in great cool lungfuls of misty air. My knees and hands began to tremble and I grew suddenly and deeply concerned about the few remaining miles to Memphis.

At that moment, I was sick of being on the motorcycle. I was sick of being cold. I was sick of the way my hands would go numb and fall asleep after hours of riding. I was sick of the same old playlist I had been listening to for a week. I was sick of the way the wind rolling over the Kawi's windscreen constantly buffeted my helmet, sick of hurrying to end my travel days before dark, of semi-trucks and their godawful wakes, and I was sick of expansion joints, grated bridge decks, and uneven pavement. I looked out across the flat ugliness of the Delta in that part of Arkansas, and then back at the waiting Kawi.

I screamed a loud primal scream against the wind and the rain and jumped up and down, stomping my feet against the pavement like an angry toddler. It felt good to release my frustration, and I smiled inside the new quiet of my helmet when I was finished.

This was the adventure I had come for. I was tired of it, but at the same time, I was in love with it. It was never meant to have been an easy run all the way. I was supposed to feel frustrated and challenged. I was supposed to have bad moments. This is why I had come, goddamit.

I stripped off my ridiculous blue plastic rain pants, rolled them up, and stashed them in the Kawi's trunk before climbing back on for the final run to Memphis, then I fished my iPhone out of its little cubby and scrolled through my playlist looking for a song to set off to, settling on John Hiatt's "Memphis in the Meantime".

The lyrics to the song are a semi-autobiographical kiss off from Hiatt to the stifling conformity he felt as a Nashville songwriter ("'cause one more heartfelt steel guitar chord, Girl, it's gonna do me in…") and his eagerness to run off to Memphis where he could get "good and greasy" with a Fender Telecaster "through a Vibrolux turned up to ten".

I never could sing or play an instrument, but as I rolled on the throttle and pointed the Kawi down the onramp toward Memphis, I felt the city's strong gritty pull in every line.

*****

In the late 1800s, a sandbar began to form in the Mississippi immediately west of downtown Memphis with locals speculating that it was the result of silt and mud collecting around a sunken gunship lost during the Battle of Memphis. True or not, the silt and mud kept building until the growing landmass became a permanent addition to the Memphis riverfront.

A nuisance to river traffic, the local government tried for years to amputate the unwelcome appendage, disking it during flood season in hopes that the high water would carry the loosened soil downriver and when that failed - trying to dynamite it. In the twenties, surrendering to the idea that they would be stuck with it for good, the city of Memphis begrudging applied some lipstick to the Mud Island sow and turned it into a city park, reasoning that if something nice wasn't deliberately planted there, something ugly would spring up all on its own.

Following what would become a decades long pattern of failed initiatives, abandoned schemes, halting half-measures, awkward reversals, and virulent civic in-fighting on all matters great and small[15], the city of Memphis eventually green-lighted construction of an airfield on the 43-acre Mud Island parcel in the mid-fifties.

The single runway facility opened in October of 1959 to great fanfare— "Memphis now has an airport on its front doorstep", "The closest airport to any downtown", "Just two blocks from Main Street in Memphis"— and then began fighting for its life while the paint was still drying in its terminal building.

The problem was the looming construction of Interstate 40, the funding of which was approved in the Federal Highway Funding Act of 1956. When completed, the east/west running I-40 would cross from Memphis into Arkansas directly over Mud Island. Proposed in the late 1950's, construction of the Hernando de Soto bridge was begun in May of 1967, less than eight years after the opening of the Memphis Downtown Airport.

For a while, pilots landing on the 3,100-foot runway on Mud Island could time the demise of the airfield with the rising pylons of the I-40 Bridge which would eventually block air traffic to the island. The airport was officially closed in August of 1970, with giant yellow X's painted across its still relatively new runway- a universal sign to pilots that the airstrip was closed to traffic.

The De Soto bridge, a nearly two-mile long steel arch bridge built by Bethlehem Steel at a cost of $57,000,000 and sometimes called the M Bridge because of its dual arches, was dedicated on August 17th, 1973 at a ceremony keynoted by the governors of

---

[15] After spending $30 million on a failing convention center- the tenth largest in the US, the Memphis city council chased a proposed new Hyatt Regency twenty miles out of town over parking concerns while the Tennessean reported on a "bleak downtown hotel situation" in Memphis that had officials "seeking legislative authority to issue bonds to build a luxury hotel at the convention center".

Arkansas and Tennessee and featuring, in grand southern tradition, a beaver pelt hat worn at another Memphis bridge opening by Governor James Engle in 1892. Just forty years later, inspectors would categorize De Soto Bridge as "structurally deficient" scoring an overall sufficiency rating of just 47 out of 100, with its superstructure rated as "poor" — no great reassurance to the 45,000 motorists who cross it each day.[16]

I crossed the De Soto bridge's rain-soaked deck in a heavy crosswind, its sea-foam green spans interlaced overhead. On the opposite side, I exited the freeway and worked my way in a loop around the 32-story Memphis Pyramid- another civic boondoggle, vacant and unused in 2014, but successfully repurposed as a Bass ProShops megastore the following year— then crossed a small bridge onto Mud Island at A.W. Willis Avenue.

Soon after the downtown airport was closed in 1970, city officials began brainstorming ways to repurpose Mud Island into something useful and by the end of the decade; a massive multi-million-dollar redevelopment project was underway.

Like most ambitious public works projects, Mud Island's costs spiraled upward once work started. As dredges and cranes worked to transform the island in 1977, city officials estimated the final cost of the development would run $30 million. Coincidently, the city was fresh off two other $30 million projects; The Cook Convention Center and a new justice complex. Apparently in the 70's there was no $30 million project Memphis wouldn't bite on. It's like they handed their finances over to the Rain Man. "Ray, do you know how much a candy bar costs?" — "About a hundred dollars". — "Do you know how much one of those new compact cars costs?" — "About a hundred dollars." By 1981, the Mud Island estimate was revised to $60 million, and when the project was finally complete in 1982, the final cost had run to $63 million—or approximately what the city would fork over for The Memphis Pyramid a decade later.   When the project was finally opened to an optimistic public, Mud Island had become home to the sprawling Mississippi River Museum, as well as a beautiful public park offering an amphitheater, bike trails, and a 40,000-

---

[16] A retrofit on the De Soto Bridge is in the works at an estimated cost of up to $250,000,000.

square-foot model of the Gulf of Mexico that visitors could explore on rented pedal boats.

Befitting a grand public project conceived in the seventies and completed in the eighties, Mud Island connects to downtown New Orleans not only by bridge, but also by way of monorail. (What'd I say? Monorail. What's it called? Monorail.)

A planned community, Harbor Town, has now also taken hold on Mud Island, and while the city of Memphis was twice named one of America's Top Ten Dirtiest Cities by Travel + Leisure magazine, Harbor Town maintains a carefully cultivated upscale boutique feel and caters almost exclusively to young fashionable professionals. Real estate website movoto.com practically trips over itself stressing the distinction between Harbor Town and what it calls "the rest of Memphis". Their rundown of the Harbor Town neighborhood reads like an extended Goofus and Gallant cartoon.

"[Harbor Town] is also a great place for professionals; a quarter of residents have obtained a four-year degree and another 17.5% have attained a masters. This is significantly higher than the rest of Memphis... The value of houses on the island are around $220,000 which is a fairly high value compared to the rest of Memphis... The culture of Harbor Town is very unique for the area, due to its isolation from the rest of Memphis... The neighborhood gives off a vibe that the rest of Memphis does not have... Harbor Town has become the blueprint that the rest of Memphis is looking to emulate and achieve... Memphis has a bit of a crime problem, but this neighborhood seems to be immune... [Harbor Town] is one of the few parts of Memphis that is relatively safe to walk at night..."

Reading the review, I couldn't help but picture Rest of Memphis as a disheveled and unsuccessful slacker staring at the floor and fidgeting nervously while its younger sibling was being heaped with praise. "Rest of Memphis, why can't you be more like Harbor Town?"

To be fair- Memphis after getting off to a reasonably successful start following its founding in 1819 by Judge John Overton, General James Winchester, and future President Andrew Jackson (at a time when a candidate's resume could gamely include bullet points for both "wealthy slave-owner" and "national hero") - foundered after being struck by a vicious Yellow Fever epidemic which bankrupted a local government already burdened with heavy debts. That incident permanently changed the demography of the city and saddled it with a reputation as a filthy, backward, and even deadly place for years to come[17].

Yellow Fever is a mosquito borne illness which was once prevalent in tropical and sub-tropical areas. Symptoms include headache, fever, muscle aches, and lack of appetite or nausea which arise after an incubation period of three to six days. For most infected people, these symptoms pass in less than a week, but in a minority of cases, the infection intensifies, causing bleeding from the mouth, eyes, and GI tract (resulting in the vomiting of blood), and leading to death by kidney or liver failure.

Because it had no garbage service, public waterworks or sanitation system, Memphis, like its swampy southern neighbor New Orleans, was routinely troubled by Yellow Fever including multiple outbreaks in 1855, 1867, and 1873. It was not yet understood that Yellow Fever was mosquito borne and with no effective measures of prevention, controlling the disease meant swift quarantine for infected individuals and avoidance of affected populations by those who were still healthy.

By the summer of 1878, when Yellow Fever struck Vicksburg, its neighbor 220 miles to the south, Memphis had reached a population of 47,000. To protect its residents from the fever, public health officials stopped travel into the city from the south as did nearby Helena, Arkansas.

A dispatch from Helena dated August 1st, 1878 notes, "The steamer Golden Crown[18] passed here at 11 o'clock this morning. Yellow Fever is reported on board… The boat will not be permitted to land here, nor will any of her passengers be allowed to disembark at this port. She will be hauled to at President's Island and subject to the strictest quarantine."

Named for its impressive size and upriver from Helena by

---

[17] After the assassination there of Dr. Martin Luther King, Jr. in 1968, Time magazine described Memphis as "a Southern backwater", a "decaying Mississippi river town".

[18] The Golden Crown, described in a shipping report in the Cincinnati Daily Star as "large, new, and palatial" had launched less than a year before and was one of three sister ships that were the pride of New Orleans and included The Golden Rule, and The Golden City."

about 75 miles, President's Island is a 7,500-acre oval of land squatting in a giant bow in the Mississippi just southwest of Memphis.

In 1878, the island was fresh from duty as a freedman's camp and had been transitioned into a penal farm and quarantine zone. Under full steam, it took the Golden Crown the remainder of the day to make her way north from Helena to President's Island where she was boarded by a Memphis quarantine officer, Dr. A. Laurence. Confirming that a female passenger was indeed infected with Yellow Fever, Dr. Laurence restricted those on-board from traveling beyond President's Island into the city.

Whether out of frustration, arrogance, or simple hubris, The Golden Crown's captain, W.P. Walker, dispatched a wharf boat into the city of Memphis with a handful of people aboard. One, a deckhand named William Warren, availed himself of the opportunity to enjoy a hearty Italian dinner at a snack shop operated by Kate Bionda. It would be one of the last meals ever enjoyed by Warren, whose incubating fever made itself violently known over the coming hours. After pleading for admission, he died in the quarantine hospital on President's Island in a matter of days. Bionda- a well-liked local woman, earned a death sentence for her smiling service to Warren, executed within a fortnight and making orphans of her two small children. In a desperate attempt to arrest the spread of the infection, her body was burned to ashes within five hours of her death.

Captain Walker of The Golden Crown and his purser E.L. Shinkle, apparently feeling quite put out by their cold reception in Memphis in spite of the presence on-board of a woman quietly bleeding to death in her cabin, co-signed a letter to the Memphis Public Ledger before steaming north, "…it is reported that there is yellow fever aboard here and [we] wish to contradict it. There is no yellow fever here, nor has there been."

The attitude of denial exhibited by Captain Walker and his purser extended to the remainder of the Crown's passengers and crew. A letter from one passenger to the New Orleans Times Picayune dated August 5th, speaks indignantly of the treatment the Crown and her passengers were receiving on their trip upriver.

"Dear Sir- Having leisure I concluded to drop you a few

incidents concerning our trip from your city to this place. We left New Orleans for Cincinnati on Saturday July 27, with a good trip of people and a large freight, and everything went on well until we reached President's Island, some 10 or 12 miles below Memphis. Here we were obliged to discharge our freight destined for Memphis, at which city we would not be allowed to land. After leaving President's Island, we made a landing at Hopefield, opposite to Memphis. Leaving Hopefield our next landing was to have been at Cairo, but it was quarantined against us, and as we proceeded up the Ohio River matters became worse, for at Mound City, a few miles above Cairo, the citizens of that burg had the fire alarm bells rung and would not permit us to land. We next passed Shanweetown where a skim came out from the shore and informed us that the entire population of the place was on the river front and to land was out of the question. In fact, an organized militia were on hand to dispute our landing at all hazards. This will give you an idea how the Yellow Fever scare has traveled up the river and the manner in which the Golden Crown and her officers were welcomed.

Notwithstanding there was not a case of fever on board the Crown since she left New Orleans, nor would it be likely to be at the end of her destination. There was on board a lady passenger who had chills and fever leaving your city, who died shortly after leaving Cairo, and was buried twelve miles below Paducah. The name of the lady was Costello, and her destination was Evansville. I take pleasure in announcing to the world that the time-honored and good old State of Kentucky did not prohibit the Golden Crown from landing anywhere along its banks. More honor to the State that bears the never to be forgotten motto of "united we stand, divided we fall" I will write you from Louisville or Cincinnati. Respectfully yours, EFG."

The Crown's run in with a militia in Shawneetown was also reported in their local newspaper, dated the same day as EFG's letter. "Our city authorities having seen reports in the papers of yellow fever aboard the Golden Crown, placed the militias on guard to prevent her landing. After being notified not to land, the pilot, feeling mischievous, blew the whistle and rang the bell as though intending to land, which brought the militia boys down the hill on double quick; but when opposite the wharf boat, instead of landing they fired their cannon as a salute and passed on up. They were in a jolly mood on the Crown as they were fiddling and dancing and apparently had not the fear of yellow fever before their eyes."

After a brief remission, during which she requested lemonade and root beer, taking both and enjoying a short walk on deck against doctor's orders, the Crown's first Yellow Fever victim succumbed to the illness somewhere south of Mound City, where a coffin was brought on board. Held back by the mayor and about a hundred locals, the Golden Crown was unable to land and was forced to inter the coffin on the sandy shore. The dead woman was not to be left alone however. The Crown also left behind three sick passengers, steaming away as they lay exposed and dying in the sun on mattresses dragged hastily ashore.

Five days after the Crown left Memphis, as restaurant owner Kate Bionda and others begun to show symptoms of Yellow Fever and with local officials struggling to contain panic as much as disease, the following words appeared in the Memphis Daily Appeal, "The Captain of the Golden Crown has made misrepresentations to the public, acted in bad faith in this whole matter, and deserves the severest censure. No man who is not lost to all sense of what is right, or who does not wish to subordinate everything to his own selfish purposes, would, in the face of physicians' declarations that he had yellow fever on board, try to land at any port…"[19]

As panic gripped the citizens of Memphis, almost anyone with the means to do so fled the city- running for their lives. In less than a week, 25,000 people, better than half the population, crushed aboard trains, boats, and coaches desperate to escape. They often found themselves unwelcome wherever they tried to lay up- turned away by "shotgun quarantine" as wretched carriers of a deadly epidemic. A morbid stillness settled over the city they left behind, the majority of the remaining population now down with the fever

---

[19] Although Walker appears never to have faced censure and led by all accounts a distinguished career as a riverboat captain, by the following August, his purser E.L. Shinkle was captaining the Golden Crown. Nearly a decade later, Walker's name was recorded once again on the Golden Crown's manifest— this time as a round trip passenger and special guest of Captain O.P. Shinkle. Walker died in 1901 at the age of 80 in his hometown of Cincinnati.

and dying at a rate of about two-hundred a day - health officials and coffin makers unable to keep pace with the demands on their time.

By the end of October, when the first frost of winter finally checked the disease, 20,000 people in the southeast had succumbed to the fever, another 80,000 having survived its kiss. So quickly and thoroughly had Memphis been abandoned that its crippled government lost its charter within the year, defaulting on its municipal debts. It would be five years before the city would have its taxing authority reinstated, but its ability to act independently would be limited by the state legislature and its municipal government would thereafter be hobbled by controversy and cronyism, Yellow Fever having crippled the city long after the last bodies were hauled away.

*****

A 28-room boutique hotel built new in 2007 at a cost of $9 million, the River Inn of Harbor Town is built to resemble an old world European getaway with a few southern touches thrown in. The hotel's pine floors were salvaged from a textile mill in Virginia and date from the 1800's, as does the lobby's fireplace which was rescued from New Orleans following Hurricane Katrina. There are small libraries on each of the hotel's four floors, and a fine dining restaurant including selections from an 1,100-bottle wine cellar.

In 2017, The River Inn of Harbor Town was ranked by US News and World Reports as #1 in Best Memphis Hotels (for the seventh year in a row), #3 in Best Tennessee Hotels, and #1 overall in Preferred Lifestyle Hotels (beating out resorts such as The Landings St. Lucia on Gros Island in the Caribbean, The Limelight Hotel in Aspen, Colorado, the five star Red Rock Casino, Resort & Spa in Las Vegas, Nevada, and the Michelangelo in New York, City as well as the Travaasa Hana in Maui.). Travel and Leisure voted it among the World's Top 100 Hotels in 2016 as well as #6 among Top City Hotels in the US. In 2014, Conde Nast Traveler named it among the Top 25 Hotels in the US.

It was time to stop peeing on myself in the Big Agnes and drying myself with dirty t-shirts and instead spend a night seeing how the other half lived— that is to say the half that don't pee on themselves and dry off with dirty t-shirts.

I wheeled the Kawasaki into a parking spot in the lot behind the River Inn and turned it off, grateful to be finished for the day. Not even wanting to look at the bike again until the next morning, I unfastened the grime slicked saddlebags and carried them like luggage into the elegant reception area of the hotel, setting them down and removing my helmet at the front desk looking every bit the cold, wet, frazzled mess I was.

Without so much as a bent eyebrow, I was greeted warmly and presented with an envelope containing a personalized letter from the manager of the hotel, "On behalf of the management and staff of the River Inn of Harbor Town I offer you the warmest of welcomes..."

I felt pampered and doted on from that first moment by the ceaselessly poised and friendly staff of the River Inn. The clerk who checked me in was pretty in an exotic way, with long straight black hair and deep brown eyes highlighted by long dark lashes and deep red lips. When she asked at the end of my check-in if there was anything else I needed, I asked about catching a cab over to Beale Street. She said it would be her pleasure to make the call and advised that I should just call down about five minutes before I was ready to head over. Then she smiled at me and handed me the key to my room as if soggy motorcyclists with helmet hair and filthy saddlebags for luggage were the norm rather than the exception in her reception area.

It was only about two in the afternoon, so I headed upstairs to luxuriate in the finest accommodations of my trip so far. The room was richly appointed and felt less like a hotel room than a spare bedroom suite in an upscale home, its floorspace dominated by a tall four-poster bed with pristine white linens layered high beneath delicately embroidered pillow cases.

I quickly stripped down for a long hot shower, letting the water run over my cool white skin until it was beet red from the heat and my fingers and toes were well pruned before finally emerging from the steam filled bathroom to set about organizing my things once again.

A few minutes later, comfortably folded into a plush white bathrobe, I frantically searched both saddlebags and every pocket in the sodden clothes I had been wearing before finally resigning myself to the idea that I'd lost one of the Kawasaki's two electronic key fobs. Searching my mind for where I might have left it, I remembered my habit of setting it on the seat while preparing to ride out for the day and realized that I'd probably been sitting on it when I left, cold and distracted, from the campground in Cape Girardeau seven hours before.

With no spare, protecting the one remaining fob would add yet another layer of low-level anxiety to the remaining two days of the trip.

*****

My cabbie for the ride into downtown Memphis, a late-middle-aged black man in a blue nylon windbreaker with elastic cuffs, walked the line between civic boosterism and safety advocate, telling me alternately how much I'd enjoy Beale Street and why it was important that I stick to the safety of the few tourist blocks.

"You can get yourself into trouble," he warned as he slowed to a stop at Beale and South Second between the Memphis Hard Rock Cafe and the decidedly cooler Blues City Cafe with its "Steak, Shrimp, Tamales, Catfish, Beer, Music, Burgers, Liquor, Ribs" signage. I paid him and stepped out of the cab onto the curb. "Have fun!" he called back to me as the door clunked shut sealing his position as Memphis's official mascot of mixed messages.

At just four o'clock there wasn't much happening behind the white sawhorses that blocked vehicle access to Beale. I was starving and also ready for a beer, so less than a full block into my exploration of Beale Street, I ducked into a bar and grill called Flynn's.

Flynn's was big and open inside with a little stage in one corner for live music and karaoke. At that hour, the place was nearly empty, and I took a seat at the polished oak bar and ordered a draft beer, deciding after looking over the menu to try a small rack of ribs. The TV over the bar nearest to me was tuned to the local Fox affiliate where an early news broadcast was reporting on severe weather in the Midwest.

The sound was off, but captions and images told a story of

flight delays, school closings, snow removal efforts and sub-zero temperatures. I ordered another beer and gnawed through my plate of mediocre ribs like a hungry bear while pondering the mess I'd be flying back to in a few days and the good fortune I'd had to miss it on the way out, even if the storm front was chasing me down the river like a roaring Bumble (the Abominable Snow Monster from 1964's "Rudolph the Red-Nosed Reindeer", not the online dating app where women make the first move).

When I'd finished the meal and paid my tab, the bartender, a stocky late-twenties woman with a warm but tired face and close-cropped platinum hair, asked how I'd liked it. "It was great," I lied, somewhat sorry to have wasted my hunger on ribs that were nothing special. "Only now I'm too full to try other stuff."

Her face lit up. "You're on Beale Street. You have to try other stuff! Have you been to Miss Polly's?" She was standing there with my empty rib plate in her hand eagerly recommending the place across the street. "You have to try Miss Polly's! Do you like chicken and waffles?"

I love chicken and waffles. "I love chicken and waffles," I admitted, "but I just ate a plate of ribs. I don't have room for anything else."

"No way, honey." She looked at me as though I were a patient desperately in need of medicine but too foolish to take what's being offered. "You're having Miss Polly's." She reached behind the bar for a cordless phone and punched in a number. "Hold on."

I looked around sheepishly and finished the last of my beer as she laughed and joked with a friend of hers working across the street. When she hung up the phone, she looked at me and asked, "Are you ready to go?"

I slipped off my stool. "Alright, I'll head over. Who do I ask for?"

"Oh, I'm taking you." She asked another bartender to cover for her and came around from behind the bar, taking me by the arm and leaning in to me flirtatiously. "I'm Tina by the way, and we're gonna get you some real food." She was short, the tips of her spiky blonde hair coming no higher than my mid-chest as she walked me across the street, her hips, breasts, and elbows grazing my body as we strode in tandem like a happy tourist couple.

Miss Polly's Soul City Cafe was tiny compared to Flynn's-not much more than a little yellow and green storefront covered with a striped awning. Tina led me under the Miss Polly's sign (a sassy looking chicken wearing an apron and surrounded by the motto "Love, Peace, and Chicken Grease"), nudged me ahead of her through the front door and sat me down at the near end of the counter.

"This is him?" her friend asked. She was nearly Tina's twin, only black.

Tina nodded and patted me on the back like a lost child she'd found wandering down the street. Then she leaned in and gave me a quick peck on the cheek before heading for the door. "Thank you!" I called after her. She answered with a wave over her shoulder.

Tina's friend looked at me after she'd left. "She's crazy, but I love her. You want some chicken?"

Tina had arranged for me to get a half order of Miss Polly's famous chicken and waffles. Half-orders weren't on the menu, which I looked over while I waited. A fried bologna sandwich called "The Jailhouse Special" was. It shared space there with catfish, fried chicken livers, and fried green tomatoes.

A hand-lettered sign behind the counter said, "If you order to go food, you must eat it off premises." The word must was underlined twice. I wondered what in the world was going on with the to-go orders. Two televisions and a photo of B.B. King also hung behind the counter.

When the food came, I immediately wished I'd gotten a full order, two full orders even. You don't have to be hungry to enjoy Miss Polly's. My single chicken breast was juicy, and the homemade breading was a perfectly crispy golden brown with flecks of spicy goodness dotting its surface.

Two thick wedges of Belgian waffle nuzzled up against the chicken breast, the deep pockets on their surfaces filled with warm maple syrup and half-melted butter. On the other side of the plate a small shallow bowl was brimming with collard greens.

Tina's friend told me the chicken and waffles were on the house, then she paused and smiled at me with a mischievous glint in her eye, "but only if you try the greens."

One of the defining features of adulthood for me has been the freedom not to eat my vegetables. It's a skill I've been working on since I was ten years old and sat stoically at my mom's kitchen table one night until it was time for me to go to bed. The offending dish was sukiyaki and I didn't like the look of its slimy, shiny vegetable components.

If vegetables are generally bad, slimy vegetables are universally worse. My frustrated mother threatened to serve me the sukiyaki for breakfast but didn't have the heart. I'd won a key battle in the dinner table wars and would routinely get away from the table having only eaten a Lilliputian portion of whatever veggie the rest of the family was eating. I'd made it four decades on the planet without ever eating cooked spinach, and the greens had a very spinachy look about them.

"No worries," I said, jabbing a fork smack into the middle of the pile and coming away with a good amount. "I'm sure they're delicious."

I put the whole forkful into my mouth, moved it back toward my molars, and began to chew mechanically. The greens were wet and brothy, with a light spiciness. The flavor wasn't bad, but the texture was definitely not for me. I couldn't get the combination of chewy and limp out of my mouth and down my throat fast enough. I swallowed hard and immediately took a big swig of Diet Coke, careful to do it nonchalantly and hoping to pass for someone who was enjoying his greens.

"They're not for everybody," the server said. "At least you tried them."

When she walked away, a white teenager in a Memphis Grizzlies jersey a few chairs down from me at the counter looked over at me and said, "It's okay, man. I don't like 'em either."

I ignored the rest of the greens and tucked in to the chicken and waffles which were simply amazing. It was one of those food experiences that make you sad when it's over. There wasn't a morsel of stray chicken breading that didn't make its way to my mouth. When I was finished, I left a $10 bill beside my plate and thanked my server from across the counter. When I walked back outside, dusk had descended and a constellation of neon had come to life in the sky just overhead on both sides of the street.

I thought about heading back over to Flynn's to thank Tina for the hookup but decided that would be awkward so instead ducked into a funky souvenir shop called Tater Red's, savoring the syrupy, spicy, malty flavor of my own breath as I made my way up and down the aisles of Memphis themed merchandise.

Tater Red's had a decidedly cool vibe and lots of what they offered was dark and racy, voodoo themed or otherwise dripping with Memphis hip. I bought myself a charcoal colored T-shirt with the silhouette of a guitar on the front and a gray Sun Records tee for my daughter.

Near the register on the way out, there were Tater Red's magnets on offer featuring a pinup blonde in platform shoes. They could be had either topped or topless. I chose one of the topped ones and added it to my purchases. Magnets, like tees, bumper stickers, and can cozies, travel well.

The rest of my evening passed quickly. I had a couple of pints in the Beale Street Taproom and a couple more at Coyote Ugly, where a striking, rail-thin bartender named Zuki cajoled me into buying the previous year's calendar because her picture was in it. She autographed it to me with little butterfly wings next to her name and I moved off down the street to bob and sway to the gospel infused blues sound of the Chris McDaniel Band at the Rum Boogie Cafe Blues Hall.

Eager to catch the King Biscuit radio show the next morning in West Helena and with my Nashville hangover still fresh on my mind, I alternated between draft beer and Diet Coke and stepped back out into the cool damp night air on Beale around ten o'clock to work my way back up to Second Street to catch a cab back over to Mud Island.

Although Beale was busier than when I'd arrived at four, it was still relatively quiet which made the heavy police presence extra noticeable. Four cruisers were stationed on each block, and uniformed Memphis police officers milled around near the corners-returning in force to old fashioned beat patrols to keep a small strip of downtown safe for the tourist trade.

I don't know where I'd ever seen so many police in such a small area outside of a holiday parade or big political event. This was a quiet Tuesday evening in a mid-sized American city. I strolled back up to Second, called a taxi, took a self-conscious selfie in front of the Hard Rock Cafe while I waited for it, and then retreated back to Harbor Town.

Goodnight, Goofus. Goodnight, Gallant.

CHAPTER NINE

"You can run, you can run,
Tell my friend-boy Willie Brown
And I'm standing at the Crossroads,
believe I'm sinking down..."
- Crossroads, Eric Clapton

The light was weak and thin when my alarm sounded the next morning and I lay in bed for ten or fifteen minutes after turning it off. The mattress was thick and comfortable, the bedding soft and warm. After the previous day's soggy frustrations, I was in no hurry to climb back onto the Kawi and hurl myself against a damp wall of cold air for hours on end— if the bike would start at all.

It stood to be a good day, however; there was King Biscuit to look forward to, a blues radio show broadcasting continuously out of the Mississippi Delta since before Bert the Turtle knew how to duck and cover, and then the Devil's Crossroads in Clarksdale, Mississippi where Robert Johnson was said to have sold his soul to the devil.

Unless something went wrong, it would be my last full day of riding and that night was going to be my last one spent sleeping outdoors for the foreseeable future. As nice as the bed felt, there was simply too much excitement ahead to dawdle for long and within thirty minutes I was packed, showered, and seated downstairs enjoying black coffee and orange juice and waiting for an order of pancakes and bacon.

An older couple at the next table exchanged pleasantries with me over breakfast, interrupting my ability to focus on the simple luxury of eating in the warm dining room, but also distracting me from my worries about the key fob, the KiPass system, the cold and wet, and a dozen imagined worst case scenarios. In that way, they were welcome benefactors.

It was about 8:15 when I fastened the saddlebags back on the Kawi, my fingers leaving trails in the grime wherever I touched its flanks or fairing. Hoping that I might be able to sneak up on the sleeping KiPass system, I donned my gloves and helmet before swinging a leg over the cool, damp seat and settling in behind the gas tank as nonchalantly as possible.

People got on motorcycles every day. And those motorcycles almost invariably started. I casually placed the Kawi's one remaining fob in the plastic cubby on top of the tank and leaned forward to turn the big plastic ignition knob. "Nothing to see here." It rotated limply in my hand, with as much effect as the temperature dial on a Fisher-Price oven.

This time I didn't pitch a fit, or curse, or stomp my feet, or act out in any way. I was twenty paces outside of a luxury hotel three hours before checkout time in a decent sized city on a weekday morning. As far as strandings went, this was an utter non-emergency.

I took off my helmet and unzipped my jacket so I wouldn't get overwarm while I did it and then I pulled back the black plastic panel at the top of the Kawi's fairing and reached down into the blackness for the wiring harness. It was easier to find and disconnect than before, and I waited a long couple minutes before reconnecting it, walking small circles in the parking lot and taking deep misty breaths.

Once I got the harness reconnected, the ignition regained its backbone, the gauges sprang to attention, and the Kawi burbled back to life on the first try. Provided I didn't turn the bike off at fuel stops and took my lunches standing next to it, I only needed it to start twice more. I didn't know how many more times the harness trick would work and couldn't help feeling a little like a gambler who has let a winning roulette bet ride when they should be collecting their chips and heading for the cashier's cage.

As for the prospect that the KiPass might launch a full-on rebellion in the middle of nowhere and simply shut down the engine— that scenario I pushed off into a quiet recess of my mind reserved for plagues of locusts and sinister, knife-wielding clowns.

The sky was the color of skim milk and the air was thick and damp as I made my way off Mud Island, through downtown Memphis and onto Highway 61 - which was pulling double duty as both The Great River Road and The Blues Highway.

It was only 38 degrees out and the cold November wind picked up its chisel and returned to work on my face, neck, and hands with the workaday persistence of a journeyman mason until I was only too eager to pull over to side of the road after only twenty minutes to snap a few pictures of the Journey Motel Court.

Built in 1945 and with its stately two-story brick office and service station literally just a few feet from the Highway 61 traffic lanes, The Journey Motel is a study in the beauty of urban decay. The office itself is square and imposing, its architecture a 1940's nod to the colonial with a columned portico and white framed windows contrasting with its brick edifice.

The name "Journey Motel Court" is spelled out in all caps in a craftsman style Avenida font - each individual letter standing apart from its neighbor and seemingly unsupported, all of them lined up formally at the edge of the roof's ledge facing the road, like soldiers of the French Foreign Legion surrounded and forced to embrace a dignified suicide rather than face capture. They stand out in sharp contrast to the sky behind them, silhouetted and proud— and it is the dignity of these letters, I think, that lends the whole image its quiet sadness. More so than the little formal portico, or the windows with the dozens of stationary-sized panes- all intact.

An internet search readily produces images of the hotel taken by others before me, each compelled to pull off US 61 to stare at it and then to snap photos trying to capture the lonely way it made them feel. The Journey Motel Court even made the cover of a novel by the same name by author Jeff H. Martin.

To the right of the office across the weedy broken concrete driveway is a row of a half dozen or so rooms, tall grass growing up in the spaces between their door frames and the sidewalk, vines crawling up one end- the untended lot returning to nature like in an episode of Life After People.

My instinct for exploration tugs at me to pull up in front of the derelict motor court and to peer into the rooms, maybe even try one of the doors, but I'm afraid to follow through on the impulse, suspecting that someone else has already done the exploring for me and has made the place a temporary home.

For the second time in as many days, I felt as though I were being watched by unseen eyes and the sensation made me uncomfortable. I toed the Kawasaki into first gear, looked over my shoulder and merged back onto 61, moving up through second and third a little more sharply than needed, the sensation of a spectral pursuer familiar from boyhood dashes up the basement stairs.

Out of reach of some imagined demon, I soon found myself back in the clutches of a real one; the cold, bony fingers of the wind probing and exploring the seams of my altogether not good enough gear. The wind made its way up my back and down my neck as the cold seeped into my thighs and buttocks, the hard coal-colored pavement of Highway 61 stretching forward beneath me as I tried to convince myself that I was warm, or at least tough.

I focused on the tiny balls of heat at my toes where the chemical warmers kept the cold at bay. I felt their warmth on the back of my hands too, where I had shoved them into my gloves. The distance from the back of my hands to the tips of my fingers was too great though for their heat to carry and I returned to my Sunday trick of alternating a single hand controlling the bike while burying the other in the relative warmth of my crotch.

It was an hour before I stopped for my next picture, this time in front of the Gateway to the Blues Museum and Visitor's Center in Tunica, Mississippi. Standing alone beside Highway 61, the Tunica Visitor's Center occupies a former train station dating to 1895. The rustic whitewash on its clapboard exterior is faded and flaking, left untouched as part of a restoration that aimed to update the facility while preserving its patina.

The museum was locked, its grand opening still two months away when I moved the Concours into position for a picture beneath the its mammoth neon sign, the sound of the Delta blues nonetheless raining down at me from unseen speakers tucked into the building's lighted overhang.

I couldn't have gone inside anyway. I was hell bent on catching the King Biscuit program when it broadcast live from Helena in a couple of hours and I wouldn't turn the bike off again until I arrived. I'd wanted to sit in for a live broadcast of King

Biscuit Time ever since Shannon had discovered it during her brief flurry of internet research in the couple of days she had before I'd left. It was a tent pole in my trip, every bit as important as the St. Louis Arch had been, or the French Quarter was to be. The King Biscuit show was the longest running radio show in American history— with more broadcasts than The Grand Ole Opry or American Bandstand.

Earlier in the year, King Biscuit had marked its 17,000 broadcast. It's kind of hard to rack up 17,000 of anything. If you have eaten three meals aday, faithfully; 17,000 meals takes you over fifteen years into your own past. If you attend weekly church services (even more faithfully), you'd have to drop a dollar into the collection plate every Sunday for 342 years to get to 17,000.

Airing at 12:15 every day, a time chosen to coincide with the lunch breaks of black workers in the Delta, (Former editor of Living Blues Magazine, Jim O'Neal, quoted online for the Blues Festival Guide said, "The King Biscuit hour was the thing that really crystallized blues music in this area. Muddy Waters and B.B. King would come home from working in the fields every day just to listen to the King Biscuit hour"), King Biscuit had been broadcasting for just shy of 73 years when I'd rolled out of my driveway and started south down the river the week before. For 63 of those years, the show had been hosted by Blues Hall of Famer, "Sunshine" Sonny Payne, an octogenarian who started work at King Biscuit's home station KFFA two days before it started broadcasting, working as a custodian and errand boy.

Payne began cutting ads for KFFA as a teenager before lying about his age to join the fighting in the Pacific in 1942. After the Army, he toured as a bass player before returning to KFFA in 1951 where he has been announcing the King Biscuit Hour ever since, earning a Peabody Award in 1992 after forty years on the air.

As a young boy and the only child of a young single mother, I spent a lot of time in the care of my Great Grandmother, Sarah Manzanares- "Manzie" to friends and family. She was equal parts strict and doting and I imprinted hard onto her and the tiny modest home her late husband had built.

My maternal grandmother, her daughter, lived just a few miles away in a Denver suburb and after my mother married a military man and we moved away, we would sometimes make it back to Colorado to visit. I remember on one of those trips, having arrived at my grandmother's house and being stricken by a low-level panic that Manzie (who was 73 when I was born and who I had only ever known as an old woman) would die before we could make it to her place to visit.

Desperate to see her before it was too late, I borrowed a bicycle and rode the few miles between Lakewood and Golden, pedaling furiously along sidewalks and surface streets until I finally arrived at Manzie's place where I found her alive and well eating a toasted bologna sandwich. As an adult, I made similar frenzied visits by car, eager to see her once more before time snatched her away—something it finally did in 1995, the same year my daughter was born and more than a decade after my first desperate bicycle ride.

As I rode south down Highway 61 with the river off in the unseeable distance on my right, I felt a similar desperate urge to get to Helena to see Sonny broadcast the King Biscuit Show. If I missed it today, there was no telling when I'd be back and Sonny, well… Sonny had already been on the air at KFFA for over sixty years and was pushing ninety.

Outside of Tunica, Highway 61 was a broad, glass-flat four-lane divided blacktop with stands of trees periodically lining the roadway. Beyond, in the low fields that stretched away into the distance, the stubborn remains of unharvested cotton bolls clung to their plants.

The speed limit was sixty-five and the extra ten miles per hour of travel brought with it an extra serving of cold damp wind, trying to pick the last nickels from any pocket of warmth that remained on my frigid body. The sharp pain in my fingertips made me certain that I'd damaged them during my early morning ride from Cape Girardeau to Metropolis and I tried not to focus on it, but rather on the music coming from my speakers and the promise of New Orleans the following evening, the relative warmth I expected to find in the French Quarter, and the first-class flight home I'd be taking in forty-eight hours.

I wondered earnestly if I'd ever again want to ride a motorcycle let alone take a trip of any serious distance away from the comforts of my couch, my bed, and my fireplace. I cursed myself for not preparing better, and then, when I was tired of feeling sorry for myself, I settled into the saddle for the last few miles of road between me and Helena, shut off my hectoring mind and became a passenger on my own motorcycle.

I rode in a daze through Tunica and Evansville until I saw the sign for Helena. Then I turned right on the faded and broken concrete of Highway 49 running north toward the Mississippi River and the Arkansas border, where I'd make three states in a day before ten in the morning— a first I could marvel at despite the numbing cold.

A couple of miles south of Arkansas I passed a blue highway sign for the Senator Delma Furniss Hospitality Center and Welcome Station. Remarkably, the Hospitality Center has its own Facebook page while Senator Furniss does not. Judging by internet entries, in fact; not only is the Welcome Center that bears his name immensely more internet savvy than Senator Furniss, it also seems generally more remarked upon. Not that Senator Furniss was unremarkable. From a 1992 re-election ad in the Clarksdale Press Register:

"The State Senator post is one of the most important positions in state government. The office demands that your State Senator be dedicated, committed, and well-qualified.
Delma Furniss meets these requirements!"

According to the ad, not only was Delma (who had served 8 years as a State Representative at that point) the holder of "high-quality, specialized formal education", but he was also endowed with "good common sense", the kind one earns from "many years of practical living experience".

The reader is further informed that Delma is both a "working man" and a "family man", before offering "two more good solid reasons" to vote for him: "what he's already done" and "what he'll continue to do" for the people of Coahoma County. Not one to get mired down in a lot of petty details, that Delma Furniss. No, Sir. Too busy working hard FOR YOU.

Kidding aside, Furniss, who was first a farmer and then a train conductor, went to college as an adult to earn his BA from

Delta State University with a triple major in English, history, and politics thirty years after he finished high school, graduating Summa cum Laude. He went on to serve twenty years in the legislature earning the nickname "Fireball" through his unrelenting work ethic. That work ethic helped him earn a patent for an efficient system of standardizing bible page numbering, and also to secure funding for the roadside convenience area that bears his name. Delma married his high school sweetheart, Edie in 1953 ("I thought all of her looked real good, but I was especially struck by her smile") and the two were married for fifty-one years before she passed away in 2004.

It wasn't the inviting little roadside stop with Furniss's name that most caught my attention, however; but rather a small sign affixed just beneath the one announcing the rest area. It stated quite simply, "24 HR SECURITY PROVIDED".

I did a quick double take before I passed it, just to be sure I'd read it properly. 24-hour security? Out here? I was reminded of a comment that someone had made to me over a beer in Memphis when I mentioned I was heading to Helena to sit in on the King Biscuit show. "You're going to Helena?" they had asked incredulously, "Do you have a gun?" I didn't, and the bear repellent was proving utterly superfluous.

It was the second time in as many days that someone had questioned my travel plans- and using nearly the same words. Counting the park ranger outside of St. Louis, the cock had now crowed three times.

I rode into Helena, Arkansas on US-49 over the Helena Bridge, a steel girder cantilever structure a decade older than I was. Distracted travelers on its two-lane blacktop surface were saved from a plunge into the waters of the Mississippi by a low concrete jersey wall that ran the entire length of its nearly one-mile span.

On the Arkansas side of the bridge, I turned right on Biscoe and rode past the Morning Star Baptist Church, a humble white building with a gravel turnaround in front but no parking lot, and then on past an abandoned and shuttered gas station and motor lodge on the right.

At semi-regular intervals along the road, vacant concrete slabs gave proof of businesses long ago failed and razed. A little further on was the recently opened Freedom Park, managed by the Delta Cultural Center and dedicated to the memory of escaped slaves, many of whom joined the Union Army at the Battle of Helena on July 4, 1863.

I turned right on Missouri Street toward the Delta Cultural Center, stopping to snap a quick photo of the bike parked in front of the dilapidated and crumbling remains of a soul food restaurant. The building was long and narrow, two red brick stories with a dead gray plywood awning over the entrance.

The restaurant's roof had collapsed inward and the single window on the street side upper story was broken out. A smiling mammy with broad happy features was painted on the side of the building. She wore a green housedress with a white collar over an ample bosom. Atop her head she wore a red scarf. There was a soup pan in her hand and the words "Home Cooking Served Daily" were painted next to her in jaunty, right-leaning letters. Less jauntily, but still professionally painted, the admonition "NO Loitering" occupied its own space on the covered window next to the entrance door.

Just ahead stood a fully restored 1912 Union Pacific railway station now functioning as a museum. I didn't bother stopping for a photo there and wondered how many others had similarly foregone the Depot, favoring instead the husk of an abandoned soul food joint a block and a half away. There is real history, restored history, and manufactured history. People instinctively know the difference.

*****

I was nearly two hours early for the King Biscuit show when I pulled the Kawi into a parking spot in front of the Delta Cultural Center on Cherry Street. The blue awnings of the Cultural Center faced out on a tidy little park featuring a newly built pavilion and stage which hosts the King Biscuit Blues Festival, a multi-day event that has taken place annually since 1986. The Cultural Center, the restored Depot, and the park and pavilion together made a pretty comprehensive list of the attractions in downtown Helena.

The street was dotted with empty lots- where buildings too far gone to be saved had been bulldozed and removed- and other buildings on their way to the same fate, their windows covered with plywood, their rotting awnings sagging from age and neglect.

Commercial space was more likely vacant than occupied and the addresses that did have tenants were home to shoestring operations like antique shops and independent restaurants.

Down the street and opposite from the Delta Cultural Center, the historic Malco Theater remained in use, operated by the public school system and used for various events. Its prohibition era architecture and Art Deco marquee, grand and forlorn at the same time, lent themselves to an exterior shot in 2005's "Walk the Line" about the life of Johnny Cash. In the scene, a frustrated June (played by Reese Witherspoon), finds Cash (played by Joaquin Phoenix) and his band drunk in a theater before a show. The exterior shot is of the Malco, but the interior is Hume High School in Memphis (the school Elvis Presley attended).

Eager to get out of the cold, I ducked inside the cultural center and looked over the exhibits, waiting for my body to regain the heat it had lost on the two-hour run from Memphis, during which the wind chill had brought the near freezing air down to an icy 18 degrees. I was wearing thermal underwear, jeans, uninsulated chaps, a long sleeve t-shirt, a fleece, a lined leather jacket, plain leather boots and a scarf.

My hands looked fragile and pink and I could feel the crimson flush in my cheeks as I moved between the exhibits, the muscles of my thighs and buttocks cold inside my pants. Every day, I'd fallen into the same mental trap— the idea that the weather would be warmer the farther south I rode. Each time I'd been proven wrong, I chalked up one more day that new gear wouldn't do me any good so that now, with just one day to go, I had pushed myself into a corner, the type known to Texas Hold 'em players who'd gone through three rounds of betting without any good news, but were reluctant to cut bait now. As I walked around the exhibit space, a trickle of thin snot ran out of my nose now and again, unannounced and unwelcome, causing me to moisten the end of my shirt sleeve continually dabbing it away.

The Delta Cultural Center's museum was faring better than I was, its space divided among three permanent exhibits dedicated to the heritage of the Delta's people, the Civil War as it played out in the Delta, and finally, the Delta Sounds exhibit which traces the musical history and influence of the Delta from traditional spirituals up through blues legends like Albert King and country stars like Johnny Cash.

The poverty and hardship I'd seen in the Delta region seemed a natural descendent of the misery that had marked the area since its first permanent settlements, and particularly moving were the stories of African-American slaves brought to life through multimedia exhibits that brought home the back breaking labor and degradations they faced. Those experiences eventually gave birth to the Delta blues and the museum's exhibits on the that heritage didn't disappoint. Among them were an acoustic guitar used by Elmore James and another bearing over 100 signatures including Albert King, "Pine Top" Perkins, Rufus Thomas, and Robert Lockwood Jr.

One end of the center was reserved for The King Biscuit show, Sonny Payne's broadcast studio set off from the remainder of the space by a low Plexiglas shield and a half-wall broken up by a little swinging door. A couple of benches waited just outside the studio for visitors wishing to sit in on the day's live broadcast of King Biscuit Time. The rest of the room featured a variety of exhibits dedicated to King Biscuit including a timeline of the show, and of Sonny Payne.

The room was being painted and thin transparent plastic sheeting was draped over many of the displays making them hard to read. After spending about fifteen minutes exploring there and reading what I could, I turned my attention to the museum's small collection of fine art pieces that reflected the spirit of the Delta.

Among them was a series of photographs entitled "Delta in Blue" produced by local photographer Beverly Buys. One showed the dilapidated soul food cafe I'd posed the bike in front of just the hour before. Here again was the smiling mammy flanked by the words, "Home Cooking Served Daily" which was also the title of the piece. The print, a cyanotype, was for sale with an asking price of $1,200. Buys' exhibit- like my iPhone- didn't have any shots of the restored depot.

The museum's guest book was filled with recent entries from the UK, Japan, Australia, Switzerland, Holland, and — Seattle. My guess is that all of them were more interested in the crumbling cafe with the smiling mammy on the side than the railroad depot up the street. And somewhere among them was a person for whom a $1,200 cyanotype might seem a fitting souvenir from a struggling town in a struggling state in a struggling region populated by struggling people who didn't look or talk anything like anyone back home. As much as I wanted to appreciate the Delta, I couldn't shake the echo of the minstrel show and its dabbling and bemused white patrons. Was I one of them? How could you sort from among the visitors? And would it be better or worse if the tourists didn't come?

David Sedaris wrote a piece about the Anne Frank house and how despite its history, he couldn't help seeing its potential as a great home for himself and his partner Hugh. Sometimes tourism feels tawdry. Suffering and history and entertainment get mixed together until visiting children walk away from the sunken wreck of the USS Arizona wearing happy red Pearl Harbor backpacks ($9.95 in their online gift shop).

With time to kill and no sign yet of Sonny, I walked back out onto Cherry Street and up to the depot. Although I'd spent an hour getting warm, the wind cut immediately back into me. The interior of the depot was tighter and more intimate than the space at the Cultural Center. It was also warmer, for which I was grateful.

I spent about twenty minutes watching a DVD on the Delta blues that was playing on a loop on a rear projection big screen TV in a small dim room with a comfortable double chair. By dumb luck I caught the segment about Robert Johnson, the legendary blues man who was said to have sold his soul to the devil at midnight at the Crossroads in Clarksdale for fame and success as a bluesman.

The video featured a black and white photo of Johnson from around 1935. It was a studio shot of him seated, wearing a dark pinstriped suit and holding a guitar across his lap, his fingers ready on the strings. A hat with a wide band sits atop his head at a rakish tilt and his expression- looking straight into the camera with one eyebrow up— is one of cocky determination. It is one of only a few verified photos of Johnson.

With about thirty minutes before King Biscuit was due to air, I made my way back up Cherry to the Delta Cultural Center to lurk around outside Sonny's studio. Ten minutes or so before his show was due to begin, the energy in the cultural center rose. An intern made his way behind Sonny's console and made a few adjustments. The museum's curator came by to check on me. Sonny, a diminutive and cherubic octogenarian, made his way into the studio, smiling and greeting as he went, his colleagues all but shouting their good mornings at his nearly deaf ears.

He was dressed sharply for work, a gray and black checkered shirt tucked neatly into taupe slacks held up by a shiny black belt. He walked with the slow deliberation of the elderly, his diminishing body aided by a black aluminum cane and thick plastic rimmed glasses. Obviously proud of his work, the Delta, and of KFFA, he smiled in determined relish of yet another day behind the console. Undeterred by the cold, he was ready to add one more broadcast to his enviable tally.

Shannon had called ahead to ask whether or not I might be able to sit in with Sonny. That was before we knew that his studio was basically in the open and that watching him broadcast was an opportunity open to anyone. Watching him work live had been the goal. Meeting him would be a bonus. Getting to share the air with him would be a coup.

I was sitting quietly on the bench outside of his studio when Sonny looked at me and asked if I was the only one sitting in. When he invited me into his studio space and sat me down across from him, I felt my anxiety rise. I liked the blues, but not enough to have informed opinions about it. I wondered if I'd be caught out, made to sound like a dumb Minnesota tourist on America's longest running radio show.

Of course, that wasn't the Delta. It wasn't Helena. And it certainly wasn't Sonny. He was generous, kind, open, and congenial, teasing me about having brought the cold with me and nudging me gently along through my brief and nervous sounding on-air comments. I mentioned the number of states I'd ridden through, commiserated with him about the cold, and thanked him for the honor of joining him for the show.

When his short broadcast was over, Sonny posed with me for a photo and gave me his business card, printing his email address carefully on the back before putting on his coat and heading out into the unseasonably cold November air; the 17,132nd King Biscuit show in the books. Although it had been only a walk-on, Sonny had granted me a part in King Biscuit history.

Five minutes later, and as warm as I would be until that night, I climbed back on the Kawi and attempted to coerce it into starting by appearing to forget a problem had ever existed. My ruse failed once again to trick the recalcitrant KiPass system. Disconnecting and reconnecting the wiring harness behind the fairing would be the only thing that could goad the bike to life. So, I walked through the process again, awakened the Kawi, and rode out of Helena past the soul food mammy south toward Clarksdale, just one harness-start away from the end of my journey down the GRR.

The sun was shining brightly as I crossed the bridge from Arkansas back into Mississippi but by the time I passed Senator Furniss's welcome center, Nuri's chill was once again creeping into my fingertips.

*****

In my mind's eye- no small credit to the Ralph Macchio film of the same name- I pictured the Crossroads as a desolate windswept dirt road intersection with barren farm fields receding in all directions, deserted except for a single tree, stunted and skeletal. It was there that musician Robert Johnson, desperate and heartbroken, would offer the devil all that he had- his immortal soul- in exchange for fame and fortune as a bluesman. If the legend were true, the Devil made good on his end. Johnson went down as one of the greatest bluesmen to ever live, inducted into the Rock n Roll Hall of Fame in its first ceremony and placing 5th on Rolling Stone magazine's list of "100 Greatest Guitarists of All Time" sandwiched between Eric Clapton and Chuck Berry. As with most Devils' bargains, Johnson's came with an Faustian twist. After recording sessions in San Antonio and Dallas in 1936 and 1937 that would cement his legend for among legions of scholars and fans, Johnson died under mysterious circumstances the following summer. He was just 27 years old.

Unlike the romantic dirt road image that had taken root in my mind, North State Street, the busy four lane blacktop that led into the heart of Clarksville, was lined on both sides by independent businesses with names like Toney's Barber Shop, Krosstown Trade & Pawn, Momma's & 3 Sons Soul Food Restaurant, and the Annie

Bell Lounge.

If Johnson had met the Devil at these crossroads, Old Scratch might well have still been digesting a brisket plate from Abe's Bar-B-Q, where the sign announces with pride, "Serving You Since 1924"— this immediately above a cartoon image of a pig, standing on his hind legs and wearing a red bow tie. The pig is black with white facial features, giving him a distinctly blackface vibe and adding insult to injury.

The actual intersection of highways 49 and 61, only about a hundred feet west of Abe's Bar-B-Q, is a bustling multilane affair. In the center of one of its turn lanes stands a monument to Johnson's legendary meeting; a trio of electric guitars extending from a simple steel pole topped with highway marker signs. Underneath is a white rectangular marker identifying the spot as, "The Crossroads".

A small copse of manicured bushes surrounds the base of the pole, while nearby and rising out of the same landscaped patch of earth are two old wooden utility poles, crowding their way into nearly every picture of the monument like drunken photo bombers. Not designed for easy pedestrian access (and with nothing more for someone on foot to do or see once they made it out to the little triangular island of grass), the crossroads monument in Clarksdale is mostly something to be glimpsed from the window of a passing car.

On the southeast corner of the intersection, immediately across from the monument, there's a vacant lot that once held a gas station. Its surface is all but entirely covered by smooth concrete. Toward the back of it, the slab from a forgotten c-store endures the slow advance of determined creeping weeds.

I pulled the Kawi off of State Street and into the vacant lot to snap a picture with the monument even while still reconciling my own disappointment. Leaving the bike idling in neutral, I walked backward toward the abandoned c-store curb trying to get the motorcycle and the twenty-foot guitars in the same frame, but it was no good. I was too close to capture the monument's full height with the motorcycle in the foreground. With no better place to pull off, and determined somehow to fit everything in the frame, I got down on my side and lined up a dramatic upward facing shot of the Kawi, bulky and angry-looking from that angle, with the electric guitars jutting skyward above the seat.

As I was positioning myself on the concrete, half on my back with my iPhone in hand, I heard a voice call out from across State Street. Glancing over, I saw a gaunt and angular black woman with unkempt hair and ratty clothes looking back at me. Catching my glance, she waved and called out again before starting off quickly across the busy street, seemingly heedless of oncoming traffic.

Not sure what she wanted but fearing the worst, I quickly snapped my picture and climbed back on the motorcycle, tucking my gauntlets underneath me as her approaching voice grew louder.

I raised the kickstand on the bike in a fluid motion, balancing the Kawi's bulk between my legs as I rushed to stash my iPhone and its wallet case containing my credit cards, money, and ID hurriedly into the odd shaped shallow plastic cubby on top of the gas tank.

In the few seconds it had taken me to get up off the ground and onto the bike, the woman had reached me, her eyes wild, her speech a nearly unintelligible rapid fire hard luck story. As I struggled to squeeze my bulky phone case into the cubby's narrow opening, she folded her thin arms around me, pleading and probing, despair mixed with aggression.

I shook my head and told her no. "No," I said, growing increasingly frantic myself, "No, no, no!"

There was almost nothing to her. I could feel the angles of her tiny body pressing into me, nearly climbing up onto me in her desperation. Bracing against her insistent push with my left leg, I began to panic, picturing her toppling us— the Kawi falling over lamely on its side, she and I and it in a tangled heap as she continued to grasp and beg.

The Concours is a big bike; 1400 cc's and nearly 700 pounds. I would struggle to get it upright again if she pushed it over and if it died; panic rose in me as my mind flicked to the failing KiPass...

I raised my voice, hoping to startle her. "Get off me!'

Instead she grabbed for my phone, half in and half out of its spot on top of the gas tank. I batted her arm up and away and then elbowed her hard in the chest, connecting solidly with her narrow breast bone and forcing her back a step.

In the split-second delay as she processed the blow, I gunned the bike and started forward, lunging toward the curb in a mad dash to keep her from taking me down. She yelled a curse at me and with barely a glance to gauge oncoming traffic, I hit State Street and tore away, accelerating quickly up to third gear, the Kawi letting out a banshee shriek that belied its sport-bike lineage.

After a few blocks, I slowed to the speed limit and shifted into fifth gear to quiet the raging hornet's nest I had excited in the Kawi, and the worked anxiously to get my phone tucked safely away into the stupid-ass narrow cubby. I kept an eye on my sideview mirrors as I backtracked east across town onto Martin Luther King Boulevard and south up the on-ramp to US 61. I cursed myself as I rode.

A stranger in a strange place, I'd climbed off my idling bike and laid down on the ground at a busy intersection to take iPhone pictures— a dumb tourist traveling alone in a dirt-poor town with electronics and money in easy reach.

As I followed 61 south from Clarksdale, I felt isolated, exposed, and unwelcome. Suddenly everything around me seemed strange and foreign. I rode through the town of Alligator where I crossed East New Africa Road, and past that, over Booga Bottom Road and into Hushpuckena where I finally had the presence of mind to pull over and put my gloves back on, my hands red and stinging from the cold, my fingertips hurting with everything they touched.

The road itself became a stranger, cracked and undulating for miles on end. It bucked against me in a steady, harassing rhythm that made the Kawi's saddle uncomfortable and kept me from wandering into reverie or enjoying the music music from the bike's tinny speakers.

I nicknamed the rolling broken tarmac "Mississippi Speed Bumps" and found some temporary amusement in that as the miles rolled by, the river paralleling me about five miles west along Mississippi Highway 1. In my eagerness to see the crossroads and my haste to get out of Clarksdale, I had wandered off the Great River Road once again. I thought about the campsite I was supposed to occupy that night and decided against it just as quickly. I wanted to sleep in a comfortable bed far above the alluvial soil of the

Delta— soil that had yielded the plaintive and mournful wail of the blues.

*****

By the time I swung the Kawi onto the frontage road and up the sloping driveway into the parking lot of the Holiday Inn Express & Suites in Vicksburg, Nuri's icy breath had seeped into every part of me. My fingers and toes were brutally chilled and my whole body ached from the a week on the road in the deep persistent cold. I wheeled the Kawi into a spot overlooking a row of low bushes in front of the hotel's columned registration canopy and turned off the ignition with a sense of finality. I only needed the bike to start one more time.

Without even bothering to remove the Kawi's saddlebags, I made for the hotel's welcoming entrance deciding to forego fresh clothes and toiletries until after I'd had a chance to get warm. My aching fingers were still working the chinstrap on my helmet when I made my way through the front doors and approached the desk, getting myself free just in time to return the friendly greeting of the desk clerk, a short, bubbly black woman about forty years old with a mischievous glint in her eye.

"You've been out riding around in this cold?" she asked me playfully while still conveying concern.

I nodded, "And boy am I glad to see you." In an instant, my mood had begun to lift. We were flirting.

She went about the business of checking me in, thanking me for being an IHG Rewards member, verifying my rate and so on, and then when everything was complete added, "Go on up and get warm and then come back down and join us in the breakfast area for our guest reception. Have yourself a complimentary glass of beer."

I gave her a curious look. I'd never been invited to an evening guest reception at a Holiday Inn Express before or been offered a free beer. She introduced herself as Gail and invited me to let her know if I needed anything at all. As I rode the elevator up to my room, a big smile grew on my face. I'd rode into the lot full of disappointment and defeat, resigned that the cold had beaten me into submission and sent me scrambling to the shelter of a chain hotel when I should have been proudly encamped outdoors a few feet away from my faithful mount, but Gail had made me feel like a welcome family member, returning home after a challenging trial.

A "guest reception" couldn't have made a bigger impact on me at that low moment and when I got to my room, I immediately stripped down and got into a hot shower, eager to shed the cold and hustle back downstairs to the breakfast area to claim my plastic chalice of ale.

After a long shower and with the heat in the room turned all the way up, I flipped on the TV to the local news while I dressed and checked in with Shannon. It was only a few minutes until the weather forecast, so I waited to see it before going back downstairs, more out of sense of morbid curiosity than anything else.

It wasn't like anything in the forecast was going to change my plans for the following day. Still, the news rolled over me in its irony. All I had waited for the entire trip was to get far enough south to be free of the cold that had plagued me since the first day when I had stopped at Kohl's and bought a scarf to try and keep the wind out of my jacket— and now that I had made it deep into the Mississippi Delta, the WAPT meteorologist was pointing deftly to a giant blue air mass overlaid with bullet points in all caps; "PERSISTANT PATTERN" (the local graphic tech had misspelled "persistent", offering the chance to take a cheap shot at the Mississippi public school system which ranked last in the nation in 2014), "15-30 BELOW AVERAGE", and "PROLONGED COLD SNAP". Incredulous, I took a cell phone photo of the screen to memorialize the irony. The seven-day forecast contained an icy animated "COLD" graphic pasted onto Thursday and Friday where lows were expected to be in the 20s and 30s, with highs only reaching into the 40s. It had been warmer in Minnesota when I stopped for that scarf. I turned off the TV and stood pondering for a long moment. One day left. All I had to do was start the bike one last time and then ride it the rest of the way to New Orleans. Just one day.

I went downstairs to enjoy one of Gail's free beers still unsure of what I was going to do about dinner.

Back downstairs there was a small crowd of eight or ten people in the breakfast area drinking draft beer from a couple of clear plastic pitchers that had been placed on the breakfast bar where the bananas or the peanut butter might have been in the morning. The guests at the reception were all men; roughnecks and industrial business travelers, the kinds of guys whose jobs kept them away from home, but whose suitcases were more likely to contain safety glasses than silk ties. It was a group I belonged to and felt comfortable in, and I walked right up and poured myself a beer from the meager remains of one of the nearly empty pitchers.

"Ms. Gail, we're almost out again," one of the guys called out toward the direction of the front desk.

Gail quickly made her way over to the bar, brushing the men out of her way like a cowboy moving through cattle in a corral. "That's because y'all are a bunch of heathens."

Gail scooped up the two pitchers, deftly refilled the nearest cup, and disappeared into the little prep room behind the serving area to refill them. When she returned a minute or so later with the pitchers full to the top, the same guy who had announced the deficiency leaned in and gave her a friendly hug. He was wearing dark work jeans and a baseball hat. "You know we love you, Ms. Gail."

"When I have beer, you do", she teased, and started back to whatever it was she'd been working on at the desk. She paused and made eye contact with me. "How are you doing? You getting warmed up?"

"Yes, ma'am. Thank you."

My stomach was empty and the beer did its job. I soon fell in with a couple of friendly salesmen wearing matching golf shirts. They said they'd seen the bike out front and wondered who the hell was riding in that cold. They peppered me with questions about my trip so far and what was yet to come and together we went through a whole pitcher of Ms. Gail's free Budweiser. "It's shitty beer, but you can't beat the price," one of them observed.

They invited me to dinner and almost before I knew it, I was waving goodbye to Ms. Gail and headed out the front door with them— their companion, guest, and entertainment for dinner. We piled into their rented Impala, them apologizing as they slid things around in the backseat to make room for me. "What do you feel like?"

I didn't know the town and didn't know the food. "I don't know. Something I can't get in Minnesota."

They consulted between themselves for a minute and settled on a nearby restaurant and lounge called The Beechwood. An unassuming brick building painted yellow with white trim, The Beechwood's western style sign features an enormous shrimp, a marbled cut of beef, and a smiling cartoon martini.

Serving Vicksburg diners for more than fifty years, The Beechwood is the type of place hungry locals go for good food and live music. The dining room is lined with wood paneling - the kind your grandma had in her basement— and lit by a row of tract house chandeliers that runs down the center of the room. The tables are identical tidy four-tops with their tablecloths sheltered under clear glass, the chairs that surround them standard banquet hall fare.

We were seated by a smiling blonde hostess still too young to order herself a drink and set about doing our part on her behalf, with my hosts ordering a red wine and vodka in turn, while I chose a local beer called Southern Pecan. Brewed by the Lazy Magnolia Brewing Company (Mississippi's oldest packaging brewery) , Southern Pecan is a nut-brown ale made with roasted pecans and has a sweet, malty flavor which earned it a bronze medal in the 2006 World Beer Cup.

My hosts were down to earth family men and we talked and laughed about work, children, and the joys and frustrations of married life while we worked our way through another round of drinks and a combination of Buffalo wings, deep fried dill pickles, onion rings, and oysters. One of the guys ordered a steak and another round of drinks came and went, with vodka being replaced by rum.

I learned that the two of them were employed by Ball jar and traveled together off and on. When the bill came they insisted on paying and we exchanged contact information- a traveling custom that isn't so much about keeping in touch as it is about edifying the brief friendship with a personal memento— the way Don Greenwood had done when he'd made me a sketch on a cocktail napkin in Cape Girardeau.

Back at the hotel, the Ball jar guys said goodnight and headed for their rooms, while I lingered in the lobby where the guest reception was winding down, having dwindled to three or four guys sitting and chatting around a granite high top. Seeing us return, they invited me over for a drink- the Kawasaki in the parking lot drawing a lot of attention as the cold wind rattled and blew.

"Ms. Gail, we're out again", called a familiar voice.

"Y'all can get it for yourself," came the reply as Gail gathered her things and prepared to leave for the night. "I'm going home to see my daughter." She stopped and looked in our direction with an expression of matter of fact maternalism. "Only one more round. And make sure that door gets locked when you're finished."

We nodded and mumbled our agreement as a group.

The guy who'd called out for a refill took up the business of filling the pitcher again and locking up the door to the room behind the breakfast bar before returning to pour me a fresh beer and top off the others. The group was discussing their love lives, and one of the guys - a former Captain in the Army who'd served multiple tours in Iraq, showed off a tattoo on the inside his forearm.

It was his wife, captured in a classic pinup pose, laying on her back with her hair flowing out around her head, her scissored calves long and tapered. She was wearing a red dress and the artist had done an almost photorealistic job of capturing the folds and shadows in the fabric as it clung to the curves of her body.

He said she was the love of his life and that she'd gifted it to him to remind him of her when he was in the desert on the other side of the world. With nothing to add that could rival that, I headed off to bed.

CHAPTER TEN

"Wasted arms; wasted legs
Wrapped round this machine…
Get me off this backwards ride"
- Ecstasy, Rusted Root

I slept with the heat cranked all the way up again and woke up early the following morning splayed out on top of the crumpled blankets like a starfish stranded on the beach. I'd have just one night in New Orleans, so I got up without delay, grabbed a lukewarm shower and reapplied my layers, wishing I'd stopped somewhere for hand-warmers the previous day. Wishful thinking had left me without any and I was pretty sure I'd be paying a real-life penalty for it.

Gail was back behind the front desk when I came downstairs. She greeted me and wished me well, and just like with the guys from Ball jar, we exchanged contact information as a gesture of goodwill- and in Gail's case, maybe a sense of affection that could have propelled us to an awkward first date in other circumstances. As it was, I was beginning to sweat inside my jacket and headed outside without even bothering to wolf down a complimentary breakfast sandwich, settling instead for a couple peanut butter packets which I pocketed for a snack later on in the morning.

Outside, I spotted the Ball jar guys' rented Impala and remembered what they'd said the night before as we talked about the electrical problems with the Kawi. "If we come out in the morning and your bike's gone, we'll assume you're good."

It wasn't much, but it was reassuring to know that someone close at hand had at least some interest in seeing me make it to the end of the line. I mounted the frozen black seat and reached for the plastic ignition switch without so much as a hitch of hesitation. To hesitate would be to give the bike power, to acknowledge that it might not decide to start. I was going the other way. My deliberate motion was meant to overcome the caprice of the universe. Today was a new day. By believing the bike would start, I would make it happen.

The ignition switch once again spun impotently in its housing and I felt the icy breath of morning on my neck. "Goddam, son of a bitch, motherfucker!" I climbed off the bike to pull back the plastic cover and reach down inside the fairing.

I had to take off my gloves to undo the harness and the cold plastic resisted until I was an angry, anxious, sweating mess. When I finally got the harness open, it was with trembling fingers. One time. I only had to get the bike started one more time. I waited two or three minutes, pacing a tight path around the parking space before reattaching the harness and once again willing the universe to give me a break.

This time the Kawi came to life, gauges maxing and resetting, its engine settling into an idle, little puff-clouds of white exhaust burbling out into the cold morning air. I plugged the stereo jack into my iPhone and shuffled my Great River Road mix. A staccato drum beat kicked up as I rolled the Kawi backward out of its overnight resting spot and aimed toward the frontage road. "Ecstasy" by Rusted Root— a song I'd been introduced to by an ex-girlfriend. A song I'd heard for the first time when we still danced in her kitchen. A song I'd come to like before I slept one night with every door in the house locked and a loaded pistol on my nightstand. It was fast and fitting and I started it up again when it ended.

*****

My goal for the morning was to see the recovered wreckage of the USS Cairo, one of seven Union Navy ironclad ships built for river service during the Civil War and one of only four remaining Civil War ironclads. Raised in three sections from the muddy bottom of the Yazoo River in 1964. Originally, the Cairo's salvage team had hoped to raise her intact, but when one of the steel cables being used to lift the ship cut deeply into the soft wood of her hull, a decision was made to continue the cut and to recover the ship in three more manageable segments. Following her salvage, the Cairo was partially restored and placed on permanent display at the Vicksburg National Military Park in 1977.

I've always been fascinated by ships and shipwrecks, so the chance to see the remains of this Civil War leviathan before leaving Vicksburg was at the top of my day's to-do list. The list itself was remarkably brief. Item 1: Go see the Cairo. Item 2: Get to New Orleans.

I had read online that the Cairo was on open air display along the sixteen-mile tour road that winds through Vicksburg Military Park. The road takes visitors past an astounding 1,300 monuments and markers associated with the siege and capture of Vicksburg by Union Forces in the summer of 1863 and is popular with locals and visitors alike.

Although I had read that the Cairo was on display somewhere along the road, I hadn't bothered to research the park's hours of operation and found myself the sole patron in its empty entrance lot a full forty minutes before the park was to open at 8:00 am.

Like most national parks, there was a little Fotomat-sized ranger's station beside the entry road where visitors could buy a day pass or get information. The station was still closed and the tour road just ahead was blocked by a metal swing arm that blocked passage beneath the Memorial Arch at its entrance. Carved from Stone Mountain Granite and rising about thirty feet above the road, the arch's Romanesque edifice lent a solemnity and gravitas to the park entrance.

It was only about 37 degrees and a persistent and unsettled wind harassed the landscape. Still trying to decide whether I could stand to wait around for better than half an hour, I pulled the Kawasaki into place beneath the arch and took a picture. I considered riding around the arch in the grass on either side, but a short unobtrusive cordon had been placed just behind the curb on one side, stretching all the way back to the visitor's lot, and an unruly copse of trees ran all the way up to the arch's edge on the other.

I considered trying to squeeze past on that side, but besides breaking the rules, I imagined the difficulty I'd create for myself if I got myself tripped up somehow off-roading the Kawi around the arch and ended up flopping it over on its side on the dewy morning ground like a dying fish.

In the end, I decided that the Cairo was too good a sight to pass up and that I'd just have to wait for the park to open. I thought forlornly about the warm room I'd just left and the complimentary breakfast I'd left uneaten in the lobby of the Holiday Inn. Unwilling to kill the engine on the Kawi again until I reached the French Quarter, I resigned myself to the cold wait and rode into downtown Vicksburg for a quick sightseeing tour.

Besides the military park, Vicksburg is also home to the Biedenham Coca-Cola Museum. It was in the summer of 1894 that Joe Biedenham, the 28-year-old co-owner of a candy company and soda fountain first hatched the idea of premixing Coca-Cola syrup and soda water, bottling the mixture and distributing it for sale away from the fountain at a cost of seventy cents a case.

Within a few years, a trio of attorneys from Chattanooga secured exclusive national bottling rights from the Coca-Cola Company for just $1, with the exception of Biedenham's Vicksburg operation. By 1909, the three lawyers had sold bottling franchises to nearly four-hundred plants, and by the end of the 1920s sales of bottled Coke had surpassed the fountain version.

If the story had ended there, poor old Joe Biedenham might be the source of your sympathy— the unfortunate country boy with the good idea outmaneuvered by shrewd big city attorneys who, although they hadn't had the idea, knew how to properly capitalize on it.

That could have been the story, but Biedenham wasn't quite so quick to lay down. Though the rules of the game had changed, Joe wasn't ready to quit playing. In addition to his Vicksburg bottling operation, he and his siblings acquired licenses to operate Coca-Cola bottling plants in Louisiana and Texas. Then, in 1925 along with his son Malcolm and a few outside investors, Joe bought a crop-dusting business and with the addition of eighteen more planes, made it the world's largest privately-owned air fleet. The company operated from Monroe, Louisiana before eventually moving to Atlanta in 1941 under its present name, Delta Airlines. A

Biedenham family member remained on the Delta board through the 1990s.

The Biedenham family home and gardens in Monroe is a museum as is the Biedenham Candy Store and offices at 1107 Washington Street in Vicksburg. I backed the Kawi into a streetside parking stall next to the building and pressed my face against the glass to peer into the soda fountain beyond, the sleepy downtown not yet awake. As at the Memorial Arch, I took a quick snapshot of the bike in front of Bidenham's to commemorate the stop.

Downtown Vicksburg is steep and hilly and quaintly old; a miniature San Francisco on the Yazoo River just above its confluence with the Mississippi. After a couple circuits of Vicksburg's quiet streets, I wandered down through an opening in its muraled floodwall on Levee Street and left the Concours idling in a no parking area while I walked to the river's edge.

Except for the soft burbling of the cycle, there was no other noise as I stood and watched the murky brown water of the Yazoo slip past, its waters destined to join the great southward flow of the Mississippi just a few thousand feet downstream— where, just like me, it headed on to New Orleans.

*****

Back at Vicksburg National Military Park, I found the lift gate up, but the ranger's shack unoccupied. I did a slow circuit of the parking lot waiting for someone to appear, but when they didn't, I rode through the Memorial Arch and onto the tour road without paying the $16.00 entrance fee.

When I was 19 years old, an in-processing clerk behind a battleship gray government-issued metal desk convinced me to enlist in the Air Force for six years rather than four, drawing my attention to an available $4,000 bonus. "It's a one-time deal," he said. "Take it or leave it." At that point in my life, like most 19 year olds, I had more time than money. I took the deal.

I wasn't entirely comfortable stiffing Uncle Sam for my hour-long ride through the park, but my overall sense of guilt might have been less than you'd expect.

The tour road was a drive-by eulogy for the some 20,000

men who suffered and died for the fate of Vicksburg— a city of such strategic value to the Civil War that Lincoln described it as the key to ending the conflict while Jefferson Davis described it as "the nailhead that holds the South's two halves together."

Stretching off in all directions on either side of the narrow winding tour road there stood monuments of varying description. Some honored individual states, units, or men, while others detailed specific skirmishes. They ranged from small weathered stones to imposing granite facades and the hundreds of informational placards that accompanied them were kept secure by silent cannons beneath the unseeing vigil of statuary officers.

Several times, I pulled over and dismounted the Kawi to get a closer look at an important looking feature or monument. Each time that I did it the gravity and solemnity of the place grew, and I found myself riding through the park as quietly as possible, coasting where I could to keep the bike's engine at an idle- my attempt to honor the dead.

It was under this reverent spell that I first spied the dark hulk of the Cairo, her imposing black angularity made all the more ominous beneath the gossamer white canopy erected to shield her from the weather. Built for a war fought before machine guns, tanks or airplanes, the Cairo has the muscular stance and crisp modern lines of an M1 Abrams tank.

More than half a century before bubble gum was invented, the Union commissioned a family of warships — the *City Class*- that would look at home on the set of a Dark Knight film; comic book phantoms brought to life from a bizarro world where Abraham Lincoln commissions a time-traveling Nicola Tesla to fashion a stealth destroyer for use in the shallows.

I maneuvered the Kawasaki into the empty parking lot next to the Cairo Museum, chose the nearest spot, and simply left the bike to idle as I walked up the sloping pedestrian ramp enveloped in a sense of stupefied awe at the object on display. More than any cannon or rifle or uniform I'd ever seen from the Civil War, the fearsome magnificence of the Cairo brought the ferocity of the human endeavor home to me.

That such a thing - itself one of seven - could be completed, commissioned, manned and sunk in a single year seemed a terrific and terrible effort. The Cairo was the height of American steam-era might brought to bear against itself, and six generations later it was still fearsome.

I walked around and through the Cairo alone, the absence of other patrons along with their commentary and cameras allowing me to be fully present in that moment, silent and solemn. It was ten or fifteen minutes before another patron appeared, a white guy in his fifties with a bushy white mustache, dad jeans, and a green windbreaker. We nodded to each other without speaking, and having had the chance to experience the Cairo on my own, I headed back down the concrete walkway to the softly idling Kawi.

As I followed the tour road out of the park, my focus shifting to the ride ahead, I felt the cold settle back into me and wished for the millionth time that I could be warm. While I was pushing south at the leading edge of Nuri's frozen bow wave, residents of Denver, Colorado and Casper, Wyoming were waking up to their coldest November mornings on record: -14F, and -27F respectively. On the Upper Mississippi, navigation had been stopped entirely. It was the earliest time that had happened since the year Neil Armstrong walked on the moon.

*****

I followed US-61 south out of Vicksburg, trying to distract myself from the cold by singing along with the songs on my GRR playlist, throwing myself into the spirit of the trip and attempting to recapture the excitement of my first day out, but I was tired and chilled and the scenery was a boring monotone of divided four-lane tarmac with woods on either side. It wasn't long before I began to fidget in the saddle, struggling to find a comfortable riding position while managing the insistent groping of frigid air at my neck, back, feet and knees.

I became overly aware of the intense cold in my fingertips and took once again to riding for short periods with my left hand balled into a fist and wedged into the meager pocket of warmth between my crotch and the gas tank as I had outside of Metropolis.

I wanted badly to switch off at regular intervals and warm my right hand in the same fashion, but of course, on a motorcycle, your right hand controls the throttle, so with the exception of short downhill stretches of a mile here or there spent coasting as the Kawi's speedometer gradually wound down from 60 to 50 to 45, there was no way to effectively get my right hand some relief from the relentless frosty wind while the bike was in motion.

As the chill in the fingers of my right hand changed to a steady biting pain, my internal dialogue became a protracted debate on the merits of determination, the prudence of self-care, and the symptoms and effects of frostbite.

With a real outside temperature struggling to reach 40 and a wind chill in the low 20s, I settled for a short time on a dangerous compromise. I leaned low and forward on the gas tank, brought my hands together behind the protection of the Kawi's windshield, and pressed my elbows against the handle grips to hold the bike steady as I rolled on down the road. To get myself into that position I had to accelerate up to 65 or so and work my right arm slowly inward, keeping steady pressure on the throttle as I did it and then trying to modulate the Kawi's speed with my forearm and elbow.

I bought myself a few miles of relief hunched over the gas tank like that, steering with my forearms, right elbow pressed tight against the throttle, but I knew I had little real control over the bike and my worried mind quickly shuffled frostbite to the back of the queue and occupied itself instead with the pavement rushing by below and how easily the bike could get away from me in that position. Fear won out and I carefully got my hands back where they belonged, a maneuver every bit as difficult as it was to get them into position behind the windshield in the first place, and then rode a few more agonizing miles until I spotted an off-ramp.

At the top, desperate for relief in my fingers and with no idea where a gas station, store, or restaurant might be, I lowered the kickstand on the bike and knelt down next to it warming my hands in the white puffs of exhaust coming from the engine's single tailpipe. After a lifetime of riding motorcycles with chromed exhaust, it took me a minute to get comfortable with the idea, but soon I had my hands resting directly on the business end of the Kawi's carbon fiber pipe.

As superheated carbon monoxide burbled out of the Concours, I crouched down on the asphalt for long minutes holding my hands in its flow like a hot spring until my fingers were finally warm again. Finding that new source of warmth made me happy and proud. As simple a solution as it was, it meant an end to my prolonged bouts of determined suffering and I resigned myself to stop as often as necessary to keep my hands from hurting.

That was the worst of it. By 10:30 or so, just north of Natchez, Mississippi, the clouds gave way and the sun shone strong against a clear blue sky. It was still cold, but the sun brought noticeable relief. Finally aware of my hunger, I pulled over once again beside the road— this time atop a forested hill with the lush deep green of pines disappearing off in all directions beyond the wide stretch of grass that bordered the highway.

After warming my hands again over the exhaust, I opened the trunk on the Kawi and fished out the peanut butter packets I had taken from the Holiday Inn Express that morning, took off my helmet, and made a late breakfast out of the two tablespoons or so of dry sticky peanut butter, using my finger to spoon it out of the shallow plastic containers. When I finished, I popped five ibuprofen and washed everything down with a Five Hour Energy shot and a partial bottle of water that had also been in the Kawi's trunk.

With my breakfast finished, I stretched and stomped and rubbed my hands together. I ran my fingers through my helmet-matted hair, tousled it vigorously, and drew it up and away from my head into a mad scientist's halo. I breathed in deeply, satisfied that I'd come so far and - faithful that the sun would bring even more warmth- feeling as if I'd survived my last great challenge. With just a few more hours of riding, I'd reach New Orleans.

On the north side of Natchez, where US 61 had taken on the character of a small-town Boulevard with a pleasant median and trees close in on either side, I pulled off into a Shell station and filled the idling Concours with premium fuel before heading inside to pay. I decided to visit the men's room while I was stopped and was conscious all the while that I was out of sight of the still running Kawi.

The risk that it would be gone when I emerged leant my brief excursion inside the station an edge of anxiety that was completely foreign to that benign activity repeated hundreds of times throughout my adult life. As I stood staring ahead at the men's room wall, reveling in the indoor warmth the station offered, I considered the unique nature of my imagination's would-be motorcycle thief.

They would have to be a person willing to steal a vehicle, able to operate a motorcycle, and who also happened to be at that particular service station at that particular time, having also apparently gotten there with no vehicle of their own to be abandoned as evidence.

I smiled, and upon exiting the men's room spotted the Kawi right where I'd left it, patiently exhaling little puffballs of exhaust as it waited nonchalantly next to the pump.

I grabbed a small can of Red Bull and a Snickers bar, paid, and enjoyed my quick snack standing just inside the door of the station, watching the Kawi through the window while I ate. On the opposite side of town, I spotted a Town & Country Farm and Hardware store and pulled into their lot, grabbing a parking stall in front of the main entrance.

I hopped off the bike and walked in without taking my helmet off, spotting what I was looking for right there in a display next to the register— Hot Hands activated charcoal hand warmers. I bought enough for both boots, my gloves and all my pockets, opening them then and there and getting them into place. They took a few minutes to get completely hot, but by the time I was five miles out of Natchez riding south on 61, I was as warm as I had been since I'd said goodbye to Ms. Gail at 7:00 that morning.

Less than an hour later, I pulled over to the shoulder of the road and snapped a selfie next to a big blue welcome sign at the Louisiana State Line. The words "Welcome to Louisiana" were printed in arcing letters above a yellow fleur-de-lis. Beneath that, the sentiment was repeated in French. "Bienvenue en Louisiane".

I didn't bother taking off my helmet for the photo. In it my smile looks forced and my face is a rosy pink reminder of the morning chill. But behind me and the bike and the sign and the trees, there is the late morning sun, breaking into the frame and spraying a rainbow lens flare over everything else. I had made it. Louisiana was my tenth state in nine days and it was here that both my trip and the mighty river would reach their ends.

*****

I rode south on US-61 through Wakefield, St. Francisville and Port Hudson, never spotting a single sign to indicate that I was still on the Great River Road though confident that for now, I was. There was little for scenery, the river flowing southward a couple of miles to my west beyond a swampy morass. US-61 remained a divided four lane highway, and with its 65 mile per hour limit, I was fast descending through the state and onward toward New Orleans.

As I neared Baton Rouge, I pulled into a vacant dirt lot beside the highway and worked in vain to pull up the internet on my phone. I wanted to know which side of the river made up the national route and wanted to review the turn by turn directions for the GRR between Baton Rouge and New Orleans[20]. I recalled reading on a travel site that the road was virtually unmarked in Louisiana and knew that I had likely seen my last Great River Road sign somewhere back in Mississippi.

Unable to get a signal, I decided to abandon the idea of having my hand held the remainder of the way and decided on my own to cross the river in Baton Rouge and then hug it the best I could as it traveled southward. A regular map showed that US-61 was too direct, making an efficient four-lane beeline for the Big Easy miles away from the river, while smaller roads meandered down both sides. Crossing the Mississippi in Baton Rouge would allow me to ride parts of both the east and the west sides of the river in Louisiana- a novelty unavailable since Minnesota, the river acting as a state border the for rest of its run.

Baton Rouge, now Louisiana's capitol city, was once part of the Republic of Florida, an independent state which broke from Spanish rule and existed for less than a full year before its flag was solemnly lowered for the last time on December 10th, 1810, the territory having been surrendered to the United States after a bold President Madison used the US Army to quickly grab control of it before Spain could muster a response.

Madison, who was both concerned by and criticized for his decision to deploy troops without congressional authority (the body

---

[20] Turn by turn directions for the entire route from the headwaters in Minnesota all the way to the Gulf of Mexico can be found on the Federal Highway Administration's website at www.fhwa.dot.gov

was in recess at the time), thus cleverly put an end to years of tense back and forth between the US and Spain regarding the territory then known as West Florida while simultaneously setting a precedent for unilateral use of the military by future presidents whenever they deemed the situation too urgent to dally around getting approval from congress. Spain meanwhile had bigger fish to fry, being under occupation by the French at the time with King Ferdinand VII under house arrest in Valency while Napoleon's older brother Joe stood in for him, under the imaginative royal title of Jose I.

Joe Bonaparte, after putting an end to the Spanish Inquisition and then commanding the French army at the Battle of Paris as Lieutenant General of the Empire, retired to Bordentown, New Jersey (where one might imagine him standing outdoors in socks, sandals, shorts and undershirt, holding a garden hose and yelling at the neighbor kids to stay the hell off his lawn). He eventually returned to Europe where he died in Florence at the age of 76.

The petrochemical industry is the beating heart of the Baton Rouge and soon its machinery and apparatus and sundry infrastructure came to dominate the scenic highway. There were rail yards and tank farms and rusting metal buildings longer than city blocks. Smokestacks, water towers, and exposed pipes of every size twisted and jutted among a dystopian patchwork of related enterprises no doubt manned by regular people who played in football pools and competed in friendly games of break room cribbage and who had long ago grown accustomed to the view.

About a mile south of the Made-to-Go convenience store, an ExxonMobil Chemical facility sits on the opposite side of US-61 from Crestworth Elementary School, their mutual sightlines obscured by stands of trees. Online, ExxonMobil Chemical ("Powering progress around the world") touts their commitment to "inspiring and preparing students to take on the important and rewarding engineering career path".

Fifth graders at Crestworth, whose swing set sits just about a thousand feet from four mammoth white ExxonMobil Chemical storage tanks, may or may not be inspired to pursue a technical career there, but their preparation is surely in doubt. At the time of this writing, they rated just 6% in science proficiency according to

GreatSchools.org. Fifth graders at nearby Progress Elementary, just south of the plant, mustered only a 4% proficiency rate.

Beyond the ExxonMobil Chemical plant, US-61 offered the now familiar mix of vacant, weedy lots and ramshackle mom and pop businesses that managed to hang on along a river and a road that would never again regain their former glory. At Airline Highway, I turned west and rode along beside an elevated rail bridge toward the river, where it crossed over between the trusses of the Huey P. Long bridge (one of two in the state), while vehicle traffic crossed over along the sides, the bridge handling its cars and trucks like a workman carrying a two by four board in each hand, broadside down.

Built in 1940 for a cost of $8.4 million, the mile-long structure, which locals call "the old bridge" carries about 22,000 cars a day. Like so many of America's bridges, it's late into its twilight years. Its superstructure condition is rated "Serious" and its overall sufficiency rating is just 9 out of a possible 100— one of the many challenges that will be laid at the feet of Crestworth's underprepared fifth graders.

On the other side of the bridge, I headed south on Louisiana 1, past a sprawling ExxonMobil tank farm and the towering cactus-like stacks of the Placid refinery. A little further on, I crossed over the Port Allen lock, itself a part of the Port of Greater Baton Rouge, which enjoys Foreign Trade Zone status and is the northern terminus for ocean going deep-draught Panamax class vessels on the Mississippi.

The Panamax ships, so named because of they are designed to the limits of the canal's locks, are limited in length to 965 feet, width to 106 feet, and to a draught of 40 feet. As crude carriers, the Panamax ships are smaller than their largest cousins, the supertankers, by as much as 500 feet, but a mid-sized Panamax carrier is still not the type of object one might expect to find sitting out in the street upon opening their front door in the morning.

By way of comparison, a Panamax carrier capable of operating in the lower Mississippi River might be ONLY 965 feet long, but the USS Ronald Reagan, a nuclear-powered Nimitz-class supercarrier toting around a compliment of 6,000 service members and 90 aircraft, is ONLY 1,092 feet long— a difference of just a little over a hundred feet. I had reached a point on the Mississippi accessible by the much of world's ocean-going fleet.

A little further on, I rode past a sprawling Dow Chemical facility, the air around it heavy with an unpleasant chemical tang, and on into Plaquemine, where I turned left on a street of the same name and made my way over to the levee road. I rode south for a block or two along its narrow tarmac before the charming tidy colonial homes one block over on Church Street enticed me to slide back west. Riding past the palm trees and covered porches there, it was easy to imagine the locals wiling away their evenings eating fresh caught fish and drinking cold beer beneath a blanket of stars on a warm summer night. Suddenly the cold and the chemicals fell away behind me and I felt like I had found Louisiana.

South of Plaquemine, I found the River Road and followed it again until it became Louisiana 405. Just north of the town of White Castle, it led me past Nottoway Plantation, the largest surviving plantation house in the south, boasting an impressive 64 rooms spread over more than an acre of floor space.

Its handsome white-columned backside mooned out toward the river and I passed it by without stopping for a photograph. Now a man on a mission, I followed 405 at the posted speed as it curved along with the river past villages and farmer's fields all the way down to Donaldsonville, where I once again had to jog east to keep alongside the Mississippi, this time following Louisiana 18.

Almost immediately, Louisiana 18 led me past CF Industries, a sprawling complex of pipelines, smokestacks and silos covering some 1,400 acres. As North America's largest nitrogen operation, CF produces ammonia, granular urea (yep, urea), and urea ammonium nitrate.

The road led under half a dozen different sets of pipes and conveyors reaching out to the river like the bony silver fingers of some metallic giant sprawled on its stomach and low crawling toward the water. I pressed on past a great bow in the river and passed under the western supports of the nearly 10,000-foot-long Sunshine Bridge before following a frontage road along its approach and using it to cross back over the Mississippi on Louisiana 70 about fifty miles out from New Orleans. I was tired, bored, and anxious, and I hadn't had anything to eat or drink since I'd stopped in

Natchez. I'd heard of marathoners who pushed their bodies to the limits at the end of their races, going as far as moving their bowels while hurling themselves onward. So close to my goal, I nearly understood their all-encompassing focus.

I'd meant to find US-61 on the east side of the river but met Interstate 10 first and took it. After merging into midday traffic and accelerating up to 75 to keep up with the flow of locals, it wasn't long before I was sorry to have done it.

The freeway seemed too fast— frenetic and dangerous after so long spent cruising along at 55 or 60. I couldn't hear my music anymore and I became acutely aware of how exhausted I was when each passing vehicle jangled my nerves. I felt exposed and vulnerable and began to dread the maze of intersecting roadways I could expect as I rode into the center of New Orleans. I wasn't a marathoner. I didn't want to poop myself for the cause. I wanted a big greasy meal, a strong cocktail, and a warm bed.

The traffic carried me eastward over and through the broad green expanse of the Maurepas Swamp, including a couple of miles of elevated roadway outside of La Place that turn the interstate into a Cajun[21] version of Bear Country USA, only with prehistoric alligators standing in for the cuddly black bears of South Dakota.

Along the elevated roadway, a stubby concrete guardrail and good common sense is all there is to stop passing motorists from hurling themselves headlong into the brackish black water fifteen or twenty feet below. On a motorcycle, I felt particularly susceptible to being flung right over the edge. No doubt there were alligators there. Official accounts put the wild alligator population in Louisiana somewhere around two-million, while the Louisiana Black Bear had been on the threatened species list as recently as 2010, with less than a thousand remaining. The odds of needing the industrial sized can of bear spray that had been taking up precious space in the Kawi's

---

[21] The word "Cajun" is actually an Americanized version of the French, "Arcadian" and is used to describe the unique and heavily Franco-inspired culture in Louisiana. The Acadians were a group of French immigrants to Canada who were largely deported by the British following the French and Indian War in what came to be known as The Great Expulsion. The largest enclaves of Arcadian descendants are to be found in the Canadian Maritime Provinces and in Louisiana where many were settled with the help of Spain, and where even non-Arcadians have adopted the name.

fiberglass trunk for a week were dwindling faster than... well, the Louisiana Black Bear population. 4,624 miles away at a London pub, seated comfortably next to a fire enjoying a Guinness among friends, Bear Grylls let out a soft and all but inexplicable snort.

I was all fascination, horror, and nerves by the time I was finally able to exit I-10 onto Main Street in La Place. Once there, I rode the Kawi right up under the awning of the Holiday Inn Express and left it idling, knowing it would be safe there as I went inside to use the bathroom in the lobby and gather my wits for the final push into New Orleans.

I warmed up for a few minutes, washed my face, got a drink of water from a fountain, and did some stretches before climbing back into the saddle on the Kawi. I punched the address of the hotel where I'd be staying in the French Quarter into my GPS and turned the volume on the bike's speakers up to maximum before rejoining the maniac flow of cars on I-10.

East of La Place, I-10 resumed its elevated course over the Maurepas, supported on concrete pylons for miles before swinging out over the open water of Lake Pontchartrain, which despite having more than 600 square miles of surface area, averages little better than 10 feet deep. In a satellite photo, Pontchartrain rides atop the city of New Orleans like a damp heavy mushroom top— its great mass of water only just held in check by the city's tired sea walls.

Local traffic was anesthetized to the sight of both lake and swamp, rushing along the bridge in a frenzied routine. It was all I could do to keep pace as I barreled along with the late afternoon rush as alternating swaths of green swamp and open channels flashed beside and below me before the roadway crossed over a levee wall into the town of Kenner at the west edge of Jefferson Parish and the concrete beneath me was once more resting on dry land. Kenner gave way to Metarie and I struggled to hear my navigation instructions as the roadway spilled out beneath me into the city.

Unable to get into the correct lane quickly enough, I missed one turn and eventually followed the irritable ("Turn right. Turn right. Turn right!") GPS off the interstate onto some small artery, and then through a series of ever more baffling direction changes until I was on Poydras riding right past the Mercedes-Benz Superdome, rising out of the ground like the ridged top of a magnificent copper urn, the wide avenue out front divided by a grass median dotted with palm trees.

I had made it. Only blocks from my destination, I was elated. I threw open the visor to my helmet to soak it all in without the filter of the face shield. After more than a week of riding, I had finally made it.

New Orleans felt new and cosmopolitan, especially after Memphis, and I delighted in its French southern majesty— concrete and glass skyscrapers brushing shoulders with wrought iron and stone. The GPS turned me left onto Carondelet and I was stuck riding the precariously narrow blacktop strip between two streetcar rails as I passed among the classically elegant facades of upscale downtown hotels and restaurants that lined the claustrophobic path.

At Canal Street the streetcar rails stopped and Carondelet became Bourbon Street, pedestrians lining its orange bricked sidewalks; bars and restaurants crammed in together on either side, the second and third stories of their antiquated buildings supporting elaborately railed balconies. The street was terrifically narrow, with commercial trucks and vans lined tail to snout along its low curbs, a flurry of activity surrounding nearly all of them as the tourist blocks prepared for their nightly rush.

Reflective sawhorses were stacked at the intersections and it was obvious that the street would soon be closed for the evening. I had only just made my chance to end my journey on the Great River Road by riding right down Bourbon Street but was nearly too overwhelmed to enjoy it. It would end up being the type of thing that a person gets to enjoy only after the fact, when the excitement and anxiety of the moment can finally give way to quiet reflection.

The motorcycle drew smiles and nods as I tiptoed it down through the French Quarter searching for my hotel, and I felt conspicuous and celebratory- a conquering general riding through the streets of a foreign place. I nearly missed my turn at Conti, and even more narrowly, almost missed the entrance to the Le Meridien's underground parking structure located immediately across the street from the hotel. It was a narrow opening along a yellow curb— little more than a double garage door cut into the front of a four-story redbrick building.

I rode down the ramp into the dim light of the underground

garage and found a tight spot for the Kawi against a wall next to a late model Vespa.

I angled the Concours into place, walking it back and forth a couple of times to get it fully out of the travel lane and then thumbed it off for the last time. I sat there for only a few seconds, reveling in the quiet and the triumph of what I had done. I'd made it. I hadn't failed, and I hadn't fallen. For the moment, the achievement was mine alone. No one around me knew what I had just done, and no one back home yet knew that I'd made it.

I climbed off the bike, took off my helmet and headed across the street, having covered 2,487 miles over the course of eight days passing through ten states. It occurred to me that if I had only gotten lost one more time, I might have logged an even 2,500.

*****

After checking in at the Hotel Le Marais, I walked upstairs and checked out my room before cleaning up the best I could with all my clothes and toiletries still on the bike across the street. The room, small due to the limits of the building, was newly remodeled and chicly modern and it was a relief not knowing when I'd have to sleep on the ground again. Once I was presentable, I headed down to the lobby bar for a celebratory beer.

The bartender fished around behind the counter and found one of their last Oktoberfests after I asked hopefully if they still had any and she served it to me in a tall beer glass with a side of nibbling snacks in a low metal bowl that could have doubled as an ornate ashtray.

It was still bright outside, but the bar was bathed in a gentle purple light and I savored the beer and the moment, extremely satisfied with what I'd done. When I finished the beer, I ordered another and texted some friends and family while I drank it. I posted a picture of my half-finished drink to Facebook and said that I'd made it safely to the French Quarter- the entirety of which has been designated a National Historic Landmark. The Quarter also has the distinction of having an elevation of just one foot above sea level. As the oldest part of New Orleans, the French Quarter occupies some of its highest ground and thus escaped the worst of Katrina's wrath in 2005.

When I finished my drink, I walked back to the parking garage, retrieved the saddlebags from the Kawi, and went back up to my room for a long, hot shower. My snack at the hotel bar had activated my appetite and I made a beeline to Felix's Restaurant and Oyster Bar, the first recommendation of the concierge at the Le Meridian. I was hungry and eager to sample a couple of different things, so I ordered the fried seafood platter which came with shrimp, oysters, and catfish- all obviously fresh and coated with a light breading that had just the right amount of Cajun spiciness. There was also a big mound of French fries and four or five hushpuppies along with a scoop of coleslaw. I washed the whole thing down with a couple of pints of IPA and left feeling full, buzzed, and satisfied.

I'd had regular business in New Orleans a decade before and remembered enjoying a courtyard bar with a colleague so went off in search of that. It was called The Beach and I found it easily enough, just a few hundred feet from Felix's. They do 3 for 1 domestics at The Beach which had surprised me the first time I walked up to the bar, ordered a couple of beers for me and my colleague and got handed a six pack. This time there was no surprise when the bartender lined up three bottles of Bud Light in front of me. I sat and drank two of them slowly while I watched the small Thursday night crowd strolling by on Bourbon, abandoning the third when I got up to leave.

It was nearly 9:00 and the fatigue of the week and the sedative effect of the alcohol and food was setting in harder than I'd expected. I'd remembered New Orleans for its live music and I wandered up and down Bourbon popping my head in here and there, listening for a few minutes at a stretch. I once described New Orleans to a friend by saying, "Imagine you're in the best bar you've ever been in, enjoying some great live music and then you reluctantly decide to step out and find another place. Two doors down you find an even better bar with even better live music. That's New Orleans."

All by myself and in a contemplative mood over what I'd accomplished- maybe even a little melancholy to see it completed, I had trouble finding the vibe I'd felt before and finally decided to grab one more drink before calling it a night. I found a spot at the bar at a place called Beer Fest that was surprisingly intimate for Bourbon Street. The walls were exposed brick and covered in places with salvaged wood. A football game was playing on a TV over the bar and I looked the drink menu over for a couple minutes before deciding to try Absinthe for the first time.

Absinthe is an anise flavored spirit peppered with various other botanical flavors. Once thought to be hallucinogenic and highly addictive, absinthe was banned in many places and is still illegal to produce and consume in Australia. A romantic aura surrounds the drink due in part to the ritualistic preparation that includes an ornate slotted spoon on which a sugar cube is set ablaze and then extinguished in the absinthe before drinking. It smacks of a more hardcore drug and makes for a beautiful visual, the sugar cube burning a brilliant blue that shimmers against the glass and the milky liquid below.

I took twenty minutes drinking the sweet thick mixture which tasted like nothing if not an alcoholic black jelly bean. I imagined myself in the shoes of Oscar Wilde and Ernest Hemingway (both fans of the green fairy) as I tottered back to my luxurious room at the Le Meridian and fell asleep on top of the covers with all my clothes on. It wasn't yet 10:00 pm.

*****

In the morning, I woke up early and showered away the fuzziness of the previous night. The sun was shining brightly outside and I had the Quarter to myself as I walked along its all but deserted streets which were wet and shiny from a fresh hosing down— the daily cleanup ritual of a city known for "huge ass beers" and 3 for 1 specials. I made my way down to the riverside and watched the sun play over the water before picking my way down the riprap to scoop some of the Mississippi up in my hand. Then I headed off toward Cafe du Monde for a plate of steaming hot beignets.

Cafe du Monde was established in 1862 in the New Orleans French market and has offered a menu essentially unchanged ever since. They serve a rich dark roast coffee and churn out plate after plate of too-hot-to-touch French style donuts covered in heaps of powdered sugar that will send you into coughing fits if you make the mistake of inhaling in mid-bite.

I ordered mine and sat down at one of the cafe's dozens of small round tables. Cafe du Monde is essentially an open-air eatery covered with an awning and open 24 hours a day year-round with the exception of Christmas Day. Because of the November cold, plastic curtains had been unfurled along the open sides of the restaurant transforming it into something like a reception tent. They did little to keep out the chill of the morning, or the birds, and a small family of pigeons patrolled the floor pecking around for fallen bits of beignet. They got none from me.

When my breakfast was finished, I walked back through the French Quarter, stopping now and then to window shop and admire all the architecture and history that had eluded me the night before. Along the way, I spotted a building for sale. From the balcony on the second floor a metal realtor's sign hung from a post. At the bottom of the sign, a smaller sign was attached. It was the type you might commonly see advertising a special feature like "pool", an incentive like "price reduced", or a triumphant "sold" notice. This one simply said, "Haunted".

Back at the Le Meridien I gathered the things I wanted to take home with me— not much, a couple of souvenirs and my helmet in its protective cover —and carefully packed everything else back into the Kawi's saddlebags for the return shipment home. A shipping company was supposed to come and pick it up the next morning, so I walked the saddlebags across the street, reaffixed them to the bike, and took a few minutes to snap pictures of it from all angles in case I had to make a damage claim.

The Concours was filthy, covered with days of grime and roadspray, but it looked suddenly quite handsome to me. It felt weird to be abandoning it now at the end of the journey. The journey had been mine, but the bike had been my partner the whole way. Back across the street, I handed off the single key fob to the concierge at the Le Meridien and he called a cab to take me to the airport.

I rode to Louis Armstrong International in the back of a tired yellow Toyota Sienna minivan. The thin black driver took a call just as were pulling away from the hotel and managed to talk on the phone all the way from the French Quarter to passenger drop-off, handling all of his driving duties with his single free hand. He spoke in Arabic, a language I had learned two decades before while serving as an Air Force linguist and which had slipped from my memory like starchy water through a colander almost immediately after I'd stopped using it- leaving me with a only few odd phrases like "his stomach is like that of an elephant", or "he is clean, and nice too", and "I speak Arabic, but only a little".

Sometimes when a clerk or cabbie holds a conversation in Arabic in front of me, I like to leave them with an appropriate salutation in their native tongue. "Thanks," I'll say in perfect Arabic, "and have a good afternoon," I always do it on my way out the door, leaving them to replay the last few moments of their conversation wondering how much I'd overheard.

After more than a week spent traveling alone on a motorcycle, it felt strange to watch the scenery slip by from a flat upholstered bench while another man took on the driving duties, nonchalantly holding a phone conversation as he navigated us through the Friday morning traffic. It seemed surreal. Pedestrian. When we stopped beside the curb, I offered him my credit card and he asked me if I had cash, waggling his cell phone in the air and saying his reader wasn't working. I pulled the fare from a roll of bills in my front pocket, included a small tip which was more for me than him, and stepped out onto the curb with a muttered thank you. I said it in English, deciding at the last second not to bother with the Arabic. What difference did it make?

Inside the airport, I moved quickly through security and found my way to the only empty stool at a crowded bar where I drank two pints of beer and ate a basket of chicken strips, keeping to myself except when a young financial planner in a powder blue dress shirt sat down next to me and asked about my helmet on the bar. It wasn't a genuine question, just a prelude to telling me about himself and I listened politely for a few minutes until he was joined by a colleague who opened their conversation complaining about a hangover and claiming to have barely made it to the airport. He sat down, ordered a Bloody Mary, and relieved me of my conversational duties.

I felt more at ease on the wooden barstool than I had in the backseat of taxi, but it was still jarring to be off the bike and headed for home. Although it had been just nine days, I'd grown accustomed to a routine of waking, loading out, and climbing onto the motorcycle to follow the road southward down the river. I'd been solely in charge of when to start, when to stop, and what to see in between. Except for yesterday, each day had promised only more of the same for tomorrow. Now I was shuffling along with other people on a fixed timetable on my way back to my other life, the one with schedules, customers, and a variety of obligations.

I remembered a sign I saw once in an antique shop. It said, "You never see a motorcycle in front of a therapist's office." Spending a week on the Kawi had liberated me from my daily worries. The first days had been spent in rhapsodic enthusiasm for the boldness of what I was doing. Each new mile brought with it fresh scenery and the promise of more. I ate restaurant food and wondered what new experiences awaited me in the days to come. I patted myself on the back for my sense of adventure and fell asleep by firelight pretending I was a cowboy.

As the ride became a routine, I spent hours in reverie while the bucolic scenery rolled by. I thought about my life and luxuriated in the remembered details of my good experiences. I thought about lost loves and Christmases past. I listened to music all day and appreciated my good fortune.

When the cold became an all but unbearable companion, made all the worse by its incessant probing and prodding, and when the Kawi's KiPass system started to threaten the trip, I was forced to focus on the smallest most immediate problems- starting the bike, warming my fingers, making it to the next stop. I began to countdown the miles and tick off small victories in the achievement of my broader goal. Twelve miles to the next town, forty miles to the border, ninety miles until you can stop.

All of these things kept my normally brooding, worried, and ruminating mind at bay. I didn't think about my budget, or the difficult engineer at the steel plant, or whether or not grubs were damaging my lawn.

When I boarded with the other first-class passengers and took my window seat, I sighed and let go of the trip. I was on the plane and soon it would carry me back home, following almost the same path in the sky as the one I had taken on land.

I was sipping orange juice and enjoying the warmth and comfort of my seat when I glanced out the window after an hour or so of flight. The world below was a mottled patchwork of green and tan and a river snaked through it. I wondered for a moment if it was the Mississippi, and then as we approached a city, my wonder turned to certainty. Far below, I could make out buildings and bridges and the distinctive shape of the Memphis Pyramid. Next to it was Mud Island. It had taken me two days to ride from Memphis to New Orleans and only about an hour to cover the distance on an Airbus operated by Delta.

When I'd started my trip, I liked it in part for the reasonable challenge it represented. I'd never ridden solo more than an hour or so from home and with almost no planning had flung myself down the Mississippi through unknown country confident that some low-level challenges would present themselves. I was glad for the KiPass failure and the cold and the rain and even for nearly falling.

A couple of months prior while preparing to leave for my first trip to Sturgis, I was trying to secure the Kawi on a flatbed trailer with four ratchet straps. I'd always struggled with ratchet straps and hated the way it seemed like every other guy had no trouble with them. With each passing minute I was growing further behind schedule and the clock was closing in on noon. The August sun overhead was a merciless witness to my helpless fumbling and my shirt was soaked through with sweat.

My neighbor, a balding engineer maybe five years older than me, was busy tending some bushes in his side yard twenty or thirty feet away as I fought the stubborn straps. Finally, when my frustration and desperation had grown great enough to overpower my ego, I approached him sheepishly.

"Hey, could you give me a hand?" I asked. "I'm trying to get my bike tied down and these ratchet straps are kicking my ass." I included a little self-deprecating laugh at the end as if to soften the admission and recognize right from the beginning that I was asking for help with something ridiculously easy.

His answer surprised and delighted me. "Oh, god. I wouldn't be any help." he said. "I've always fought with those things."

I thanked him anyway and headed into the house to pursue plan B - YouTube. The first video I pulled up explained that if not properly maintained, ratchet straps can indeed suck to operate and then set about providing instructions on proper maintenance. Mine were old and seized and had been put away wet. I turned off the computer and headed to Walmart. Thirty minutes later I was back in my driveway with an entirely new set of straps that worked like a champ. The lesson most people would have taken from this would be to properly maintain their ratchet straps. The lesson I took away was that a lot of other men felt just as clueless as I did about the stuff that was supposed to make us manly.

When I'd gotten back to work tying down the bike, I took my time getting it set up on the trailer, working and working at it to get it as straight and level as possible. Still, I found myself glancing back in the rearview mirror all the way to Sturgis waiting for it to flop over on its side. When it didn't, I counted myself lucky.

Days later, when it came time to strap the bike on the trailer for the trip home, my dad helped. As had always been our rhythm, I deferred as he took charge of things. When he was finally satisfied that the Kawi was strapped down well enough, I couldn't keep my concern quiet. The bike was cockeyed on the trailer and leaning at an angle that made me nervous it would fall over on the trip home.

Dad stood back, sized things up, and announced that it would be fine. "You worry too much," he said.

He was right.

AFTERWORD

"Times have changed and times are strange
Here I come, but I ain't the same
Mama, I'm comin' home"
- Mama I'm Comin' Home, Ozzy Osbourne

The day after I returned from my trip was my 42nd birthday and my girlfriend Katie had arranged a full day of celebration for me beginning with an hour-long massage at a local salon. As the day wore on, she led me from place to place, pampering and treating me, but the truth was I was tired and wanted to be at home.

I share a birthday with my niece and my family had arranged to get together for cake at my sister's house that evening. I didn't want to go and was getting sullener about it as the time approached. Then Katie suggested that we stop off at my place on the way so we could freshen up. I was happy to oblige.

When we walked into my darkened living room and turned on the lights, a chorus of cheers erupted. While I had been away, Katie and Shannon had carefully planned a surprise party for me, pouring themselves into the smallest details and somehow managing to keep the whole thing under wraps.

Later, enjoying ice cream and cake and surrounded by people who loved and supported me, I felt good to be back home. The freedom and independence of the road and the joys and challenges of the trip had changed some small part of me forever, but it's not good to be by yourself for too long. Especially not when you have people willing to love you whether you fail or succeed, whether you fall off or not.

*****

Three years after riding the GRR, my fingers are still hypersensitive to the cold. Almost as soon as I start doing anything that exposes them to a chill, they get tender and a sharp stinging pain starts in the tips. My right hand is worse than my left.

It was so annoying the first winter back that I researched frost bite a couple of different times, certain that I had gotten some level of it on my trip— probably the morning I rode to Metropolis out of Cape Girardeau. But frostbite is marked by frozen tissue damage and has specific symptoms (including blistering) that I never experienced.

Still convinced that I damaged my hands during the trip, I continued researching and eventually learned of a condition called NFCI or Non-Freezing Cold Injury. Caused by prolonged exposure to temperatures just above freezing and usually associated with being damp as well, NFCI has been studied in soldiers and other workers whose jobs sometimes have them suffering cold exposure for hours at levels just above frostbite temperatures; fisherman for example. One of the markers of NFCI is long-term chronic hypersensitivity to cold. Military members diagnosed with it can collect a disability. NFCI is accompanied by an overactive vascular response that constricts the tiny blood vessels in the fingers, robbing them of needed circulation and heat just when they need it most. By trying to protect itself from some greater damage, the body is basically offering up the fingers for sacrifice at the first sign of trouble.

I recently bought a pair of electrically heated gloves - 36 months too late.

ACKNOWLEDGEMENT

"If you wish to make a complaint
We can handle it, we're well prepared to handle it…
Of course, you may have to wait"
- Thanks for Your Time, Gotye

When I planned my trip, I arranged with a Florida based shipping company to pick the bike up at the Le Meridian and ship it back to my home. When I hadn't gotten a confirmation from them by Monday that they'd made the pickup, I called the concierge at the Le Meridian who verified the bike was still in their parking garage. I apologized profusely and told him I'd follow up with the shipping company immediately.

When I was finally able to reach someone at the shipping company they told me they couldn't pick up the bike in the French Quarter because the streets were too narrow for their hauler, but they were working on alternate arrangements and would keep me informed. I'd already paid them a large deposit, so I reluctantly went ahead and let them work on the problem. First days, then a full week passed as they drip-fed me a series of lies and broken promises. All the while, the management of the Le Meridien was patient, courteous, and reassuring, but their parking rate was something like $35 a day and I was horrified to imagine what kind of bill I was running up and when their patience might run out and they'd simply have the bike impounded.

The week of Thanksgiving, I finally took matters into my own hands and contracted HAUL BIKES to get the Kawasaki back to Minnesota, but they also wouldn't go into the Quarter to retrieve it. I worked with the local Kawasaki dealer, Hall's Motorsport in Harvey, who turned me on to an independent towing company they sometimes used, B&M. When I called the number Hall's had provided, I had trouble understanding the man on the other end of the line, Michael. His Cajun accent was so thick I found myself simply agreeing with whatever he said and hoping for the best.

The next day Michael texted me a picture of the Concours safely on-site at Hall's where it would be picked up by HAUL BIKES in a few days. He called me for my credit card information and apologized profusely when he told me how his helper had stumbled getting the bike up the ramp onto their truck. The Kawi had nearly fallen all the way over before they could get it back up. Michael was concerned the extreme angle it had leaned to might have allowed oil up into the cylinders and wanted me to know it shouldn't be started for a day or so. The charge for the tow from French Quarter to Hall's was about a hundred dollars.

It was mid-December by the time the Kawi made it home, delivered by a semi towing a long, two deck trailer with a hydraulic lift. The driver got the bike completely unloaded and parked it for me curbside before going over the paperwork with me. Christmas was coming up and I tipped him a twenty-dollar bill. He seemed surprised.

I had a surprise of my own when I called the Le Meridien to follow up and find out what my parking charges would be. They thanked me for staying and told me there would be no charge, that the bike hadn't taken up much space, and that they were always glad to of service to their guests. Their great service, that of the towing company and the Kawasaki dealer, all served to wipe the sour taste out of my mouth left by the first shipper. Most businesses, like most people, are trying their best.

When the HAUL BIKES driver (who had met me a short distance from my home due to his concern over getting the rig down my street) handed me the Kawi's key fob and pulled away, I climbed into the saddle and pretended once more that nothing was wrong, hoping to trick the Concours into starting up for the short ride home without disconnecting its wiring harness.

It was below freezing and the ground around me was covered with snow, the pavement beneath my boots a chalky white from dried road salt. I held my breath for an instant as I reached down and turned the chunky plastic ignition switch. When I did it, the Kawasaki's instrument cluster lit up immediately, the needles on the tach and speedometer arcing to their redlines before returning to zero. I pushed the starter button and the motorcycle's big four-cylinder engine sprang to life beneath me, burbling softly before I revved it twice and rode away.

The KiPass never failed again.

With the late, great, "Sunshine" Sonny Payne (1925-2018)
Helena, Arkansas

More photos from Welcome to Metropolis
available on Instagram @kochauthor